BOOK ONE IN

VOICES

Women Braving It All
to Live Their Purpose

BOOK ONE IN THE VOICES SERIES

VOICES

Women Braving It All to Live Their Purpose

Co-Authored and Edited by

Chloe Rachel Gallaway

CHLOE RACHEL GALLAWAY
KAREN DOREY LOVELIEN, TBG
CONNIE C. COX, LCSW
SHELLEY A. RAEL, MS, RDN
LORI CHERAMIE
RUSANNE JOURDAN
JOAN TEAGLE BRUMAGE, LCSW
ANDREA ROBERTS PARHAM
NICOLE "NIKKI" BRUTON-PHILLIPS
KAREN ANN BOISE
M. JACQUELYN SIMPSON

Library of Congress Cataloging-in-Publication Data

Gallaway, Chloe Rachel with Karen Dorey Lovelien, Connie C. Cox, Shelley A. Rael, Lori Cheramie, Rusanne Jourdan, Joan Teagle Brumage, Andrea Roberts Parham, Nicole Bruton-Phillips, Karen Ann Boise, and M. Jacquelyn Simpson

VOICES: Women Braving It All to Live Their Purpose, Book One

p. cm.
Paperback ISBN: 978-1-947708-36-5
Ebook ISBN: 978-1-947708-45-7
Library of Congress Control Number: 2019919919

10 9 8 7 6 5 4 3 2 1
First Edition, December 2019

 CITRINE PUBLISHING
Murphy, North Carolina, U.S.A.
(828) 585-7030
Publisher@CitrinePublishing.com
www.CitrinePublishing.com

Dedicated to the Braving It All women
who helped to raise me

Ida, My Foster Mom
Riva, My Mama
Grandma Sally
Grandma Ogreta

Contents

Woman

She will rise
Up from the ashes
With love in her eyes

She will lift her soul
To heights unknown
Be shown the path
That awaits her

No more running
No more shame
She carries with her
All the parts of her name

She has found a lighter self
A new way to breathe
An acceptance of past
A life that will last
Beyond the old story

She will rise
The tears in her eyes
Flowing
A deep knowing
Of her inner Power

A knowing of each step
Wisdom beyond fear
She is here
To lead you home

—Chloe Rachel Gallaway

Dear *Braving It All* Woman,

How far have you traveled to come home to yourself?

Perhaps you are still on the journey, or even a deeper matter, you don't know where to begin on the journey of seeing yourself, of honoring yourself and your past. Oh, the mountains you have climbed, the rivers you have traversed in being human, in being a woman.

Born to this earth we all came in with a voice. A loud cry echoed throughout the room, and a baby wrapped up in love was handed to a mother. We all arrived at some point and the beginning fibers of life offered us each a unique start. As a storyteller I believe we all share a beginning, a middle, and an end—or some might say, a first act, a second, and a third.

My own mother is now in her third act at seventy-nine with a hip injury that has stopped her from running her three miles a day, which she did up until the age of seventy-six. This Third Act phase and all the weathered moments behind her have stopped her from being out in the world, stopped her from being the unstoppable woman I have always known her to be. She is my model for braving it all and I sit in tears thinking of what her life has been. In the late '60s, my mother appeared on the cover of *TIME* magazine as a poster woman of the "Flower Children." Shortly after this she left Haight-Ashbury and the world behind and with it a life full of worldly possibilities. Instead, she chose to follow my father into the Northern New Mexico wilderness, where she birthed and raised six children. Once a ballet dancer, a beauty of her time, she was a woman whose artistic expression shone brightly in many forms…and she gave it all up for a whole other life. For a moment, I want us to go back, I want her to have another shot at life. On her wise and wrinkled face, and in her ocean-blue eyes, her strength shines reverently, and it begs the questions:

Who did this woman want to be?
Did she have the life she wanted?
And most importantly:
Has she come home to truly see and love herself?

I also ask these questions for you and me.

The *Braving It All* story is the raw and real journey we each face from that moment at birth where we cry out, to all the other moments of life offered up to us with the possibility of expressing our truest self.

How do we get here?
What are the challenges we have faced and how do we overcome them to stay the path and walk ourselves home?
Must we wait until our Third Act to face this?

These final questions spur a rolling hill of tears up from my heart and I realize it's not just about my mother. I, too, want another shot at life. There is something profoundly powerful in stopping right where we are at and claiming our lives. My mother is claiming her life and just recently she started a new process of using herbs to heal her body. No surgery, no doing it the way everyone else has told her to do it.

This is a new beginning for her, and an opportunity for each of us to claim our lives right here and now.

Finding our voice and seeing our braving-it-all story clearly is a path to becoming whole, to becoming our truest self while claiming our lives. It is time to pick up the torch of truth and seek the life you desire wholeheartedly. I believe this begins with honoring and seeing the greatness in your own story. Recognizing how far you have come, and finding a soul-deep communication with yourself, is the start of something beautiful… it is the start of the life you deserve.

Chloe Rachel Gallaway
December 2019

In these pages, ten women carry the torch of the *Braving It All* story. You will come to know them and witness their unique start to life; their paths took different, winding turns, and their stories reflect a deeper truth that beckons an awakening in each of us. The soul speaks, the heart opens, the child inside cries out again, and the woman inside rises up to meet herself. I have journeyed alongside each of these brave storytellers, and this book opens with my own *Braving It All* story of finding my voice and becoming a writer.

—CRG

Becoming a Writer
and the Birth of the VOICES Book Series

Chloe Rachel Gallaway

"The Soul Knows."—Chloe Rachel Gallaway

I was seven years old standing in the front yard of our wilderness home, a two-room cabin built by my father. Truly it was the wilderness, four hundred acres of wild land perched high atop a mountain in Northern New Mexico. Our cabin was surrounded by cliff dwellings and a multi-green forest of pinion, juniper, and cedar trees that blew in the wind on that late-August afternoon. It was a typical day that found me outside, a child of the earth, playing in the trees or in the dirt, making friends with all creatures.

I looked up and saw my tall, sturdy father a hundred feet from me at the hilltop where the dirt road entered our property. He stood in the glowing sunlight, his white cowboy shirt rolled up to his elbows revealing his strong forearms. Zooming up the hillside, I ran closer to him. I paused in the road and watched him pour a bucket of wheat by holding it high in the air and slowly letting each golden wheat grain be filtered by the wind as it made its way to another bucket at his feet. He was chaffing the wheat, a process that removes the shell of the wheat, blowing it off, leaving only the best part for us to eat.

Much like wheat, we humans have an outer shell and it is our realness that is found deep inside. My entire childhood forced me to seek the realness from the inside and discover what it meant to be human.

That August day, I felt free as a bird as I lifted my arms into the sky and twirled around in the wind. Floating like the wheat my father put through the chaffing process, I was limitless. There were no words spoken between my father and me; he was my hero and I a gift from God, as he had said all children were. The wind picked up and blew even stronger as we stood on the hillside.

Time changes rapidly on the mountain and within minutes I felt the heaviness of a storm coming in from behind me, the light in front of me changed from a bright gold to a dim piercing orange. I turned my body around to face the storm and to the far north, the sky was an ominous black and gray. It didn't scare me one bit; it was in fact, so stunningly beautiful that I stood in awe as the clouds became a pressured force rolling toward us. The warm air lifted and a dense wind beat at my small body. I looked far, far beyond the north and a deep feeling sank into me, a message sounded from all sides and rang aloud from the spiritual world: *Someday you will leave this land and become the greatness you were meant for.*

Along my journey I faced many storms and somehow in the midst of them, I lost this message from my childhood. I forgot that which I knew. I forgot how special, talented, and prepared I was to become everything I was meant to be. All of life's pain, trauma, and change brought with it a force that became a barrier to my *knowing*. The outer world seemed masked with layers of temptation, chaotic busyness, and a relentless seeking prompted by its own outside forces. Amid the noise, I'd lost touch with the call of the inner voice that draws us deep within.

At twenty-two years old, I was in my second year of college. Formal schooling a new thing for me, I had missed school in the world from ages six through twelve and believed this was a great disadvantage for me. I felt lost in the world much of the time. I had entered it abruptly through the foster care system when I left the mountain under traumatic circumstances.

Through the weathering of my life I was continually motivated to fight to belong, to be a part of it all, and somehow be myself, the wild child inside that knew how to draw a straight line from her heart to every star in the sky, the girl who could sit alone in the dark, feet dangling off a tree branch with no traceable fear. This reconnecting to myself would come last, as I didn't realize it was the most important piece; because at one point or another we all face the desire to fit in versus the call to be ourselves. This desire to fit in contrasted against my soul trying to heal old wounds and this conflict grated against my lungs and heart, leaving me in a profound spiritual battle. Initially I was unaware of this battle and its connection to bits of anxiety and depression, not severe, but like a constant drip of water from the kitchen sink that you can only hear late at night once all has grown quiet. It dripped and dripped away, one little drop at a time. Lacking connection to self, I could not stand strong in my truth, and thus made choices that were more harmful than healthy. This particularly affected my sense of self-worth in intimate relationships.

Yet there was, and always is, a way back to the soul. I had started writing poetry in high school as a means of letting my soul speak of my pain. It was the most natural form of expression for me. Writing it down meant giving voice to it and thus freeing myself from the pressure to fit in, from the pressure to stuff the pain; and for just a moment I was more connected to me, the real me, the girl with a voice that had wisdom to offer the world. Even in those early years there was an ache in my heart to be a writer, but the dream of being a writer seemed far-fetched. My years of missed schooling meant spelling and grammar issues in everything I wrote. *How could I ever be a writer?* Simultaneously, my outer world fed me a message, "You can only be it if you do it this way." My inner fears and expectations collided against the expectations of the outer world and right there in this explosion of doubt, my voice was paralyzed. I no longer felt the seven-year-old twirling on a hilltop that lived inside of me. I was no longer free as a bird; I was imprisoned by expectations and fear.

There is a light that feeds the soul from beyond. We have an opportunity to dig deep, find faith, find courage, and take steps forward right in the midst of our own fear. At age twenty, I signed up for a creative writing class where I was attending college at the

University of New Mexico. My story lay heavy on my chest. I had no remembrance of the warrior I was, no recognition of my own strength given how many storms I had faced so bravely. This is what happens when we cannot see ourselves clearly. In two decades on this earth, I had already lived the most riveting braving it all story, but I could not see it.

What does it take for us to see it?

When it came to the dream of being a writer, I thought it was all about the untouchable, unreachable *craft*, the elements of writing that all known writers had studied, for years perhaps. Or maybe they were born into families that had taught them from day one. I read *Bird by Bird* by Anne Lamott, who spoke of growing up with a writer father. She recalled the early days of being in her father's office listening to him write, as he typed on an older type-writer. She heard the *click-click* of the words pounding onto paper; she watched the light bounce through the glass window. Being a writer fell into her lap, as she played on the floor at his feet.   I wish I knew then that comparison is the thief of connecting to our unique self.

I don't have this, I thought. *My father was not a writer with a typewriter.*

Did I stop then to consider how he was a storyteller via his music? How he wrote songs almost daily and played them after a hard day's work in the woods? No. This I couldn't see as part of my path to becoming a writer. I had filled a box with academic concepts and my own limiting beliefs about what it meant to be a writer and anything outside of that box didn't count.

This was my headspace, but there is a heart-space, a soul con-nection that knows better. Eventually, I realized, because of my childhood and being raised in nature, so deeply connected to inner voice, my limiting beliefs and expectations were not enough to completely keep me from hearing the whisper of my own truth. I'm very, very fortunate, I know.

The soul knows and the head tries to interpret. Initially I approached writing from this headspace when I first entered creative writing class at UNM with Professor Daniel Muller, a published author! And I thought that this was *it*, anyone who was published was the be-all-and-end-all of writing and would get me to where I needed to go.

It was the first day of the Fall 1998 semester. I sat in class watching the afternoon light stream across the tables and chairs when Mr. Muller stepped in the room. He was tall and husky looking with a five o' clock shadow and wore jeans and a baseball cap with the front tilted upward. This guy was a rebel, a no-suit-and-tie kinda fella. I liked him right away.

The semester flew by like a bird overhead—in one big swoop I had learned about the beginning, middle, and end of storytelling. I had learned about using metaphor and narrative to write a story. I remember writing a memoir piece about falling off a cliff and breaking my leg when I was ten years old. The heaviness of my story and wanting to tell it had been pressing down on my shoulders for ten years. I had just turned twenty-two.

I felt nervously elated turning that paper in and not so elated when it came back to me. I first saw the red marks all over the page, most of them for grammar corrections and some for spelling. Somehow I missed the remarks at the end that said, "What a captivating story, completely drew me in." My mind rushed to the surface of the red marks. *Grammar… it will be the death of me.*

The rest of my story flooded my mind, *about how I'd grown up in the woods with no worldly advantages and I'd never be a real writer.* This is what happens to us writers; old, limiting narratives about who we are start to take over, creating a heavy resistance to writing and finding our voice. In that moment, I realized that learning craft was only a small piece of telling one's story; facing the emotional pain was the much harder part of the journey.

Again, the soul knows and calls us home toward wholeness, but are we listening? Can we hear the deeper message beneath the surface?

I let go of the dream of writing my story for many years. Besides my poetry, writing was something I did silently in my own private time. When I shared it now and then with my father, a tiny crack in the wall of forgiveness broke through in our relationship. The times I read it to my mother, she nodded in affirmation that I had something important to say. *Was I a writer?* I dreamed of writing a book, learning the craft and becoming that *something great* that was given to me in that spiritual message of my childhood. At the time I didn't remember that moment, though. It never crossed through the layers of memory; everything that passed through was intertwined with the many layers of pain, like a barbed-wire fence all woven together tightly to keep out the wolves. I was the small child who could not cross that fence without being snagged and dragged backwards into an abyss of an unhealed story. I needed more years and more life under me to face it. I wasn't behind on my journey, I was simply finding my way. However, my mind chattered on in self-judgment about how I was behind and how I lacked the determination to complete my task: to become a writer.

When I turned thirty-one, I got married. I turned thirty-three and had my first child. I could have shoved myself into a box at age thirty-three and said, "*Well, that's it you're too old now to start,*" but thank goodness, instead I was cracked wide open by the birth of my child and the daunting task ahead of me, being a mother. I call these God moments. You may or may not have experienced this, when you have a soul connection to the spiritual world and the voice of God speaks to you. It happened to me at age seven, and now at age thirty-three, while nursing our newborn baby in the back of my husband's new pick-up truck.

In these moments, time stops, and you feel as though you are floating outside of your own body, but you are not. You are deeply present to the moment. My three-month-old daughter nursed as I watched a soft rain fall from a gray sky, just outside the two-room cabin where I'd grown up. There I was back in the yard again, after all these years wanting to remain in connection to my father, as he had lost his hero status to me during many turbulent years and the falling apart of our relationship. As a teen, I had questioned his intentions and motives for having his family live out a life in the wilderness and I resented him for his unresolved anger that he most often displayed in fits of rage toward my mother. My heart cracked from wall to wall inside of my chest, but love has a way of bringing us home. I loved him deeply and longed for understanding between us. I had brought my darling Sofia Azalea to meet him, almost like a peace offering to bridge the gap between us. Before this moment, life had been zooming past me. I was on the trajectory of the "normal life": get married, have children, work in some job that will pay you, find a way to make your marriage happy, even when it's not… keep moving, outrun the tiredness, the doubt, the fear, the broken pieces of your past, make more money and outrun it all, until that God moment of sitting in the front yard of my childhood home stopped me in my tracks.

My father came to the window and looked out to us. His age showed so deeply upon his face and in his eyes, his hair, his gait of leaning forward. He was no longer the sturdy rock I'd seen at age seven; he was now clearly in his third act of life. That feeling of *I must stop time from moving forward* came pouring over me. *I must stop time. I must heal my heart. I must love my father.* It all piled onto me and poured out into my daughter as she nursed. A moment so big it broke me through all my fear and my insides came alive with the message *"I must write my story."*

There was much work to do after this realization; however, it was that moment that gave birth to me as a writer, reminding me that for many of us the truest version of our self may be born from pain. For some they may be born from joy, I'm open to the possibility, but for me it was the pain that asked me to dig deep to find myself and stay on the path to becoming who I was meant to be.

Once I made the decision to write, doors opened up, but I was still in my headspace, and off I went to sign up for my first memoir class. I stayed with it for five years—yes, five years of memoir classes. I came back time and time again writing just one piece of my story at a time. It was all I felt I could manage alongside being a new mother, a wife, and now I had a son, Jonah Oliver. There was no good time to write a book, no perfect time at all, but this was as good as any and my heart was in it.

I had not forgotten about my God moment on the mountain with my Sofia, and wore it close to my chest so I could feel it moving inside of me. I was only on the verge of finding out how much my heart needed to be in it to finish. Any power in my life was leaking away, as I nursed my babies, stayed up nights and wobbled through my days folding laundry, doing dishes, and drying tears of little ones. I felt my dream slipping through my wet fingers. My husband was supportive of my writing career and this helped a great deal with my continuing to go to classes, while I left my babies a few hours with a nanny. As much as I wanted to write, I secretly wanted to find some corner space to sleep in; the loss of sleep for me was the most challenging part of being a mother, unless you recognize the patience, love, and genuine kindness that you need to present to everyone while you are completely exhausted and just trying to remember why it all matters. This larger lesson, though difficult, helped me to see what I was capable of, and a tiny hint of recognition of the warrior who lived inside of me began to show. My husband continued to cheerlead my writing; being a creative and working in film himself, he understood this part of me and admired it. However, we had many struggles and faced opposing core values that broke our marriage apart daily. This heaviness on top of the heaviness of my past was about to drown me all together.

Can you come home to yourself if you stay inside the storm?
During my childhood I learned to face the storm quite well, the earth storms that is, but the storms of human life showed me just how fragile we can be. Despite my commitment to writing, the emotional turmoil of this time moved me further away from my unique self and further away from my voice. When I approached the blank page in this state, writing became the barbed-wired fence again, tearing me apart. I was splitting in two, trying to make my marriage work and trying to fit in, instead of aiming to stand up and stand out by saying *this is not who I am.*

In such moments, time does slow down, it's an aching-of-the-heart time, so bitter that the conditioned inclination is to run from it… but like a bouncy ball, it keeps springing back to hit us in the face. It's not fair to young children to be in that life. I know. I once was the young child in that life, caught in the crossfire of my parents' bitter war while they danced around their own inner demons hurting one another. I had to claim a different life, a new path, so I stopped and dropped all my dreams and walked out of both my home and my marriage. It was August 1st, another August in my life proving to be a time of change for me. The transition was marked by divorce, a blur of nights with my face buried in my pillow crying, feeling like a failure, letting go of the dream of family that I'd envisioned. With it I also let go of my book. For six months I didn't write a word, my voice again paralyzed. In this whirlwind of suffering and crawling back to myself, I also had a baby and a toddler to care for. Looking into big, round, sparkling eyes and chubby cheeks of these little people I had created forced me to see the realness in this human experience. I had forgotten that my early years prepared me for just this, to seek the realness in what it means to be human.

I had to try, to risk failing, to get up, and listen to my inner voice taking one step forward at a time. The soul knows if we are willing to listen. It wasn't a fast pace forward; it was a long, slow walk toward my future. I crawled on many days, wept on many nights, and slowly began to find myself in the midst of my life's rubble. My story was there too, waiting for me.

I had to start thinking and living for myself. *What did this look and feel like?* I wasn't yet a bird flying free, but I started to believe that *it was possible, the dream of being who I truly am, it was possible.* The sunlight broke through the early morning as I woke in a new place. I started to write. Writing became the bridge, the gateway to awareness in looking at old patterns and beliefs, along with developing a new mindset for strength and courage. I took up more writing classes and went to workshops on developing craft. I listened from the inside to find my voice. It was painful to leave my children, as we now had split custody, but I found the gift in even this separation. I now had just a little time to work on healing myself and becoming a writer. I started to breathe again, connecting back to my earlier years of being in the present moment while riding my horse through the woods. I slept at night and woke with purpose. I was determined to finish my book. Writing is so much about being able to connect to the present moment, whether it's a past moment or the actual experience taking place.

With the little time I had, I flew to the Oregon coast and stayed right next to the sea, where I watched the waters rush in and out on a damp foggy beach. It was the soul calling I needed to hear, to be in the deep woods of the Pacific Northwest, to be in the wind, on the sand, and next to old driftwood washed up on the shore. To just be. I gave myself the freedom to write whatever I wanted. This was a newfound wisdom: write for the sake of writing. Write to have a relationship with myself, write to express myself, and *then* write to tell my story. Who has this much time? It was a new mindset entirely I was developing. Simultaneously I was learning more and more about the untouchable craft of writing, with Jennifer Lauck, who was known for her Zen teachings on the craft of writing memoir. Only it wasn't so untouchable; it included many elements of information that had to be integrated and articulated through my voice.

I started to see right away that there were two sides to this process of writing: understanding the mechanics of craft and the whole other side that involved facing fear, cultivating mindset, becoming aware of emotions, and processing our story. I organically knew how to write a scene, because I lived and breathed *being in the moment* throughout my childhood, when I slept under trees and felt the naked sky touch my skin during summer months. But all this evaded me when I tried to approach it from a headspace. I got what my teachers were saying, but no one ever talked about heart-space and out of nowhere I'd get writer's block. I'd write something good and connected, and then I'd overthink it and whittle it down to a few lines that had no rhythm. I was starting to get it, this disconnect from head to heart, the inner critic taking over, and the emotional body screaming to be heard, as part of the process to writing emotionally connected narrative. To find my rhythm and my unique voice I'd needed to step completely outside of that box, the one I had created earlier in my life, the box that left me feeling inadequate, the one that said, "There is only one right way to be a writer."

Stepping outside the box meant going home. And going home may mean something entirely different for you, but for me it was my spiritual connection to the land and the loss that I needed to come face to face with. This meant going back to the woods of my childhood and back to all those feelings I felt about Mom and Dad. Yes, there was a deep internal well filled with dripping sap from all the piñon trees of my childhood, but I no longer feared crawling my way through it. I no longer feared getting stuck there. I was reconnecting to the light that feeds the soul and the soulful child who lived inside of me. I stayed with her, she stayed with me, and we learned to enter the story through the heart. I was amazed, surprised, and filled with tears to learn that my very own life that I once thought of as a disadvantage had prepared me to be a writer.

Finding my voice meant speaking my truth.

Oh, it sounds so simple, but as you are transitioning from trauma to healing and from healing to empowerment, your truth is being learned just as you are being born again. Fear accompanies each word, spoken and written, each decision, the learning to say no, to set boundaries where there have been none before. Becoming a writer was a new relationship with myself, one I deeply needed; the soul-deep communication was an absolute necessity for me to finally be me. Every word I wrote counted. This was not a frivolous act of putting words on paper: it was my life, my truth, my need to convey all the pieces of myself and draw them back together inside of me, after years of brokenness. My reader would feel my very blood and tears in my words as they read my book.

It was this level of connection that broke me through to my authentic voice. The real me. From this place I was able to give birth to myself as a writing coach to support others who might feel lost wandering in a dry desert, while desperately seeking their own truth like their need for *just one* glass of water. They would need someone to come close and see them, to witness all the wear and tear on their face and beneath the surface, to invite them in for a cup of tea, to teach them the love of words, rhythm, and soul expression. I had done it for myself and now I knew I could do it for others. The seven-year-old was alive inside of me, on a new journey of trusting all of her gifts.

Even the child who walks barefooted through sunshine, in love with the silhouette of her father, grows up. All the foundational pieces of her childhood follow her right into adulthood. For the first time, I had moved on from making a relationship with a man my most prized, desired, and fought after part of my life. Since I was sixteen, this had been my pattern: find the cutest guy in the room and when he loves me then I will be someone. I wasn't aware of how deep this subconscious pattern was threaded through my being. Just when I was about to get a hold of old patterns and had the feeling it was all going to be okay, the black and gray clouds rolled in from the north. That desperate feeling I'd had of stopping time that day I took my daughter Sofia to visit my father came and went, like ocean waves rolling out to the sea.

And one day it all stopped, all of life, it stopped. I got the call that my father had died, alone, on the mountain. Someone had found his body. I was a certain "me" before this news hit and a different "me" after.

News of my father's death hit hard in my gut. The very core of my existence shifted, the earth tilted over and spun 'round, my body felt ill, and I wanted to get time back. Then a new truth started to climb its way up from my belly; a new warrior was born in the midst of my grief.

At first, I couldn't see this and it felt like I was drowning. I stopped writing and had to give all my attention to getting out of bed, breathing, making food, and eating it. On some days, I had to lay and stare out the window. Evenings brought the most sadness and the most solace, as I watched the doves fly past in a golden light. "Oh, Dad, it's you," I'd whisper. He sang all the time about the doves. Grief turned over and over inside of me like the sea, a remembrance of the sound of my father's guitar strumming rolled over me along with the waves of loss.

The soul knows and this time round I was in touch with my soul. I never let go of my story; it was brewing inside of me. I wished for things to be different, for my father to be alive... I was in the process of forgiving him when he died. *I was coming home to him.*

Spiritually his death helped me to be a better writer, to dig deeper, to search every corner of lost self and bring it forth. After he was gone, I wrote the hard parts of my story, the parts I'd resisted, the parts I'd wanted to shove in a closet somewhere. I wrote and wrote until the last page, the last period. I let my story go just as I'd let his spirit fly into the wind. There were no more August days standing on the hilltop together. He had flown north, and I'd found my compass to guide me while staying here on earth.

In a short span of time, I had lost my husband through divorce, my father through death, and soon after that my paternal grandfather. Three of the most important men in my life were gone. I sat with my grief over and over, and I continued to lead others through soul-deep writing.

Helping others write their pain out onto paper gave me great purpose, focus and deliverance from my own sorrow. I was beginning to see that we were all in this together, this process of facing fear, in both life and in becoming writers. We were walking each other home. I leaned into my mother, so grateful for her presence. She was still alive and together we were a transcendent team making every moment count. For the first time, I felt the strength in being a woman to its full capacity. I became filled with feminine strength I never knew was there—I was capable of taking care of myself, becoming myself fully, and leading others. The box I'd put myself in as a woman had burst wide open. So often as a child I'd wanted to be a boy. Cowboy stories taught me it was a boy's world and besides that, I had four strong brothers and a very masculine father. With the departure of my three strongest male figures, the gifts of being feminine were just starting to open up to me. It was at this time that I met someone. A man. My world was about to shift.

I felt just good enough to strap on my boots and go out into the world. I felt just good enough to smile every now and then. I was beginning to love my life and open my heart just a little when I met Steve, which was one of my favorite guy names. It was February 3rd, right in the brisk of winter. We talked on the phone for three weeks before we had our first date. For hours on end, I'd lay on the floor in my living area next to a burning fireplace listening to his voice on the other end of the line. I grew fond of this voice and we connected on all fronts of life. We had both endured divorce and loss, and had strong roots in the love of nature, God, music, and being raised in a small town. I read him aloud pieces of my memoir over the phone, which still shocks me till this day. *What was I thinking?* I wasn't thinking. The soul knows.

On our first date we met and shared a piece of cheesecake at a local café. He was tall, 6'1" with a muscular build, broad shoulders and strong hands. His hands stood out to me and reminded me very much of my father's working hands. But there was nothing like his eyes, a deep blue with kindness pouring from them. He was a gentle giant unlike anyone I'd been in relationship with. After hours of talking, he walked me to my SUV. We stood under a black sky with a few stars peeking through. It was cold and I clasped my hands together to stay warm. He then pulled me into his chest with a deep hug. No kiss, one hug. We embraced and time stopped. I felt glued to him, an energetic pull like I'd never experienced. Pulling away from him felt like prying apart two magnets. We looked at each other. "Good night," we both said and walked away.

On our second date, we kissed. This kiss lasted two hours, but still it was only kissing. We both agreed that time was an important factor in true intimacy. It was a new experience of intimacy, of a man putting my needs before his own desires, giving of his heart openly, and communicating deeply. I was still grieving the loss of my father and felt emotional often.

About four months into dating, we came back to my house after dinner. We stood in the kitchen talking, our exchange of dialogue often finishing each other's sentences, the clock on the wall ticking behind him, and out of nowhere I burst into tears. I wanted to cover them up and hide, as in my experience with men they just never knew what to do with my tears. I felt the need to protect men from my feelings and protect myself from their response. In this moment of wanting to pull away, Steve grabbed me and pulled me into his chest, my head falling right below his neck and perfectly at his heart. Then he said these words: "The only thing you need to know about crying is that it should be done on my chest."

I really couldn't believe the words I was hearing. I couldn't believe there was a man with a strong masculine side that also held such tenderness. At the same time, I found myself sinking deeper and deeper into him. I was falling into the arms of love like floating in a warm ocean, slowly drifting toward a truer version of myself while being held by a man.

This moment marked a new beginning for me and for us. We were bonded in true love and Steve called me his soul mate. I had a hardwired, life-experience kind of resistance to love being a lasting event for me. I found myself pushing back at his idea of us as soul mates.

"There's no such thing, ya know," I'd throw my words at him in my fiery way. He would grin at me and step in for a hug. The more I understood this dance of love, the deep connection, the vulnerable communication, the showing up and owning your pain, sharing your truth and your life in front of another person, the more I came to respect and love Steve. Our lives are imperfect, and we struggle to balance it all, co-parenting with exes, juggling finances, loving our children, and trying to find new meaning for family in a whole different way than we had imagined. Almost five years into our relationship, we have faced many trials and still we are finding new ways to connect and be in love. We make time for our relationship. We take walks into the evening sunset; we dance in the kitchen to country music; we dream, play, and struggle together. When things get hard, as they sometimes do, we lean into each other, instead of pulling away. This has been one of my greatest lessons from Steve: learn to lean in, be vulnerable, show up fully, and embrace all sides of love. We lead retreats together, write together, and give birth to our greatest visions for healing the planet, together. This love has allowed me to be in love and be myself. Looking back, I now know that finding my voice truly was the beginning of a new life.

It was August, yet again. The air in New Mexico was still warm but a perfect breeze caressed the sidewalk every afternoon. I had made it a priority to take afternoon walks, to stop editing a client's work, to turn off the phone and computer, and go for a jaunt, slow and easy, feeling the wind. I rounded the corner a few blocks from home and the soft wind picked up as a golden light streamed through the streets, the trees, and the Sandia Mountains in the distance. I had felt this feeling bubbling up before and here it came, another God moment. I stopped in the street and wept. Gratitude swept over me for the response I was receiving from readers of my book and the feeling of voice sounded inside of me. Then came the spiritual message from beyond: "Every woman can reconnect to the light that feeds the soul and awaken to her voice."

Voices. Another hit landed in my chest. What about doing a book called, VOICES, where every woman tells her story and comes home to finding her voice? The golden rays of the sun held me while standing in the street; it was the same sun that soaked into my body at age seven when I stood on the hill with my hero, my dad. And this was the moment that I remembered that actual memory. The memory of how I had felt the wind alongside my father, and how I had seen those dark clouds roll in as I turned to face the storm. Time stood still and in seconds, minutes, the story was already taking shape on the page, the entire opening scene of this story flashed before my eyes. The feeling was overwhelming. In that moment, I believed the message that had echoed from beyond the mountain tops during my childhood: *"One day you will leave this land and become the greatness you were meant for."*

We—my retreat team and I, my brother Nye and my love, Steve—led the first VOICES Writer's Retreat one year later, in the month of August. The three of us together create a symbiotic balance of masculine and feminine through our leadership and service; from food as medicine, to yoga and writing as a soul-deep communication, there is a learning and a mind-body-spirit nourishment in every part of our retreats. The invitation for women to gather to tell their stories became a sacred journey, one filled with tears, hopes, and a returning to one's past through a new narrative, a new lens of seeing oneself and one's story with clarity, compassion, and vision. The context would support women to show up fully and so purely as themselves that the resulting anthology could only support and impact others' lives for the better. The bond that formed through the breaking of bread at the same table, through the rise and fall of voices coming to life on paper and throughout the room, it was tangible. You could have reached out with your physical hand, touched, and held the energy of love, compassion, and courage. Every woman birthing her story shined as a unique embodiment of feminine presence, a warm box waiting inside of the heart, waiting to be opened. As I gazed around the circle and met each storyteller eye to eye, heart to heart, I quietly wondered, *How was I so lucky to be chosen to help women birth their stories, how was I chosen for the task of midwife?*

My heart leapt with its answer in an instant: *I had listened when my soul called me to co-create the Voices Movement.* I listened even when I was scared, doubtful, and sometimes worried that I may not be strong, or capable enough to birth this book in such a unique manner, alongside these amazing, insightful, and purpose-driven souls. Each woman has become a spoke in my windmill that gently harnesses the power of our greater shared vision for impacting humanity one voice at a time. Facilitating these retreats has been a life-affirming, spiritual experience. I feel honored, blessed and filled with passion and purpose as I introduce you to each of these women carrying the torch of the *Braving It All Story,* knowing it will light your path as you read.

This book can be read from beginning to end like any other, or used as an inspirational guide to be opened to any one woman's story at a time, allowing her message to guide, lead, and inspire you to go after your dreams, to bring comfort and compassion to areas of pain and loss, and to encourage you to seek the power in your own voice.

Bestselling author of *The Soulful Child: Twelve Years in the Wilderness* and intuitive writing coach Chloe Rachel Gallaway is the founder of The Winged River Writer and the VOICES *Braving It All* Book Series. As a mentor and facilitator of the writing process, Chloe is unlike anyone in the industry. She combines her experience of growing up in the wilderness with her training in mindfulness tools and literary writing techniques to deliver a powerful process of self-transformation and empowerment through writing. She helps her people move from fear to courage, and from doubt to confidence, in mastering the dance between craft and intuition. For detailed information about her book writing programs and retreats, visit ChloeRachelGallaway.com.

Soulcraft of a Starseed

Karen Dorey Lovelien, TBG

"You are here for new knowledge to come in,
Living Light to be known, for love to be clear."
—Karen Dorey Lovelien, TBG

Totally relaxed, in fact dozing, I was curled up in a window seat when the captain came on to announce, "Prepare for landing." I could feel my heart begin to quicken. As the wheels were lowered, I took in the panorama of New York City's night sky lit up like a fictional movie set. It stole my breath! The reality was setting in. I was a twenty-year-old senior at South Dakota State University, and the adventure of a lifetime was about to begin. Arriving at the massive JFK International Airport in the dark of night, I rummaged through my carry on and found the small piece of paper with the address of my destination. Walking outside, I stepped into the bright yellow taxi at the front of a long cab line. The driver greeted me with a nod and helped with my bags. Small talk was limited for I realized he knew very little English; I gave him the small slightly crumpled piece of paper. It was at that point that my thoughts began to wander, comprehending that I did not know anyone within nearly 1,500 miles.

I was alone. All I had was the address of the dorm across the street from the school I was about to attend. My heart now pounded. *Can I trust him to take me there? Will he take the most direct route?* The drive seemed to take forever. Suddenly, a profound peace came over me; I remembered what my father told me just before I left home when I'd asked him, "Are you nervous about your daughter traveling alone to New York City?" His reply came with an assurance of confidence in my ability to navigate my life alone in a strange environment.

"No, I don't worry, because it is *you!*"

In that moment there was a resonance, a realization that I had not known before. My father could finally see *me*.

I felt as if I was sprouting wings!

I was born Karen Dorey, the third of four girls, into a family rooted in music. My early years were spent in and out of the hospital with pneumonia or bundled up so I could hardly walk, like the younger brother in the movie *Christmas Story*. South Dakota winters were brutal with blustery winds and mounds of snow that seemed like mountains, plowed high on each side of the icy roads. No matter the weather, there was one priority that could not be missed, church every Sunday. Dad was the high school and senior choir director; Mother directed the children's choir. Blizzards became a necessary adventure. We, the three older girls close in age, would be bundled up and pulled on a sled down the middle of the vacant streets in the blistering wind for the four-block trip to church.

My sisters Brenda, the oldest, Kristi, second, and I began singing together in harmony, like the Lennon Sisters, when I was about seven years old. Our youngest sister, Gretchen, came nearly eight years after me. God gave her the solo voice of an angel. When we came home after church, the kitchen was filled with the aroma of beef, pork and vegetables slowly roasting all morning in the same pan, creating caramelized drippings that went into the most flavorful gravy. Sometimes cleaning up after Sunday's lunch would take hours; we were singing in harmony and creating new lyrics to old songs while Mom and Dad were *napping* upstairs.

Our vocal training often took place at the dinner table. I remember a time when I asked, "Please pass the peas" with my little-girl high-pitched voice. Dad responded with a deep tone of authority, "Speak from your diaphragm with breath in your tone. Put your hand on your belly so you can feel the vibration when you speak." Again, this time with my hand on my belly and a much lower more full tone, I would ask with a slow hesitation on each word, "Please.. pass.. the.. peas." The cold peas arrived only after my first lesson in how to properly use my voice. This gift has stayed with me the rest of my life!

Looking back at our childhood, we were truly blessed. Our parents supported our creativity, allowing us to often literally tear up the house for props to create our explorations. Backyard dramas/plays/performances were hits in the neighborhood with bed sheets on the clothes lines as curtains. As the youngest at the time, I would always be assigned the most minor part, which was OK with me, for I was happy to be included. I was the student when playing school and the dog when singing "How Much is the Doggie in the Window?" My one line, "Woof, Woof."

While studying music at Concordia College, our dad discovered a nearby school for the blind. Legally blind and eyesight failing, he chose to also take the courses there to become a piano tuner and technician. He would often take one of us with him to work in people's homes as his "helper," giving us the job of sorting the colored paper levelers that fit under the piano keys. The sound of him tuning by ear is imbedded in my memory. I always knew when the pitch was perfect. Little did I know this was training for my life that was just beginning to unfold.

Our parents opened a music store with Mother managing the business side. She seemed to be in a hurry at all times managing the home, children and business. Mother always looked professional in a dress and high-heeled shoes. People would comment that they knew it was Evelyn coming with the fast-paced signature *ca-click, ca-click* of her heels. Someone once added, "I thought she was being chased!"

Beginning as far back as I can remember I had a recurring dream that continued into adulthood. I would walk off a cliff that seemed like the depth and expansiveness of what I now know as the Grand Canyon, free-falling with my stomach in my throat. I would always wake up just before I landed. The dream took many forms as my life unfolded. When I started to drive, I would drive off the cliff and wake before the crash at the bottom.

As a young child I felt like a fragile China doll, protected so I wouldn't break. Starting kindergarten at four years old I struggled the first few years, needing remedial help. My parents never expected much of me and I learned to make it through high school with average grades without bringing books home like the other kids. Leaving home, I surprised everyone when I was consistently on the Dean's List in college.

I now can see that parents' perceptions can create a person's reality or, as in my case, early perceptions gave me an unconscious reason to prove them wrong. When I was in my early teens, I remember my parents talking to friends about their older daughters, "Brenda is an accomplished artist. She will be famous someday. Kristi is the intelligent one. She could read at three years old. Karen, well (long pause and deep breath as if to be looking for the right word) Karen, she's do-*mes*-tic." The word domestic would come as a sigh with their voices dropping off at the end, as if in disappointment. As I heard that word, the core of my being would reel as if it were silently screaming, "Not me!" Looking back, I can see that I was the one that would tidy up and try to keep everything in the home in balance when life got chaotic. Living at home, I was quiet, an observer of life. Some people referred to me as "invisible." I had pulled back from being myself, for I felt different. Life seemed like a competition and I didn't want to play that game.

At nearly fifteen, I experienced what has sadly come to be seen in our culture by many as a *rite of passage,* a sexual assault while spending the night at my favorite aunt's home. She would leave for work at 5 a.m. I was sleeping in the guest bedroom, dreaming about meeting a boy that I had seen working in a field next to Bible Camp. He was unique, Native American and really cute. I was shy but my heart wanted to connect, to flirt. Then the dream turned weird. As if part of the dream, I felt someone was in bed with me, pressing his genitals against me, hand in my pajamas, fondling me. Waking suddenly, I leaped to my feet realizing it was my uncle. Not able to scream, for I was caring for his baby granddaughter then sleeping in the same room, I held my scream inside, grabbed a bottle of formula and the baby and locked the two of us in the bathroom. I sat on the floor trembling for hours, rocking the baby as if I were rocking the innocent little girl within me. I wasn't sure if he was still in the house. When I finally needed to get food for the baby, I opened the door and discovered he was gone. *What was I to do?* My thoughts went rampant. If I told anyone, it would break my aunt's heart. My dad would probably kill him. I stayed silent for over twenty years!

This silent scream locked inside of me didn't go away. Finally, I was able to tell my mother. Her response was, "Boys will be boys." Overcome with sadness, I continued to keep the secret and carried the damage of that encounter for years to come. There did come a time in my healing I wrote my uncle a letter telling him the impact of what he had done and the concern I had for his six young granddaughters. His response, "How can you hurt a man in his eighties this way? I was drinking at that time."

In so many ways, time has not changed the attitudes in our culture. It is amazing that now when women in greater numbers are shifting from silence to using their voices, boys can still be seen as boys and the perpetrator is often cast as the victim. As sexual assault survivors, women and men, continue to speak up, they are creating what feels like a virtual tidal wave of greater awareness and higher consciousness, cleansing and healing the long-held pain of so many.

At twenty years old, I woke in New York City feeling the excitement inside of me quicken with the energy on the street outside. Looking down from my fifth-story window, I could see people moving, weaving together like cattle urgently aiming toward their dinner. These crowds were merging and quite seamlessly weaving through the oncoming pedestrian traffic. In the street the predominant color of the yellow taxies blended with cars, bicycles, and because we were near the garment district, people pushing carts of merchandise. There I was in my final semester in college, in a dorm for the first time since my freshman year, with college students from around the country. We came together in a condensed honor study program in Fashion Design and Merchandising at the Fashion Institute of Technology.

It only took a couple of weeks for me to realize that the walls of this new world were beginning to close in on me. The students from all over the country in the same program were great, yet we all had the same schedule. We would go to class together, have lunch together, come back to the dorm together. My breathing was becoming shallow. I realized that I was a stranger in a foreign land when my insides would reel as men on the street would grab my long blonde hair and pucker up to make the sounds of kisses at me. I could no longer share my open heart, the love I had known, or look people on the street in the eye. I felt I needed to look down, put a bubble around me and keep moving with the rest of the cattle herd, so as to not attract attention.

I realized how important my time alone had become growing up in South Dakota. The reality hit: At home there were 10 people for every square mile versus New York City with 25,000 people per square mile. I began my search for a place to be alone, other than the bathroom. One day on the campus I discovered a door to a classroom building that had a sign, "Do Not Enter." So I entered and climbed the tall stairwells to the roof. Finally alone, I could breathe! I could have a bigger perspective. I could find *me* again! When no one was looking, I made a daily trip to my private spot in the midst of the seeming chaos of the city. It was here that I knew I was OK within my inner landscape, no matter what was happening all around me.

I graduated from my university in South Dakota and stayed in New York City, receiving my diploma in the mail. After a few jobs it didn't take long to realize that I had gone as far as I could in my chosen field. I went to a headhunter with a list of qualities I desired in both a company and a position.

What did I love about the work I had done? I loved to be given responsibility and the independence to create the way I would achieve the results. I was willing to step out of the comfort zone of the industry in which I was trained. More importantly, I desired an organization that had integrity, was entrepreneurial, that supported creativity and was willing to take risks. After interviewing at several companies, I accepted a job at the only one that seemed to fit, a large financial services company. A global company, it was, at the time, managed in an entrepreneurial manner. I was encouraged to be creative and take risks. I climbed the ranks quickly, always grooming at least one person to take my place so I could continue to learn and grow within the organization.

Not realizing I might be stepping off a cliff, I scheduled an interview for a position in (what I learned later was) the most old-style masculine dominated group in the organization. In the meeting I felt relaxed yet a bit queasy inside. The interview seemed to be going well when my inquisitor suddenly stood up, leaned over his desk emphatically speaking, only inches from my face, "Are – you – tough – enough?"

What could I do or say? It felt silly and inappropriate. My natural response came with a chuckle, "I guess you will have to find out."

He hired me and I said, "Yes."

Little did I know exactly what he meant.

Married with a two-year-old son, I began this new job only to discover a month in that I was unexpectedly pregnant. My heart silently screamed, "Not now. Not in *this* job!" The realization swept over me: that my staff and I needed to produce results quickly to gain credibility. I was grateful that my pregnancy did not show and with my fashion background, I thought I could dress in a way that would keep it a secret.

One day, five months into my pregnancy I decided to tell my new boss. My heart wide open, proud of the little one alive within me yet nervous about the reaction, I shared my news with my boss.

Barely able to get the words out of my mouth, I was interrupted by him in an uncharacteristic leap of excitement, "When are you due?" I told him as he darted out of the room yelling my due date in the lavishly decorated corridor lined with mahogany doors to the offices of the president of the corporation and his all-male senior management. Still sitting at his desk, I could hear the men running out of their offices, hooting, laughing and congratulating the winner. I crumbled inside as the very core of dignity began to unravel with the realization they had been betting on how quickly I had become pregnant. My joy in bearing the treasure of womanhood had been stripped away. I silently left the room entering the corridor to witness the men exchanging money at my expense. No congratulations or acknowledgement. The elevator opened and with tears streaming down my cheeks; I quietly went home. I was overcome with sadness and in my solar plexus, there was a burning ember of anger ready to ignite into a raging flame. Was I angry at them or angrier at myself for not being their definition of *tough enough* to take their blatant degradation and lack of respect? I considered taking action but I decided to continue quietly working at least until I gave birth.

Marchelle, our sweet baby girl, arrived early about a week before a scheduled C-section.

Upon return to work six weeks later, I was asked to interview someone, for what I was told was a job under me. I did the interview, made the recommendation, and she was given *my* job. One more time, I remained silent.

No longer a China doll needing to be protected, I needed to take action. I began a search for a job transfer to California. The timing for a smooth transition did not happen quickly, so I found another job in New York in the same company. Two years into this *temporary* job, I was once again standing near the edge of the cliff. In this version of my dream, I slipped off the cliff, spun around and grabbed the cliff's edge. Hanging by my fingertips, I clung to the edge with my full body hanging into the deep canyon. Waking up with my body stiff attempting to be in control and still clinging to the edge, I found myself not really sure I wanted to let go of the life I had known.

Although limited, there were a few opportunities in California that would possibly be opening up. My husband and I made a choice to move. We sold our home. It was Halloween of 1980, the used truck we purchased for the move was packed. We took the risk; I left my employer to drive west. We were in a change of seasons in our lives just as autumn was in full expression. Arriving about a week later, the air was different in California. I could once again breathe.

Within a month after arriving in California, I was offered a job in another department in the same company as in New York. It felt different; I was three-thousand miles from the implosive energy at headquarters. Once again hired, I was able to have my years of service bridged so I did not lose benefits. It felt like I was stepping forward, yet there was a lingering uneasy feeling inside that seemed to know what I could not see.

In California I, once again, felt freedom and the ability to be creative. I loved this job, for I finally felt it fit the qualities I had expressed to the headhunter so many years earlier.

By 1990 the corporation with which I had spent fifteen years, took a severe nose dive into financial difficulty. It felt as if the entire corporation was imploding. Not only were departments competing with other departments for resources, people in fear of losing their jobs began to compete with colleagues next to them. People were holding secrets rather than working in collaboration. Much like the separation and destructive competition that is happening in the world today, it felt as if the walls, the basic structure on which the corporation was built, were coming apart.

In 1991, I was experiencing great loss while going through a divorce, I was grieving the passing of both my father and of Robert, my twenty-seven-year-old male administrative assistant. Robert had been the glue that held our department together during the dysfunction of the organization. Again, overcome with loss and the collapsing of integrity within the organization, I felt a deep void in my solar plexus that I knew was out of my ability to control.

My immediate supervisor in New York had a new female boss that had just joined our corporation. She decided to hold a team-building retreat in Arizona to boost morale. About fifty of us flew in from around the country for what felt like an inappropriate, no-expense-spared ho-down. The first night began with an outdoor cocktail party to meet our new leader. The country-western music was turned up loud with a song that served as a booming drum roll introducing what was about to come around the corner into view. Decked out in flashy red, white and silver cowgirl gear: skirt, vest, hat, boots and spurs, our new leader was riding a huge white bull into the party. This bull could win an award for his beyond-enormous masculine power symbol. I am surprised he didn't trip over it.

Helped off the bull, the first order of business of our new leader was to call to the front probably the most vulnerable woman in the crowd, a boss to many of the people there. One of the men handed our cowgirl leader a stool as she directed/demanded the woman to sit on the stool and *milk* the bull. The *milk-maid* was visibly shaken and crumbling inside; she resisted as her boss insisted. At first this drew immediate hooting laughter by a few, which then turned into a ripple of uncomfortable *ha has*, moans and sighs. My heart sank to my feet with this public intentional humiliation of another businesswoman through use of a sick sexual joke and an attempt to strip her of her ability to have choice. This was, for me, a new milestone for a corporate *leader*, male or female, in order to make her role known to everyone present, using old-style masculine domination. The silence of everyone present about this episode was deafening. It was as if the culture had groomed us for this.

Back to work, numb and focused on results, I found myself being asked from New York to lie to my employees and to my senior officer contacts in the corporations with which we were doing business. Because of our company's financial difficulty, New York operations could not, at times, deliver on what was promised. I began to walk a tightrope by finding ways to handle each situation without lying. At the same time, we continued to produce fierce results so headquarters left us alone. As time went by it became much more difficult to stay upright in my high-wire act balancing on one foot at a time.

Not realizing the impact, I had set aside my own spirituality for eighteen years of marriage by agreeing to raise our children Jewish. I could not convert but I felt it important to have one primary teaching for the children. We observed the Jewish holidays and had a Christmas tree.

Something that I could not explain was beginning to stir inside of me. I drove myself to a church for the first time in years. It was a small local spiritual center. I sat down and as soon as the music began, I started sobbing inside as tears began to flow. I could not hold back the explosion of additional emotion that was ready to burst forth, so I turned to the door, held back my desire to run and walked slowly to my car with tears streaming down my face. It was the music, I missed it so much. Spiritual music and my personal connection to God had been set aside for so many years. I didn't realize that I had experienced this sadness for so long. In the car I let the floodgates open, wailing until I found a place of calm then remained quietly crying and reflecting on my journey and on how much I loved Yom Kipper each year. As my son and husband went to Temple, Yom Kippur became a sacred day in the dark. I stayed home with my daughter. Silence, sweet silence, as I entered the inner chamber of my heart, praying, listening, feeling, meditating. After people left the service, I left my car, went back in to the church, spoke to the minister and received a beautiful prayer for peace of mind and clarity on my path.

Like a magnet pulling on my heart, I soon found a new spiritual home with the teachings of Michael Bernard Beckwith. I made a clear choice to reconnect to my roots. Listening to the inspirational music and his empowering messages, I often shed tears of remembrance and joy. Once again waking up to a part of me that longed to be nurtured. My heart was cracked open. I felt like a child eager to feel it all, realizing I had become numb barely able to put words to my feelings. It was in my daily meditative practice that I began to discover I had an inner guidance system all along.

In grief of the passing of my administrative assistant, Robert, I attended a heart-opening retreat near Prescott, Arizona. On the last day a traditional Lakota Sweat Lodge experience lifted me to another level of spiritual activation. I sat opposite the entrance, the hottest spot in the lodge. The sweat lasted four hours with no opportunity for exit. The rounds of prayers were powerful. I could feel the presence of ancestors. The heat continued to build as I became more consumed with the energy of the prayers and chants.

At one point I put my hand on the ground behind me and felt cold, rich, black soil just under the skin of the teepee. I scooped up a hand full and as if on autopilot my hand came to my face. My body deeply inhaled the fresh scent of Mother Earth, moist from a recent rain shower. My lungs expanded and my arms lifted straight up and began to spin clockwise. The spin changed with each person's prayer, slowly for some and a rapid, almost anxious spin for others. I gave credit to the ancestors as if they were spinning me. No longer hot, I was transported, becoming an integral part of the cosmos.

Leaving the sweat lodge, I was surprised that when I stood up, my entire body continued to spin clockwise. Standing, I spun. When an elbow was on a table my forearm would spin. A loose foot would spin. I could not stop it. Certain that this was just happening at the retreat, I was surprised that I spun all the way home. It was not within my control and I could not explain it. At home I spun the most when I was centered or in meditation. My sister, Kristi, became angry, then concerned I was losing my faculties.

To me, it felt authentic and powerful.

I could see that my body had become a pendulum where my spin could indicate "Yes" or "No" to a question. Feeling the gift, I learned how to ask yes-or-no questions with my heart. I did not know or care who was guiding me; I was a novice. It felt clear and loving. It took about six months for me to *own* this gift, to embody it. The spin became much gentler inside me.

I could not get enough spiritual connection. Soon I enrolled in a spiritual weekend workshop. At the end we were each asked to step to the front to tell the group what we received from the workshop. Even as I stepped forward, I had no idea what I was going to say. Standing in front of the room with fifty sets of eyes waiting for my response, my two hands rose in front of me in tight fists. I looked at my two fists and began to speak, "I realized that I have been living two distinctly separate lives."

Holding up my left fist clinched a bit higher, I shared as the words moved through me with no forethought, "This has been me at home. I have realized that I have not been myself at home (as I opened my left hand). I have recently asked my husband for a divorce, for I can no longer stay in the unhealthy patterns we have created together." Next, my attention was brought to my right fist, tightly clinched. Realizing it represented my life expression at work, I nearly collapsed as I gasped in surprise. My right hand slowly opened wide on its own. My heart began to speak and fresh tears began to flow, "I can now see that I have not been myself at work either." Another loss, the feeling of sadness had been accumulating over the years, like a heavy cloak weighting me down. It was a slow death building each time I had compromised my values, not spoken up or skillfully walked the tightrope. "Yes," I continued, "I now see I have been carrying the weight of profound loss. I have lost everything I have known my life to be. I have lost ME!"

In that moment I could no longer walk the tightrope. I had compromised my long-held strong value of integrity. I needed to tell the truth and find a new path.

Returning to work, I put both feet on the ground, setting my tightrope aside. When asked to do something unethical or out of integrity with my customers or employees, I would offer my boss in New York another way of handling the situation that provided the clarity of the truth and honored everyone involved.

Six weeks later I was suddenly unceremoniously fired. I called my son Aaron to come to help me pack my belongings. As we packed, the sun was setting with hues of coral and purple. The colors were softly moving and blending like a wet fluid water color painting framed in the expansive windows of my fifteenth-floor corner office. In the sunset I could feel the loving presence of Robert from beyond the veil. It felt as if he were telling me a simple yet powerful message, "Step forward and be blessed."

Returning home, I went into my bedroom and collapsed to the floor in prayer, "God, I don't know who I am or why I am here. Show me. Teach me. Use me."

I had no clue. I had been living the so-called American Dream: an eighteen-year marriage, a big corporate job I felt passionate about, a generous salary and two amazing children, a boy and a girl! I became like a bear in hibernation, rarely leaving my room, spending hours, then days turned into weeks, my heart in the deep surrender of my prayer. The power of the unique vibration of heartfelt surrender became real to me. I was not giving up. It felt more like a way of authentically *giving the 'how' to move forward to God.*

Over time with my surrender of each new choice I began to add, "I surrender this and all." Looking back, I realize I have surrendered my entire life to God! What freedom. My need to know I was OK moment to moment shifted into simply knowing I was being blessed. During my hibernation, I was grateful that my sister, Kristi, was living with us and helped support Marchelle, then twelve, and Aaron, sixteen.

Something had happened early one morning while in deep meditation and prayer. What felt like an immersion, a sudden birth into a new reality, the veil to all dimensions of consciousness lifted. I was filled with and surrounded by an unimaginable clarity, pure light. A message from beyond anything I had experienced before came: "Become ease."

My heart full, I replied, "I don't know how."

The response, "Just say *yes* and you will be shown the way."

My choice, "Yes! Yes!" came from my voice sourced directly from the energy of my heart. I could feel it vibrate as frequency into the universe merely with the sound of my voice. Again, I went into deep surrender of my new choice with, "Show me the way."

An energy I had not felt before began to shower over me and move through me. As I let it in, I could feel a penetration of this new frequency into my cells. They began to wake up, alive in a new way.

As I continued to allow it in, to penetrate my very being, spirits of people that had crossed over to the other side showed up and to get my attention, I heard them say, "Hey, Ease!"

Back into prayer, I asked, "What am I to do with them?"

The answer, "Help them in their healing."

Again, I replied, "I don't know how."

The same answer came, "Say yes, and you will be shown."

As they continued to come one by one over time, I surrendered to God *how* to heal each one, and I was guided. I came to realize that we are all vibrational instruments that like sponges have soaked up the frequencies of our history, our family patterns and our environment. My willingness to *become* ease, to actually receive and embody ease, became my first lesson in working with specific frequencies for tuning, aligning and healing myself and others to our true nature. This was a glimpse into what was to become my new reality.

I could feel the purity of the guidance. On some level my soul knew I was finding ME. As time went on, I became more comfortable carrying the energy of ease, I began a journey into the unknown, learning while supporting each spirit that came. Many had left the earth plane, yet had not moved into the Light. In this state of consciousness there is no time. Some had been in this transitional state of consciousness for days and some for years. I was surprised when my grandfather came to me thirty years after he had passed. Because of his beliefs, I asked him if he saw the Light or if he had felt the presence of Jesus.

He immediately snapped back at me, "NO, I will be judged!"

In that moment the most brilliant translucent Light appeared. My heart nearly burst out of my chest. The purity, clarity and soft yet powerful presence was unmistakable. The presence of Christ was with us. There was no judgment, merely an overwhelming nurturing acceptance directed toward Grandpa. A novice, I became a student observing as my grandfather's old perceptions, self-judgments and fears dissolved. With his choice to move into the Light, Grandpa was gently lifted and welcomed by many loved ones.

Although I didn't understand exactly where these twilight visits from people that had crossed over would lead at the time, it was clear that a powerful new way of being was unfolding. It felt new yet seemed to have ancient roots within me. I now see how it led into new modalities of energetic/frequency healing, how to apply them in my own life and share them so others can align with their unique soul imprint and share their gifts in the world.

The profound loss of everything I knew my life to be was a wake-up call like no other. I became committed to discovering more of who I am. Meditation, prayer, and Michael Beckwith's Life Visioning process became my daily practice, asking open-ended questions in meditation, like: *"How can I serve? What is seeking to emerge through me today? What have I not seen?"* The answers came with greater and greater clarity as I personally accepted and embodied this gift. I realized that it is not about accumulating knowledge; rather it is about flowing moment to moment by allowing my heart to feel into the guidance. Rather than judging each step forward with, "Will I be OK?", I began to trust the wisdom of my heart. Conscious choice became my new navigational tool.

I began to work with friends and before long, other people on earth started making appointments for healing. Each time I begin in prayer, in deep surrender to how a session will unfold, and open for guidance. I have learned to begin each day clearing and aligning myself so I can be available for others.

One day while asking the question in meditation, "Who am I?" I was taken back in time to when I was two-and-a-half years old, in the hospital with one of my many early bouts of pneumonia barely able to breathe. Feeling it all in my recollection, it was as if I were in the room as an observer yet with vision from beyond this realm of consciousness. The little me was in a place of struggle when she was suddenly overcome, gasping for air and then in a big sigh she relaxed into a sense of deep peace. It seemed she knew that this was part of why she came here. She was surrounded and filled with the Divine Light I had become so familiar with in my work. As she made her final gasps for air, I watched the exchange. Her spirit was lifted as another Light spirit entered my frail body, as if emerging straight from the stars.

Flooded with emotions of great joy, sadness and grief at the loss of this little *me*, my heart moved in the frequency of what I learned later was *honor,* for the little girl that bravely chose to leave. Filled with love, she shared, **"See, I am still alive! I was on earth for one purpose, to bring you into the world for new knowledge to come in, Living Light to be known, for love to be clear."** WOW! I was overcome with gratitude for the journey of this little one and the clarity of my purpose she shared.

My parents were not in the hospital with me when this happened, but they knew. Although it was not spoken to me, my oldest sister, Brenda, knew. I believe now that is why I felt like a China doll that could break. They were afraid of losing me again.

Witnessing this transition and filled with questions, I began to ask my heart to energetically *honor* the star spirit that had entered my little body. I learned she came directly from the star system Sirius. I surrounded her in Light, for she had just emerged into a foreign land. Realizing I am that Starseed, I asked no questions; somehow, I knew this transition was part of a master plan.

Feeling complete in Southern California, I asked in meditation, "What now?" I was given precise quadrants on a map, longitude and latitude that pointed to Durango, Colorado. I was being asked to be lifted out of my comfort zone. One sunny winter day, Aaron, Marchelle and I went on a trip to explore this new potential destination. The snow-capped mountains welcomed us as if we were coming home from a long journey. The love was clear. I could, once again, receive the gift of a full breath of air, crisp air.

While my children went skiing on the slopes, I was taken on an adventure of discovery meeting people that would prove to be part of my journey, while exploring housing possibilities. The only clue came when I went to Oak Drive in Durango and was told, "You will live here." However, there was nothing for sale or rent on that street.

As I had been taught, I listened to the energy of my heart and said, "Yes" to the guidance of living on Oak Drive, because it felt authentic and right. My heart made the choice, "Yes, this town is home." Yet, I felt it important for my two teens to also have choice. My son, eighteen, decided he would like to stay in LA where their dad lived. My daughter, fifteen, did not want to leave her friends.

We returned to California; I was excited, yet not sure. Many times, over the next few months, when Marchelle and I were driving, we were guided off the freeways in different towns, down streets and stopped under street signs that each read OAK DRIVE! She finally told me she was willing to move because she could *feel* how important this move was. She and I traveled to find a home the following July.

Our one day of house hunting ended when we entered the final of six homes intuitively selected in the MLS book. Upon entry, Marchelle immediately said, "This is the home I saw in a dream." The real estate agent showed us downstairs and as we were ready to go upstairs, the owner came flying around the corner at the top of the stairs.

"What are you doing in my home?!" he blurted.

He had been in the shower. Our agent politely introduced herself and said she was showing us the home. "Our house is not for sale." By then I also knew this was to be our home. I explained we had looked at six houses and we were going to make an offer the next day. His was our first choice and another the second. I asked him to consider it and call the next morning if they were willing to sell.

The owner asked if Marchelle and I could stay to talk. He was curious about the mystical way we ended up in their home. He and his wife had similar spiritual experiences but did not have anyone to talk with about them. They called the next morning, we bought the house, and closed a month later. Their home had been on the market months earlier because they wanted to build a new home. They saw this as a gift and decided to rent while building. We did not know until the closing that our new home was on Oak Drive, another Oak Drive just outside of town. Yes, we were living an adventure in a way we had not experienced before.

A new beginning! A birth, once again into the unknown. A life with no agenda, only possibilities! With this reality, came one last episode of my recurring dream: This time with a running start, I leaped off the cliff into the expanse of the familiar canyon, and just before the free fall began, I sprouted wings! Like a baby bird in its first flight, I flapped my new wings, attempting a sense of control, until I discovered the unlimited flow of air currents that would effortlessly carry me. What freedom. I playfully soared in the canyon, and returned to the top of the cliff.

Waking up, I chose to become a part of the infinite flow of life. Accepting even the unusual movements, tones with inflections that were coming through my voice. I made the choice to accept it all, for it was an authentic part of my training, my journey, of me. Realizing that some people in my new life may not understand and may be uncomfortable around me, I chose to be authentic, not to hide, stay silent or try to govern what I knew could not be stopped. I also did not want to offend people. I surrendered the *how* to do this to Spirit. The sounds moving through me became quieter and the movements less severe. I learned that the more I was comfortable with myself, people were also comfortable with me, for they could feel that what was happening was real.

A fresh start. Time to step forward. I could feel the enormity of what was to come. *How do I begin?* Often taught in symbols, I bought a flip chart, for I had to allow what was moving through to express in a big way. Marker in hand, I drew a huge circle divided into sections like a pie. Each became labeled. Home, Family, Spirituality, Personal Healing, Loving Relationship, Right Livelihood in the world, Finances, Health, Play, etc. I started to write in each piece of the pie, asking myself what I desired. The word *desire* had a texture. It was similar to the way I approached a job search in New York. Back at my pie chart, my desires took the form of qualities of God, i.e. Love, Clarity, Creativity, Joy, Flow, Connection, Wisdom, Freedom, Integrity, Clear Communication. Each section of the pie took its own form. It took me two weeks to feel into each piece of the pie for the clarity of what my heart truly desired.

Since I did not know *how to* create my life in this new way, I created a personal ceremony in a park. A sunny day, I sat enveloped in the embrace of the exposed roots of an ancient oak tree I spoke my desires to Mother Earth with the vibration of my heart, one slice in the pie at a time, choosing "Yes" to each one. My heart then dropped into the familiar frequency of surrender giving my choice to God with, "Show me the way."

When complete, I heard a deep billowing bass voice from beyond, "Now you must *become* what you desire."

With my "Yes" choice to actually become my desires, I was overcome with floodgates of new energy. It felt as if I were standing in the warm sand facing the vast expanse of the ocean. The rhythm of the waves coming in enveloping my feet and ankles, I was being called to go in, go deep into this new unknown.

Wednesday mornings became a special spiritual time. New spiritual friends and I would meet to explore the wonder of nature, to hike, to meditate together. One warm Wednesday while sitting on rocks meditating in a spacious high dessert canyon, I began receiving detailed specifications for what was being called a healthy natural *wall system*. When sharing this, one in our group who was a contractor spoke up. It was Fred who said he had been receiving messages like that for a few years. Over the next several months he and I met to meditate together to see where this would lead.

Knowing construction, Fred would ask questions like, "How do we make this strong?"

The answer came, "Let go of everything you know; this is beyond current knowledge." We learned to listen with new ears, opening to it all.

Soon a friend called Fred saying that she was building a new natural home and in meditation, Spirit told her that Fred had her "wall system." With that prompt, we realized we needed to get serious for we had a potential customer. From an unusual array of natural materials, we created an energetically clear system. It was the beginning of a business partnership based on listening and creating in meditation.

At the same time, I was getting messages that were about helping me expand and grow. A typical message, "Go west at 6 a.m. tomorrow." Feeling into the blessings of the guidance, I would say, "Yes" and go into the deep heart-centered surrender. In order to prepare, I would ask, "Do I take our dog, Shanti?"

With my heart wide open receiving guidance from moment to moment, it felt like I was flowing in a cool freshwater stream not concerned if there were boulders ahead blocking my way. In this flow I knew the current would carry me around any blocks in my path. I was supported in packing, for I didn't know if I would be camping or driving to Sedona or the west coast. On these trips I would meet people that would become instrumental as I continued my journey, learning new life lessons, being shown to serve others, or trained to open or close vortexes in the planet. These adventures helped me realize that I am OK no matter what life brings.

One autumn weekend when golden apricot hues of Aspen trees were in full expression, Santa Fe became my destination. This time Shanti stayed home and I was given help selecting clothes to pack. My first stop was The Arc, a spiritual bookstore, arriving just before closing. I was directed to the bulletin board in the back of the store. My attention went to a specific sign for an all-night Bali-theme party in an industrial area, that very night. As my heart said, "Yes," I became overcome with dread. I took the flyer and I found my way to a comfortable hotel room. My thoughts began to wander. *Go to a party alone?* I knew no one. After leaving my marriage years earlier, I had only one short relationship. I sat in silence feeling into this dilemma. Once again, I decided to follow my heart and go to the party.

Yes, I was stepping into the unknown and becoming more comfortable each time, for my heart was leading the way. Upon arrival I realized it was a costume party in the Bali theme. Much to my surprise I was in costume, a full print skirt, sweater and a scarf that worked beautifully. I knew how to maneuver at a business or spiritual gathering but not in a gathering of mostly singles, perhaps a meat market. As the evening went on, I stepped out on the dance floor alone as many were, initiated conversations with women easily and let men approach me. I even began dancing with men. The shrink-wrap that I had unconsciously wrapped myself in for years, was starting to unwind. I discovered that I didn't need to be like other people; all I needed to do was to *be me*. I relaxed, connected, met new people, danced and played until 2 a.m.

My vibrational healing practice began to grow locally and with distant clients on the phone. A medical doctor from our spiritual community, who was also a client, was planning a weekend spiritual retreat. He asked me to conduct a workshop as part of the event. I agreed knowing it would unfold. As the date became closer, he was preparing the program.

He called to ask, "What is the title after you name?"

I had never been asked that. I asked him to hold on as I stepped back to listen for guidance. The response was TBG so I told the doctor, "TBG."

He then asked, "What does that stand for?" Not knowing, I again paused to listen. The message came, "Taught By God." I shared my new title. The questions ended and he printed it his program. It felt right, actually so true. Now when asked or if it is appropriate, TBG is my title.

Soon I began to feel a strong loving presence with me most of the time. It felt expansive yet grounded. This was a loving presence that was familiar, yet seemed more than I could handle. People would ask me, "Who is that blue energy with you?"

I found myself back at the shoreline, toes in the water. *Was I ready to get my feet wet, let alone dive into love this expansive? Would I be swept away from what felt safe into a possible oceanic riptide?*

I could feel the power of the guidance as it began introducing me to the qualities of the life partner that I chose in my ceremony with Mother Earth.

Working with Fred for the next year, I lived in the mystery while *becoming* more of the qualities I had chosen for my life partner. On my birthday, a chilly overcast October morning, my doorbell rang. I opened it to see Fred holding the most magnificent bouquet of yellow roses I had ever seen. A memory from California flashed before me, I was shown in meditation that my love would come with yellow roses. As he wished me a Happy Birthday and continued speaking about being in a hurry and needing to go to a meeting, I collapsed sobbing in the entry with the door still open. *I knew! He was the blue light.*

Not able to explain why I was crying, I accepted his gift and calmed down long enough for him to leave for his meeting. My thoughts went rampant, "No, not Fred. He is married." I had made a commitment I would not be with a married man for I had seen in others the potential impact on everyone involved. I sat, a steady stream of tears flowing down my face, with the vibrant yellow roses mixed with white baby's breath. Some roses were birthing as new tight buds and others were as wide open in full bloom just as my heart felt in that moment. I decided to keep the secret of my discovery, even from Fred.

Fred and I continued to work and create together. The answers to our open-ended questions were clear and they felt natural and familiar. We learned to trust the guidance. We realized we had arrived together our first time on the planet with a combined purpose. It was clear we were to work together, but were we also to be life partners? In the process we learned to be present moment to moment, to practice non-attachment and to honor ourselves and our families. Fred later shared that his wife had come to him after a reading with a psychic who asked her who was the twin flame that the psychic could see around Fred? For the two of them, this began a difficult journey of sorting out this realization and the impact on their lives. Their marriage ended in divorce and she married a couple years later.

With loving guidance, Fred and I came together in 2002. Fred's love could not be contained, for it expanded far beyond what had been familiar in my life. With each step forward, I let my heart crack open, often causing great physical pain. I learned to be grateful for each new opening; my heart had been locked down too long.

Over the years Fred and I have learned to live into the mysteries of the universe by consciously expanding, learning and growing. Stepping into the unknown became familiar. Surrender has become our friend.

Along with so many light workers at this time on the planet, Fred and I are being called to participate in what clearly feels like a cosmic master plan. Trained by God, we have stepped into the expanse of the ocean together, into our role of bringing multi-faceted high frequencies of Light to the planet. In one of several expressions of this role, we became conduits connecting Sirius Living (life-giving) Light to the core of the planet in over two-hundred locations around the globe. We traveled to many locations in person and others in consciousness, using Google Earth to guide us to specific GPS locations.

It was when we traveled with a group to Nepal in 2013 the purpose of this planetary work became clear. A sacred trek, this journey was to activate the entire planet with higher frequencies of love. The crystalline clarity of the Himalayas moved through the fourteen of us and those in our support crew with each carefully placed step on the rocky trail, often only wide enough for one person at a time. Our voices became unified echoing through the canyons as specific tones, harmonics or joyful song. The sounds, sometimes distant, were tuning our vibrational connection to each other.

Our third day of trekking brought us to the destination for our ceremony, Langtang, a mountain village tucked in and surrounded by towering snowy mountain peaks pulsating a flow of high crystalline frequencies, as if fine-tuning our hearts to the heartbeat of the planet. Our guest house owner, of Tibetan origin, was spinning his prayer wheel chanting in prayer as we arrived, in seeming preparation of the gathering space for our ceremony that evening. In our sacred sound ceremony, we traveled as a unified field of consciousness to a location near us in Tibet, now China. The sound ceremony activated four other key locations of the over two-hundred sites; these four sites then ignited the remaining two-hundred plus sites that had been opened previously. The planet was alive. It felt like the planet itself could breathe! We could feel the spontaneous shift into a higher frequency.

Following the ceremony, the message came that plants and animals would automatically shift. However, in a free-will universe, people would need to *choose* to align with the higher frequencies that are becoming available. Upon our return from Nepal, there was a flood of new online images of unlikely animal species playing with and loving each other. Lions were caring for lambs; historic enemies had become friends.

Beginning in 2009 Fred and I began to receive messages for creating a new power system, a technology to support life on the planet. With clear detailed specifications, we have been taken to the internet to purchase rare materials, many used in aerospace applications. We came to realize that the system we have been creating is a mirror of the heathy functioning of our own bodies. We have been guided to *become* each part of the system in order to receive specifications for that part. Becoming more and more in alignment with the pulse of nature, we now understand our connection to the universe.

As my work with individuals and groups in Soulular Clarity, our vibrational healing practice, continued to grow, it shifted from me *doing* each step of the vibrational healing and alignment as I had initially been taught by Spirit, to simply *allowing* specific frequencies to move through my voice as tones. Similar to when my father was tuning a piano, my voice has become a trained instrument able to release the exact tone and inflection necessary in each situation. This technique has an even broader impact when used with groups in presentations, retreats or workshops. The full body of this work will be released soon. It will include the vibrational technology with unique energetic personal practices and techniques supporting individuals in creating their lives in alignment with their unique soul imprint.

We also lead mystical tours to sacred sites on the planet, each with a specific intention for those participating and/or for the world or the planet.

Our ever-evolving work, with its many expressions, follows Helen Keller's adage, "Life is an adventure or nothing at all." Like small children on an adventure, we move forward into the unknown. When we fall down, we get up, dust off the grit of the journey and look around the next corner to see what new adventure is ready for exploration.

"Life is not a problem to be solved; it is a mystery to be lived. There is nothing that compares to the discovery of who and what we really are and taking responsibility for it."
—Michael Bernard Beckwith

The last twenty-eight years have been a profound spiritual journey dedicated to understanding the mystery of my life. Fred and I have been discovering and sharing the many ways we have been taught to live in Divine guidance. As in Beckwith's quote, we have learned to shift our perspective from fixing what is wrong to tuning into and energetically receiving the blessings that are continually unfolding in our lives.

When going through my divorce I realized that neither my married name nor my maiden name resonated for me. At the same time, I learned that in original Aramaic texts translated directly to English, the word "name" means *nature,* as in "Jesus' name."

I asked, "What is my true nature?" I then remembered that my father proudly used the original Norwegian last name of his grandfather, Lovelien, as a middle name. Like many, Dad's grandfather had changed his name when the family immigrated to America. Lovelien felt right! Yes, I became Karen Dorey Lovelien to honor my dad, my ancestors.

It is with a profound sense of peace that I now realize that my true essence has been *revealed* from within, through me. Just as when, in the early 1990s, my fists raised revealing the two aspects of myself I had been living, I can now see that I have healed and integrated the two aspects of my true nature as one. I am both Karen Dorey Lovelien and Kara Dorey Sumi, a spiritual name that came through me in a powerful sacred ceremony seventeen years ago as a mere glimpse into the vastness of my true Self. Now I know this is the name of the Sirius spirit that entered by body when I was two-and-a-half years old. My parents must have been listening when they planted a seed for Kara Dorey to be revealed when they gave me a vibrational match at birth, the name Karen Dorey. As my first little one expressed to me upon her departure:

"You are here for new knowledge to come in, Living Light to be known, for love to be clear."

As a multi-dimensional portal of sound and Divine Light frequencies, Karen Dorey Lovelien, TBG, is a spiritual leader, healer and teacher providing both vibrational pathways and a blueprint of heart-activated spiritual practices/knowledge for people to re-discover and live in their own unique soul imprint. Karen has twenty-eight years of experience supporting individuals and groups around the world. She and her husband, Fred Boshardt, have served as instruments in raising the frequency of the planet by activating over 200 sites around the world with the Living (life-giving) Light of Sirius B or one of fifteen other pulsar stars. They also lead spiritual tours to sacred sites, each with specific intentions for the planet, the world and individuals on the tour. Learn more about her work, Soulular Clarity: Attuning Cellular Frequencies to the Soul's Purpose, at SoulularClarity.com.

She Who
Rides The Wind

Connie C. Cox, LCSW

"Bone by bone, hair by hair, Wild Woman comes
back. Through night dreams, through events half
understood and half remembered..."
— Clarissa Pinkola Estes

*Insects are numbered in billions and are seen and not seen. The
Elders say it is the insect nation that holds the planet together, and it
is the river of winds above the world that courses them across the globe.*

*Those same winds urged me to leave the velvety darkness of my
mother's womb.*

*Along with her waters, I gushed into the light. Something violent
opened me to that light, and my first breath hammered my little lungs
like a freight train. My parents rewarded me with the name Connie.*

*The atmosphere applauded and unleashed a big wind that tore
up the east coast. It headed north from the Carolinas, quickly lifting
cement and bending metal. It turned left around New York.*

*By the time it reached southwestern Pennsylvania, exhaustion
and old age set in. This wisdom greeted my birth, and the weather
forecasters named the Hurricane, Connie.*

*And those storm clouds held one of the major life lessons I came
here to learn: nothing is ever totally good or bad.*

*Across time, I realized my duty to harness the opposites first inside
myself, then to assist others in doing the same, and finally to ride that
wind horse into beauty and pleasure.*

I was liberated the day I was strong enough to climb out of my crib and run into the open arms of my parents or Grampap.

They began reading to me as soon as I walked to them with a Little Golden Book in my hand, usually *The Little Train that Could* or my favorite, *The Night Before Christmas*, read to me by Mum or Dad every Christmas Eve and on nights throughout the year. When I was four years old, I pointed to the words and read each one out loud! That September Mum told me I was going to have a little brother or sister. I overhead my family say they were surprised because the doctor had said Mum could not have any more children. Soon there would be a miracle.

Mum's belly grew and, when I put my hand there, I felt the little one move. One day Grampap asked Mum and Daddy about sitters for me as the baby was soon to arrive. Dad said that his sisters or younger cousin could watch us. Mum looked at him, her eyes squinted, daggers shooting of them as she said bad words: "I'll be damned if women who think so little of me will have anything to do with my babies!"

Dad's face got red and he looked at the ground. I felt bad because I liked my Catholic Aunts and big cousin, Delphine. They let me sing and dance in front of Aunt Gina's big fireplace and clapped for me.

Dad took Mum to the hospital and two babies, instead of one, were born. When the doctor said Mum and the twins would stay in the hospital, I felt sick and started to cry. He told me not to cry because they would be home soon. They were not home soon enough and Dad never gave an answer to me about why. In the meantime, kids teased me because my hair and clothes were dirty and—sometimes—I forgot to tie my shoes. I didn't like ice cream anymore and I was always tired. I had bad dreams about being inside rocks that were pressing against me.

The day my mother's cousin Delmar came to the back door was the worst. I opened the door and he walked in. He was short like Grampap but had a butch haircut. He was the only quiet and calm person I knew; everybody else was talking or nervous all the time. He came in the sunporch, looked down and smiled. "Connie, I just want to tell you that if your Mum doesn't come home, I will take care of you," he said. "You can come live with us and your cousin Tommy."

"Why won't my Mum come home?"

He didn't say anything for a long time. I got cold all over, squirmed and my foot started tapping.

"Connie, she is very ill and might die."

My shoes froze to the floor like ice cubes in a metal tray. I looked through the screened window at the blue sky and wished I was a kite that could fly above the world. Then I started thinking: *maybe I could live with our Cleveland family; I could be with my cousin all the time, but maybe I wouldn't like the big city.* Just then Dad came to the back porch and Delmar told him what we were talking about. Dad got mad, swore, and told Delmar to leave. Delmar looked back at me through the open door and reminded me what he promised. Dad still wouldn't talk about what happened after Delmar left.

After that, my bad dreams got worse. One night in the dream I heard a fire truck siren and knew someone was coming to help me and I prayed they would hurry up. The siren noise got softer and began moving away. The rocks pushed against me harder and I couldn't breathe. I woke up and realized no one was going to help. I started to cry and Dad heard me and came into the room where he hugged me for a long time, gathering me softly against him, surrounding me with love.

I kept thinking about my cousin Bonnie and her parents and how much I liked it when they visited. But that summer passed without them. Dad said they didn't visit because it was too hectic with Mum in the hospital. I wondered how Bonnie was doing and couldn't wait till the next time I saw her.

One day Grampap told me Dad went to the hospital to pick Mum and the twins up. I began laughing, jumping up and down, and pulling on both his hands!

He smiled down at me, picked me up and said, "Your Mum was expecting only one baby and there are two. I don't know how she can manage all three of you."

"Don't worry, Grampap, we'll be fine."

Later that day I saw the car in the alley and ran to the door and opened it. Mum walked in holding one baby and Dad carried the other: I wanted to hug her and couldn't. The boys were sleeping and wrapped in blankets like hot dogs. Mum wasn't smiling and was skinnier; her face was pale and she looked tired. In that moment I knew the boys would need lots of attention and I would have to take care of my four-year-old self.

They laid the boys side by side on the couch: one was blond and the other dark. I gave each of them a finger that they squeezed and I smiled. Grampap made me a bowl of chicken noodle soup from a red and white can. It was my favorite. I looked at the counter at the hospital stuff Mum got. There was a green vine in a planter shaped like an old shoe filled with holes; out of each hole poked a child's head.

"There was an old woman who lived in a shoe. She had so many children she didn't know what to do," I sang out loud the words I remembered from a Mother Goose book. Mum frowned at Dad after he told me Aunt Gina was the one who bought the planter. I watched the plant turn brown and die.

Kindergarten was a place I was always in trouble for talking too much or knocking stuff over. The teachers were always telling me to pull my dress down: I hated wearing dresses. Very soon Mum and Dad had to talk to the teacher. I sat and listened.

"She is disruptive and talks nonstop. She appears awkward in a dress. She has problems following directions. She has spilling accidents with paints and milk."

Hurricane Connie was just too much.

After school Mum and Dad told me to act like the other girls or I would keep getting in trouble. Grampap listened quietly and after the talk he took me shopping. I got stuff in pretty colors: six skirts with matching blouses; two fancy dresses and one pair of black patent leather shoes. I picked out frilly socks in matching clothes colors. Grampap always wore perfume and ivory shirts with colorful ties and pocket hankies when we went out and now, I had nice clothes, too! I learned how to act like the other girls and stopped getting into trouble, but changed into my pants when I got home and played on my hobby horse or in the alley with the boys.

The next summer my cousin Bonnie and her parents came and stayed awhile. They walked in the door with fancy blue suitcases with gold locks. Bonnie and her mum wore pretty dresses and even their tops and pants were fancy. I wondered how they knew to take small steps; I thought they must have watched the other girls like I did! Aunt Minnie smelled good and when I asked if I could wear her perfume, she said, "You're too young." I wondered why I was too young to smell like pretty flowers.

When Mum was taking care of the twins, I had Bonnie to play with! I liked playing with her better than with the boys in the alley because she was funnier and knew girl stuff. Bonnie also brought crayons and coloring books; some were magic books. When you brushed water on the pictures, they turned colors! We played on my swing set and red sliding board and talked with the older lady next door on her porch. Bonnie would not play with the boys in the alley and liked to keep things clean—she always helped with the dishes and dusted stuff off. I was happy when she was around and when she left, I got sad again, but the coloring books Mum bought me helped.

Mum lost more weight and her tops and pants were baggy. She started smoking Raleigh's and Pall Malls. Dad stopped watching TV with us at night; he was out drinking beer. I wondered why it was OK for Grampap to drink beer at home and Dad had to go out for some. One night after Mum put the boys to bed, she and I did something we hadn't done in a long time. She sat in her chair with me and we rocked. I loved her smell and how warm she was. She started shaking and I looked up and she was crying.

"Mummy, don't cry!"

"It's not your fault, I just miss your Dad not being here at night with us."

Then I understood why Dad shouldn't go out at night.

I started getting sore throats, my ears hurt bad, and I was running fevers. Trips to the doctor and the medicine I had to take only helped a little. My nose was runny all the time and I had to come home from first grade a lot. I couldn't breathe at night. When we went to see the doctor, I found out there were two little raisins in the back of my throat that had to be removed. I wondered how raisins got stuck there and tried to feel them when I swallowed.

Grampap asked the doctor, "When will she be hospitalized for tonsillectomy?"

And the next thing I knew I was in the hospital. The walls, bed spreads, and the doctors' and nurses' uniforms were white. After supper, my parents said goodbye and that I was supposed to be a brave girl. I slept all night. Nurses awakened me the next morning and put me on a cold metal table. They rolled me into a big room with a white light surrounded by a metal cage that that hanged from the ceiling. The doctor came in and explained the situation:

"We are going to put a mask on your face that will help you go to sleep. When you wake up, your throat is going to hurt but you won't be sick anymore. You are a brave girl and if you are still, we won't put these straps on you."

I didn't want the straps, so I lay there and the nurses put the mask over my face and nose. I took a deep breath like doctor said and got sleepy. I heard two ladies in the waiting room talking and one of them was crying:

"They gave my little boy the ether mask and he died—I hope she doesn't die too."

"There must be another way to put them to sleep?"

I got really scared, pulled off the mask, and slid off the table: I didn't want to die and started to scream for help. Everyone ran back in the room. The nurses started chasing me around. I almost escaped through the door, but doctor caught me and pinned me on the table. I kept kicking at him and knocked the glasses off his face. The nurses held me down and strapped me to the table. I could not move and when the mask pushed down on my face, I couldn't breathe and just died.

I saw three nurses around my bed: they were good nurses and looked like angels in heaven smiling at me. My burning throat told me I was not in heaven and still alive. A fourth nurse came in with Jell-O and fed me from a spoon. Afterward, another nurse gave me a big cup with ice cubes in it and told me to suck on the cubes and my throat will feel better. I was always asking for ice after that and soon they let me go to a room and get my own ice and water! Grampap came to see me in the daytime and either Mum or Dad came at night. I asked to see my brothers but they were too little to visit. My Catholic aunts, and cousin Delphine, visited me too.

When it was just me and the nurses in the hospital, I got to walk around the whole place, look at all the neat things, and say hi to everybody. Pretty soon lots of nurses were coming to visit me and doctors, too! A couple doctors gave me big books with pictures of colored animals and people in them. Flowers were everywhere and some from strangers. I don't know how long I was there, but everybody was sad when I had to leave and told me what a good girl I was. On my last day, I carried my new books with me and went with Dad to a big room filled with lots of little kids.

I talked with some of them and then Dad whispered in my ear, "See that little blond-haired boy by himself over there, Connie? His name is David and he is going to be here a long time because he is really sick—why don't you give him your books to make him feel better?"

I walked up to David, who said he didn't know how long he was going to be in the hospital. His skin was bluish and his eyes had black circles around them. He was skinny and said he didn't like food anymore.

"Not even chocolate?"

"Nope, and not even ice-cream either."

He let me hold his little stuffed rabbit with lopsided ears. I knew he really loved it and gave it back to him. I picked up my books and knew Dad was right:

"Here, David, these books are for you!"

His eyes got bright and he smiled for the first time. "Thank you, little girl!"

I started crying and didn't know why because I felt good at the same time.

"Dad, that little boy is going to die, isn't he?"

He took his white hanky from his pocket and smooshed the water from under my eyes. "Yes, he has cancer, Connie, and you're crying because you did a good thing."

It felt good because I helped him. I was glad Mum didn't die after having my brothers and I didn't die because of the raisins in the back of my throat. Right then and there I decided I wanted to help people when I grew up.

My voice sounded deeper to me after my operation and Grampap said I sounded like a frog! I kept eating ice cubes and soup and eventually my throat stopped hurting and I could eat everything again. The scratchy sound disappeared but my voice stayed deep and I felt older than a first grader.

I traveled through grade school, made new friends, and watched my brothers walk then run. They always wanted to follow me around the patch and I hated it. The alley boys always asked me why my brothers were following us and told me to get rid of them. I yelled at my brothers and they stopped following me. One day one of them tried to take my bike and I knocked him down and he started crying. Soon they got their own bikes: two new stingrays, one purple and the other blue metallic. The bikes were the nicest ones in the patch, but mine was a girl's Huffy with a long, sparkly blue seat, curved handle bars, and blue tassels coming out of the hand grips. Sometimes I would put a card between the spokes and when I rode it, it made a clicking sound.

Bonnie started to spend the summers at our house. She was my almost SISTER who was happy and made everyone that way, even Dad who drank too much beer. We colored and she shared her *Nancy Drew* books with me. Mum laughed and joked more when Bonnie was there and I was happier too. Every day Mum drove all of us to Flatwoods swimming pool when Dad was at work. In the evening, we would sit outside and talk with Mum and sometimes the boys joined us. Dad was usually at the beer garden and Grampap listened to the Pirates baseball games on the radio. It was always sad when Bonnie had to go home to start school.

One night at Supper Mum was frowning and I knew Dad was in the dog house.

All three of us started to cry when he said we were going to transfer to Catholic School next year:

"Your Aunt Gina says the nuns are better teachers and everybody will learn more."

I yelled back at him: "But we can't go to Catholic School unless we're baptized Catholic!"

"That's right, so just stop carrying on and get used to it," he asserted.

"They call Star Junction Elementary kids retards and hold them back a grade!" I said.

The three of us looked at our mother:

"You would jump in front of a train if Gina said to, Ivan!" Mum said.

He kept shoveling food in his mouth and didn't even look at her.

At that moment I realized my Mum had little say over our family despite her constant presence.

I screamed at Dad: "I will NEVER go to Catholic School and be put back a grade."

I crossed my arms over my chest and slid down in the chair and scowled. Then my brothers screamed at Dad and it was just too much for him. He left his supper, put on his cap, and went drinking.

The next day I found Mum crying. It was her birthday and no one got her anything. The boys and I ran up on water tank hill behind the house and picked bunches of wildflowers. Mum was tickled pink and put them in a vase.

"What is Dad getting you, Mum?"

"The usual—nothing."

I thought about this and saw a big change between them. The happiness I remember between them, was gone. Mum was miserable all the time and my Dad was either working, at the bar, or sleeping on the floor. I wanted Bonnie to live with us full time because Mum was always happier and so was I. This, I reasoned, was a dream of a happy family not filled with arguing or drinking. For some reason, Mum's sadness made me think she might die. Some days she never left the couch except to get us ready for school and to fix our meals when we came home. She never combed her hair and tied a work hanky on her head in a triangle. She wore the same clothes all the time. My dad did too. He had body odor and Mum had to spray deodorant under the arms of his shirts. He wore the same socks and his feet smelled bad. I couldn't bring friends over because he was an embarrassment.

I was glad when my parents got sick of being home all the time and decided we needed to get away. My family traveled to Cleveland via Pennsylvania and Ohio Turnpikes. Dad was driving a navy blue Dodge Coronet 440 and there was plenty of room for all of us. We arrived in Cleveland and made a lot of turns into neighborhoods with flower boxes in the house windows. The houses were neatly kept with fresh paint, aluminum siding, or brick. The sound of mowers chirped through our open car windows. The grass in Bonnie's yard stood up at sidewalk edges and ours did not.

In Bonnie's driveway was her dad's car. He got a new one each year. Aunt Minnie had a car, too: Uncle Micky kept them washed and clean inside. His cars were flashy like him in his cool clothes, shoes, and white driver's cap. Aunt Minnie got her own new car every year; Mum used Dad's car. That year Aunt Minnie's car was gorgeous and when Mum looked at it she looked at Dad and looked at the ground. He started talking fast about how nice Minnie's car was. Uncle Micky was home every night and Dad never was. Aunt Minnie and Bonnie wore makeup and set and teased their hair. Bonnie wore Chantilly perfume and that summer she let me wear it too; me and Mum did none of that.

That summer I got to stay at Bonnie's house In Cleveland. In Star Junction, I roamed all over the hills but here Uncle Micky told both of us to stay on the block and use the nearby playground. Bonnie wore a watch so we knew when we had to go home. In Star Junction, the rule was come when called or be in before the street lights come on.

One day I went to the playground, near the house, by myself and was happy to meet some neighbor boys. We asked each other get to know me questions. They teased me about being a hick and I called them city slickers. One of them pushed me so hard my back slammed into the leg of the swing set, my head pitched, and

I fell face forward in the dirt. I couldn't pass air in and out of my lungs and I got scared. They boys looked at me lying there and took off running. I caught my breath and was glad they were gone.

I told my story at the house and Uncle Micky's face turned fire-engine red and he yelled and spit at the same time:

"These are city boys here, Connie, not like the ones you know in the alley back home! I told you not to go there by yourself and now you see what you get!" I ran into my room and cried. For some reason, I was afraid of Uncle Micky and told Bonnie so:

"He gets mad like that all the time but don't worry, he never hits anyone."

Soon Uncle Micky put a pool up in the small backyard and I knew he did it to make up for yelling at me: swimming was my favorite thing next to bike riding. When we were not in our bathing suits, Bonnie and I read new and old *Nancy Drew* books. We liked the fact that Nancy's car was nice and her clothes spectacular. She drove all over the town to solve mysteries.

When I got to seventh grade my world turned upside down. All the girls had boyfriends and some of them were dating tenth-grade guys. Not one boy was interested in me and the alley boys stopped talking to me except to say hello. I started walking with my head down and avoiding people's eyes. I dreaded going back to school on Mondays. My face broke out in pimples and classmates called me ugly. Star Junction was the end of the line for me; I would never date or be married. I began living in a world without a future. Bonnie had pimples, too, and was teased because of it. We began exchanging letters and that helped us both.

One spring day I sat in a chair beside an open window. Tears ran down my face and my chest heaved up to my eyebrows. The trees were pink with blooms and fragrance spilled in the window: beauty was everywhere and I was ugly. I looked out the window and a school kid looked back at me with open mouth, sad eyes, raised eyebrows: he heard my voice and I was surprised. That look opened my eyes—I realized something was wrong with me; more than being just ugly: I felt a weight across my shoulders like a yoke. It was daily sadness I could not control. I just acted my way through school, with friends and family. I screamed and yelled at everyone at home for anything.

The night after an explosive day, I lay on my bed exhausted, sobbing, and unable to sleep. Mum sheepishly handed me a small, blue diary. A tiny, gold key stood inside the lock:

"This might help you when you're sad."

I angrily asked her, "Where's your diary?"

She asked me if I needed a hug and I screamed out, "No! just leave me alone!"

I initially used the diary to record daily events. Eventually, the pages reflected sadness, self-deprecating thoughts, and ideas of how others disliked and despised me. In another tablet I wrote poetry reflecting these themes; eventually, songs appeared and told stories about various characters and situations, much like Jim Croce Ballads. At times, my writing was humorous and had the ability to lift my spirits; it was a barricade against hopelessness but did little to quell the raging monster's fire, blasting exclusively at home. Hurricane Connie was a burning volcano, I didn't know how to stop her.

While I despised myself, I despised my parents more. I saw them as weak and Dad as a hypocrite who hid at the bar. I was ashamed of myself for being ugly and like a boy, and embarrassed by the differences between my friends' parents and mine. I felt sorry for Mum and verbally engaged my father on her behalf whenever I got the opportunity. How could a man ignore his wife completely and how could his wife hate her husband and stay with him? Through it all I kept remembering how happy they were when I was little. I had no answers for any of it, but that was about to change.

In eighth grade health class we studied psychology and I was fascinated with the categories of mental illness and its treatment. I scoured the categories in our textbook, comparing myself to all of them and doing the same with family members and friends and a light came on when I read this in our book:

"...known in the past as Melancholia, Depression is a condition of extreme sadness characterized by hopelessness, sleep problems, and low self-esteem. It effects all age ranges and both men and women: anger is Depression turned outward. Depression cn be mild, moderate or severe."

I was both happy and sad with my self-diagnosis: it was another separation from others, but at least now I knew what was going on.

I turned thirteen in August of 1968. Bonnie had been at the house since Memorial Day. We slept in single beds on either side of my room. I woke up that morning before she did and when I got to the bathroom my panties were wet. I thought I peed myself, but when I looked down there was blood all over me. I had cramps, too. I knew what was happening because we learned about it in school. I wiped myself off in the bathroom and went back to the bed.

"What happened?" Bonnie whispered.

"I started."

We both began laughing.

"I'll tell your mother," she said.

Mum gave me the supplies I needed and I put on a pad. I went down to the kitchen. My parents were there and so were Aunt Minnie and Uncle Micky. My brothers were still asleep and Bonnie sat at the table.

Uncle Micky looked at me and said: "So, you started your period? Now you can be raped!"

Anger and shame flared through my body and I shouted:

"I will never be raped because I will hold my legs together!"

"That's what you think, girl! If someone wants to rape you, they will!"

The room went silent; I went back upstairs and laid down. Alone, I wondered if Uncle Micky were right; I reasoned against it because I held my own with alley boys and always took care of myself.

I considered the situation and thought about how my life changed with blood coming from inside me. I could have babies and would have to wear pads once a month from now on. I was crabby this morning and recognized Mum and Bonnie were crabby when they bled, too. Bonnie's boobies had gotten big since she started her period but mine were still flat. Just before my period

I grew taller than my cousin and got hair on my legs and under my arms. Mum would only let me shave after kids harassed me in school about having hairy legs. Bonnie became even prettier and was an expert with her hair and makeup: I could care less about any of that. I was so ugly it wouldn't help anyway. In the end, I knew I wasn't a kid, but I still liked the same things.

Bonnie was in eleventh grade and studying Beauty Culture part time so she could get a job after graduating. I was impressed with her ability to financially take care of herself as well as the fact that she always had money when she visited. She told me that after she graduated, she would be working full time and only spending two August weeks with us to celebrate our birthdays. My hands shook and I started crying inside. I didn't want to be a baby who cried out loud but what would I do without her?

At the beginning of her last full summer with us, she announced she was on the pill and her mother was aware.

"Well, you're level-headed and responsible, so it's a good thing" was Mum's response.

"When can I get on birth control?"

"YOU are not Bonnie!"

Once again, I felt ashamed of being unlike others and wondered if my angriness made me irresponsible. I also knew that I could get on the pill anytime I wanted after I was a certain age and needed no parental permission.

Toward the end of summer, Mum took everyone blackberry picking along curvy, narrow country roads outside town. There were two types of berries: the little ones close to the road in the sunlight and the black, juicy ones shadowed deep inside the bush. Long reaching and squeezing into patches left us scratched and bleeding, but we needed the sweetest ones for the pies Mum baked.

We went picking one day after a downpour and piled out of the car and into the bushes. The rain dropped the temperature, raising a slight mist from the hot summer ground; the musky smell of water-logged earth and plants wafted upwards. Suddenly, a crack appeared in the low hanging, blue-black sky, spilling a single ray of light into the patch we worked, illuminating shadowed berries, and awakening invisible birds into song. This was a space where tears and sadness did not exist; everyone was a part of everything and my ugliness did not matter. In fact, I was not ugly at all: the light pouring from the dark clouds turned me beautiful!

Afterward, Mum drove us to a small produce stand. The produce ledge held bright green and white-striped watermelon, red tomatoes, and husked, yellow corn. The farmer's red house stood behind the stand. Beyond that, acres of hay spiraled upwards against blue sky. The overhead sun blinked and dowsed the scene in gold, moving everything in slow motion. As we pulled away, I watched my cousin, mum and brothers turn their faces to the scene: I saw the face of God twice in one day and hoped they did, too.

I started hanging out with girls I met in junior high. What we had in common was cracking jokes, making each other laugh, listening to music and wearing cool clothes. I really liked a guy from across the patch who visited me every day after school and told me he liked my clothes; sadly, he moved out of state. I was thirteen and my twelve-year-old friends dated guys with cars and their parents approved. One got pregnant the first time she had sex. She quit school to raise her baby and the other girl made sure her boyfriend used a rubber. I told them they were too young to date. I thought I was, too, until I turned fifteen and everything changed.

My friends all had dates who accompanied them to dances and visited them at home; in fact, these slightly older boys would drive them to out of county sports activities. I was on my own, so I simply waited at the stoplight and would flag down a particular car-driving male friend. I was too ugly to be seen with him; so, we traveled together to sports activities and separated as soon as we arrived. I sat alone or with strangers and would catch a ride back with the same guy or someone else.

Summers meant being away from school and its twisted social scheme. I was always happier then and did things with patch girls.

That summer our routine was walking to the post office, hanging out and watching soap operas, going swimming, or playing records. We wore head bands, short halter tops, and faded bell-bottom jeans with a range of frayed pant-leg openings between twenty and thirty-six inches wide. Two methods of jean fraying were employed: hand-cutting or street-dragging the hems; I liked to do both and so did my friends. This look sent the message we were travelers looking for adventure; kids who knew the score and how to get there and as far away from adult expectation as possible. My disrespect of authority was based on my own parents saying one thing, demonstrating another, and remaining in a dreadful marriage; the marriage of Bonnie's parents was the opposite and she had the better life as far as I was concerned. Yet I never saw her wear jeans and wondered why she didn't.

One night, my friend and I were there alone at a local hangout spot called the Wall. A car stopped with two young men inside of it and we piled into the backseat. Soon we were drinking pony bottles of Fort Pitt beer and riding around narrow country roads with two cute guys rich enough to have cars. We parked along one of the bushes I used to pick berries from. I moved to the front passenger's seat and my friend and I began making out with the guys. I had only kissed one boy in my life and it was nice; this guy was a rotten kisser. His limp mouth and tongue poured water in my mouth and I was disgusted. He also smelled like motor oil from working on his race car...yuck! The guy in the back seat was another story: he had stylish clothes and wore cologne he called "Brut." I laid on top of my guy so his spit went back into his mouth instead of mine; also, this way I could have a better look at backseat boy. He had dark hair cut in the Prince Valiant-style and I could tell he was not drowning my friend! I drank more beer to better tolerate the jerk I was with. I felt a hand on the back of my jeans, realized it was Prince Valiant, and yelled at him to stop what he was fucking doing right now. Everyone started laughing, including him.

"When I see a nice butt, I want to touch it!"

"Well, don't, you mother fucker!"

We laughed and kidded all the way back to the Wall where they had picked us up, got out of the car and went home.

Two days later, my friends and I walked the six miles to and from Perry, a little town three miles from Star Junction and the location of the junior high and high schools. The humidity and heat smoothed sharp creases in bell bottoms and unmanaged everyone's hair. The wall was in sight and the corner store across the street had pop to drink. A car rounded the corner that ate so much gas, so quick, it sounded like a vacuum cleaner. It was the best-looking car in town and did a mile under six seconds at the raceway. Everyone started teasing me because I liked Prince Valiant. He pulled up next to us, three girls jumped in the back seat, and my best friend pushed me in the front seat and sat me next to the window. I was confused by feeling relaxed and nervous at the same time: I didn't understand the familiarity between the Prince and I. We all rode around until the street lights came on and he dropped us off at The Wall. He grabbed my arm before I could leave and whispered in my ear:

"Are you still a virgin?"

I shook my head yes, "Why do you ask?"

"Because the last virgin I dated went crazy and I won't have that happen to you. Go get a boyfriend."

My heart thumped out of my chest because I realized he knew things I didn't; I got out of the car and grinned back at him.

I had six weeks of Cloud Nine that changed itself into depression and left me at the elementary school playground with a couple friends. I was standing atop the center fulcrum of a teeter-totter, angrily slamming down one end—and then the other—against dry, cracked cement. A white car pulled up the alley and my best friend was leaning into the driver's side window. She came over to me and told me her mother's friend wanted to meet me.

"Why would your mother's friend want to meet me?" I asked. "He's an old man!"

"He's not that old; come on!"

We walked over and there he was: thirteen years older than me with a quart of beer between his legs, the smell of it spilling out the car window, and a cigarette hanging from his mouth. Older Guy spent the next couple of minutes flirting with me.

"You are a REALLY cute girl, why don't you come over and talk to me?"

I leaned down to get a better look: he had dark eyes and hair and wore nice cologne. I liked it when he complimented me.

"My mum told me not to talk to strangers and you are weird!"

I walked away from the car and went home, amazed that anyone would be interested in me.

He began calling my best friend's house and she relayed his messages to me. I was impressed by this and wondered about how my Dad had courted my mother; they were miserable now but I remember their happy past. I wondered if all marriages turned rotten and how they got that way.

"He wants to meet you," my best friend told me for the zillionth time.

"Not interested and you can tell him so."

A couple of days later I walked up the hill to her house and she wasn't home; so, I walked over the hill, was just about to circle the reservoir, and a car pulled up behind me. I smelled his cologne first: sweeter and lighter than the Prince's, but pleasant in a different way. He started telling me how cute I was and a bunch of stuff I didn't believe. The longer he talked and smiled, the softer his voice grew. I told him to "get gone" and walked home knowing it was a matter of time...

My cousin never gave me specifics about her dates, but she did like older guys she and her girlfriend met at dances. I wasn't worried about Older Guy drinking: my dad drank beer, which made mum sad and I did think about this; but being out of the boyfriend loop guaranteed Older Guy a chance with me.

I began meeting Older Guy for short make-out sessions. Later, I left the house unlocking the door behind me and met him late at night. One evening I was unable to get back in the locked door. I knocked, Mum opened the door, and told me she was getting phone calls about Older Guy. I shouldn't have been surprised. The town's oldest gossips always kept calendars on girls who dated;

this way, they could measure dating/marriage time against baby delivery dates, determining shot-gun marriages.

I asked Mum if Dad knew about Older Guy.

"No, I haven't told him because he would kill that dirty, old bastard!"

I was tired and went to my room. I loved that dirty, old bastard.

Gary Puckett and the Union Gap's song, *This Time You're a Woman Now*, played on the radio when I had intercourse with Older Guy. We were in the back seat and his buddy was with my best friend in the front. It was lovely until it wasn't.

"Where's the blood?!" he screamed at me.

"I don't know, I must have lost it [hymen] on the monkey bars when I fell."

"Bullshit! You are nothing but a lying whore—just like the rest of them!"

They drove us back to Perry, he pushed me out of the backseat with his foot, and I landed on the curb. My girlfriend said she knew I wasn't lying and so did Older Guy's buddy. She hugged me until I stopped crying.

I asked my parents if I could get a therapist and told them I couldn't handle it anymore:

"Handle what?"

"Being sad and grouchy all the time."

They said it was ok to get one; here's the phone book—start looking. Therapists abounded in the Yellow Pages, but I feared being a "patient" would subject me to more harassment.

Older Guy changed his mind two weeks after declaring my whoredom. Our renewed relationship triggered several miracles: his dick stopped working after a priest caught us making out in a pew at St. John the Baptist church, school bullies left me alone, and writing became a daily necessity for me. In the meantime, a drinking buddy of Dad's told him about my secret rendezvous. Dad drove around the patch, and to all the bars in Perry, until he found Older Guy and secured my marriage and a promise: Older Guy professed his undying love for me and agreed to leave me alone until after I graduated.

Here was his proposal to me: "Once we are married, I will slap you if I think you deserve it."

"No, you will do no such thing. I won't tolerate it and will leave you."

"We'll see about that" was his angry answer. My self-esteem was a dismal forest filled with no trees, only dried out bushes popping up in the wind. Hurricane Connie was lost at sea.

That night, I journaled a list of events leading to my "engagement on Daddy approved terms." I reread my journal and was horrified: no academic talent, and even less chance of appropriate marriage, equaled my dismal future. After several weeks, Older Guy disappeared for good. I was fifteen and my relationship with the twenty-eight-year-old man was no more.

Mum and I had an after-school visitor from the county agricultural extension. She was in her early twenties and asked several questions about the family, documenting our answers on important papers attached to a clip board. She looked directly at us nodded her head in understanding.

She agreed that I could ask a question.

"It seems like Mum is the focus of your questions."

"What makes you think that, Connie?"

"Well, she says yes to them all."

"Very good! Do you think I get the same answers in every house I go to?"

I thought about this for a long time, looked shyly at the ground and replied, "I think in Star Junction all the women are doing chores and raising kids and driving them around."

"O.K. Do you think a place exists where men share those duties?"

"Only in Oz."

"You are referring to the *Wizard of Oz* movie?"

"Yeah," I laughed, "everybody knows that women get married to raise kids and not have to work. It's only old house cleaners like my Aunt Gina, who live alone, go to college and don't have kids!"

"Oddballs, you say?"

"Yeah, oddballs!"

"Well, I am married, work for the extension, and have a child. My husband helps around the house, too!"

"Wow," I answered, "You are no oddball, that's for sure!"

Mum and the nice lady both started laughing at me and I joined in.

Afterwards, I thought about the visit and wrote in my journal…

Mum never made me wait on the boys or Dad like she did; I never had chores to do and didn't have to cook. I guess she doesn't want me to do those things… but what does she want me to do, what do I want to do? Whatever it is, my crazy moods might prevent me from doing it.

The end of Older Guy meant a new beginning with Prince Valiant. He told me to go to beauty school; that suggestion, along with my cousin being a hairdresser, pointed me toward a vocation resulting in a spectacular consequence. I learned to make others beautiful, as well as myself, and turned glamorous overnight. The Prince received compliments about me in his travels. That was important because others harassed him about dating me and our relationship was undercover until I blossomed. I learned something else about myself: I was a good listener and told by many customers I should become a therapist.

The Prince and I turned heads walking down the street: he was 6'2" and dressed like Tom Jones with frilly pink and blue shirts and velvet jackets; I was 5'7" and wore matching short skirts or hot pants and sometimes boots. My heels were high, and my earrings were gold circles that matched his big square belt buckles that he always positioned to the side of his hip. Our engagement happened on Christmas Day but my crazy mood swings ended our relationship and my hair dressing career and we never walked down the aisle. Everyone I knew was married or going to be, except for me it seemed. I began drinking heavily and engaging in spiritless relationships.

Months later, a Man-Boy leaped from a quart of Mad Dog 20-20 into my daily life. He was a genie that should have stayed in the bottle! We were both twisted and desperate: the difference was, his anger exceeded mine. After a six-month drunken debauch, we were married and I was out of Star Junction but not far enough. In marriage to Man-Boy, I reconstituted the chaos in my family of origin by failing to recognize a clue: the males in his home verbally abused women they lived with. The '70s T.V. series *Those Were the Days* was a dark comedy showing the abuse of women by a bumbling male; Man-Boy, his younger brother, and father applauded it. I was oblivious to this and to the fact that my freedom was slowly curtailed. Man-Boy disallowed me use of the car and monitored the time I walked around the neighborhood. Eventually, I received no phone calls or visits from others.

An old friend and I discussed the situation.

"The reason friends and family stopped calling you is because they can't stand hearing about the person you have become: you are unrecognizable!"

"I don't understand…"

"Connie, you just told me he screams at you all the time, accuses you of cheating on him constantly, and dictates what you do…you are home all day without a car and even your mother can't stand to hear what you are going through…I don't know who you are: you used to be a tough girl!"

Just then he walked in the door.

"Who the hell is that on the phone, one of your slutty girlfriends?"

He kept up his spiel and I reminded my friend that he never hit me.

"It's only a matter of time until he does…you need to get out of there now."

I gently put the receiver back in the phone cradle while he screamed in the background.

Numbness started in my right hand, climbed to my shoulders and through the rest of my body: dry ice had nothing on the cold coursing through my veins. The hard chill pointedly moved to my left eye and filled it with water. I was confused by the track of heat the tear left on my cheek. I spoke this under my breath, quietly, so he wouldn't hear:

"Now I have to take care of my Self…I am the only one who can."

The sound of breaking glass slowly penetrated me. My eyes opened to see Man-Boy standing over shards of my favorite mirror. I was determined not to return to my family a failure as a divorcée and dug my heels in place.

One afternoon I heard a knock at the door and the old car my dad bought me was sitting in front of the townhouse. I was thrilled! I didn't ask my dad to do this, he just did and told me he thought I might need it. I had forgotten, and now remembered, him caring for me during Mum's hospitalization following her birthing the twins. Thereafter, he sang to me and took me for rides with him to his job sites, to *real* playgrounds outside Star Junction, to get fresh eggs from the farmer and for ice cream. He bought me a metal Palomino pony that I bounced on so long and hard that the springs broke. The most important thing I recalled was me returning love with nastiness and anger. My cousin showed my parents, and hers, that she loved them. I needed to start doing the same. I threw my arms around Dad's neck and gave him a hug and cried. Someone loved me despite my craziness! Man-Boy wanted me to return the car, but that was a definite no!

In our building's laundry room, I was approached by the manager of a donut shop about waitressing and accepted! Our serendipitous meeting happened because she and her husband lived in the same complex we did. I was twenty-three years old and this job was my first employment commitment that would last seven years, giving me a window in which I could feel my self-esteem rising up from the ashes. I was somebody, and that little girl that ran the streets knew it somewhere deep inside. My start date was in a week and I excitedly told Mum about it on the phone. She immediately questioned my decision based on my husband's dislike of working women.

I had the conversation with him under cold gloom of a November day.

"I am selling that car your Dad gave you!"

"That car is in my name and you will not sell it!"

"I forbid you to work; you will whore around with your customers!"

"Watch me go to work, you" was my triumphant reply.

I was surprised when my curt reply ended the discussion, but then came Sunday night before my start date. He was determined to thwart my employment. He purchased three cases of beer, bought pizza, and invited his friends with guitars to play at the house and smoke weed. Of course, I couldn't sleep and the partying kept on until 1 am. I went down stairs and screamed loudly:

"I need you upstairs, now!"

He came in the bedroom and glared at me.

"You have to stop the noise; I have to work tomorrow and can't sleep."

He laughed at me, and said it was his house and he would do as he pleased; he then told me I should fuck myself and started heading back downstairs.

My next course of action was clear: I shrieked for help as loud as I could.

He leaped onto me with knees straddling my neck. He used one hand to shake my head by my hair and the other to shake his fist in my face:

"Shut up right now, you bitch, or I will kill you!"

I kept screaming for help and finally the music downstairs went silent. A male voice asked if I were O.K. I said I was...more silence. The group decided to take the party to a bar and he left with them, denying out the door any harm coming to me. He was back within the hour.

"Think you're smart, don't you bitch? I want sex, now!"

"Oh my God, how could you want that after what just happened?"

He started taking his clothes off and I realized I had no control over what was about to happen.

"Just so you know, this is a rape, so get on top, do your business and be done with it."

"It's not a rape; a man can't rape his wife—he owns her."

"Don't you watch T.V., stupid bastard?"

He looked confused.

"*Oregon vs. Rideout,* he got sixteen years for raping his wife."

He laughed again, "So take me to court, slut!"

My thrashing was ineffective. He tore my PJs off and thumped himself atop me, pinning my arms back. He thrust me into my imagination, away from his stink, to that golden summer day years past. I recognized Mum, my brothers and Bonnie inside the car, next to the fruit stand. I was there, too, and everything was golden. Just as we pulled away from the scene, Man-Boy rolled off me in a drunken stupor: a wake-up alarm ending my protective reverie.

Dirt and slime covered my skin the first day of work. I smiled brightly, taking direction from my boss, co-workers, and customers.

I had not yet found my way out, but the day in the blackberry patch in which God visited me came back to me in my dreams now and then. I'd wake seeing beauty in my reflection, but the darkness still reigned over my life. I had to find a way out. Man-Boy kept up with his overbearing abuse and finally upped his game by having an affair.

A co-worker that I admired had divorced her husband. She proceeded to birth light upon her story of another man who promised much but left her single with two girls. I intently nodded understanding. Her face glistened with tears; I learned over the counter and hugged her. After a time, she thanked me for listening, telling me I should be a counselor. I never saw her again and wondered if she was O.K.

I didn't have two kids but I DID have a job. The deep October blackness was cold; I looked into my reflection against the large, plate glass windows; a twenty-six-year-old woman stared back, begging me to help.

I began my walk to freedom by going on a date with Saint, a handsome, sweet boy that I knew from work. I spent time in the evenings with him, walking the streets of summer, holding hands and visiting with friends. I had moved back into my parent's house and Saint dressed in a suit the first time Saint visited. He fit right in with everyone at home.

The enormity of my behavior changes dimmed family fears of me. I was appreciative of everyone and returned any demonstration of affection. My mother and I engaged in shared activities and spent quality time together. I continued to work at the coffee shop, seriously dating Saint and grateful for his presence and support. Saint rarely raised his voice and, like me, loved to hike amidst the splendor of Greene and Fayette counties: the stable energy amidst towering hardwoods and ferns was HIS reflection. In summer, greenwoods surrounded us and whimsically changed red, amber, and gold in autumn; often we viewed these changes high above the canopy in his four-seater plane. The flights we took introduced me to perspective and how small things looked from afar.

I left Man Boy and moved back in with my parents.

Something strange began happening at work: younger customers harassed me. At first, I didn't know why: I was efficient and courteous with them. One eventually made the giggles and pointed her finger at me:

"You are so stupid you have to be a waitress!"

Once, they kept changing their orders to confuse me and cause me grief. After they left, I began to cry and the only person at the counter supported me:

"You don't have to do this job…you're a smart girl and can do anything you want."

We talked for a while, I asked him if he was a pastor and he said yes. He was like my parents, compassionate and forgiving. Other customers began telling me I needed to go to school. Once I decided to do so, the harassment magically stopped. I talked to my brother, Carl, about this:

"Go to a real college, Connie—not secretarial school."

"But my grades were never good."

"Believe me, as long as you pay them you will get a C; they need to make a profit."

Mum agreed that I could do whatever I wanted and Dad was my biggest supporter.

I became a twenty-six-year-old college girl with nearly straight A's. Unfortunately, my encompassing negative thoughts continued and subjected me to multiple realities: the one inside my head, the one happening around me, and the horrible outcome when they collided. I learned in psychology classes about cognitive-behavioral therapy and became my first patient! I named the voices Brain Dictator and quelled them though self-organization and steady focus; also, when I studied the thoughts were interrupted. I began reframing things in a brighter light, trying to see the good in everything. I continued to journal and now ideas began to seep into my writing along with complaints and angst.

I took all the psychology courses offered at Penn State, Fayette Campus, in Uniontown Pennsylvania. One of them was a *Psychology of Women* course taught by a feminist. Her no-holds-barred approach exploded our heads and hearts with statistics, examples, and study reports clearly defining embedded misogyny in American culture.

With the realization that my depression was not just because of me, I considered my options and had a social worker assessment. I saw a female psychiatrist who prescribed a mood stabilizer. I avoided the medication, wrongly thinking my taking it would prove I was crazy. The impressive therapist helped me to see difference between anger and rage; with her help, I learned the time out concept. To this day I don't think my family recognized I began taking meals in my room because the screaming and yelling at dinner time overwhelmed me.

I became a volunteer in the Day Treatment program of the agency providing me with therapy. I first observed and led guidance groups helping schizophrenics orient themselves to place and time. I did not lead mood therapy groups, but appreciated the gift of being able to watch social workers as therapists who improved self-esteem and mood in mixed groups. I wondered what a Therapist could do for groups of women struggling as I did with depression.

I completed Bachelor's and Master's degrees in Social Work at the University of Pittsburgh. At the suggestion of my undergraduate advisor, I invited Saint to monitor several classes. He did and enjoyed himself because he was supporting me and I loved him for it. His mother was against college for him and said so. His dad admired education but was not supportive of it for Saint.

Saint kept my sanity when I experienced an unrecoverable loss prior to Thanksgiving in 1984: Mum died of cardiac heart failure my first year of undergrad at the University of Pittsburgh. Dad and I were at a table having coffee and wondered why she was not up at 10 a.m. I climbed the eight stairs to the second story of our old company house, now called a duplex. Her door opened against my hand into a room filled with blackness. I took a breath and recognized the smell of fresh linen and HER smell; warm and musky. There was a light feeling in her room that replaced heaviness usually there. I paused, fumbled for the light switch, and stopped: a recent dream she described pushed me.

She was walking across the old, swinging rope bridge in Layton; her steps swaying it back and forth, her arms grasping rope rails that squeaked with her passing. In her dream, the bridge stretched across the world. As she walked, she noticed a figure approach her from the other side, arm extended forward, and hand grasping a light, or something…

"We met in the middle, Connie: it was me, carrying my own head by the hair."

"With blood, spinal cord and muscles hanging from it?"

"Yes, but no blood."

"Mum! That is so violent!"

I burst into laughter because of my horror; Mum was not outwardly violent!

"It's meaningless: haven't you every had a crazy dream?"

"Yes, but not like that."

My finger pressed the switch releasing light into the room. She lay horizontal across the bed, knees bent and feet dangling just above the floor. Her soft face bloomed and her eyes shone as she peacefully looked at what I could not see.

Death had cut off lifelong troubles. There was a broken childhood and caring for and tolerating an alcoholic father, son, and husband. There was the unbearable disdain Catholic relatives placed on her and us kids: all non-Catholic. How she tolerated my adolescent anger and disrespect, I will never know.

I wondered if the reaper took her sadness. She loved being a young mother, summertime and swimming with her family, roller skating with my dad at the Perry roller rink. She loved acting in school plays and being a girl scout leader with me in the troop. Most of all, she loved her sister, Minnie, who raised her. She loved my cousin Bonnie. Mum loved the drinkers, too and said so.

One day she added this remark about Dad:

"Connie, when they made him, they broke the mold."

And now I had to climb down the stairs and tell him what I found. He told me to check again and see if she really died so I did.

"I am going to miss you and am glad you were my mum. I am checking on you again because Dad's broke up and crying in the kitchen. I am sorry for my teenage craziness, but I promise you I will make up for this forever in my life, somehow. I am so happy we got to be best friends when I moved back in."

One never forgets the final moments of the living, once dead: the days that follow, are like slow molasses pouring out from the heart. I let mum go as much as I could into the mist of the forest, into the night sky, into her final safe place away from all that had chained her down.

My heart held my grief for exactly one year and cracked itself open spilling unmitigated rage into my body. I screamed curses, jumped up and down, and beat pillows on Saint's couch for over an hour. I gratefully began crying. I moved on to complete my Master's degree.

As far as I was concerned, my marriage with Saint began in 1977. We lived together in Pennsylvania until I left the state in 1989 for Michigan social work employment and he stayed behind. I genuinely engaged in therapy beginning in 1990 and reliably took meds, the first one being Prozac. It literally rearranged my brain cells and stopped the incessant crying following me since age thirteen. I was able to feel things, but commensurate with incidents; for example, a perceived slight from a co-worker no longer triggered a four-hour crying jag. I stopped awakening in tears and my exhaustion lifted. The most important benefit was cognitive: negative thinking was easier to control. This improvement cemented knowledge with therapeutic treatment skills I learned from co-workers. I learned about medication and treatment team operation from Muslim doctors I worked with. Most of the time I was in disbelief of their confidence in me.

Once I moved to Michigan, Saint spent long weekends with me, returning to Pennsylvania afterward. He began discussing something troubling to me. He was a Class A machinist, helping engineers and co-workers do better, despite their poor treatment of him. When he complained, I would ask him why he didn't go to school and become an engineer.

Something developed at work. Its impact was both immensely positive and destructive to me. I fell in love with one of the docs. He financially supported his wife and children living abroad in a Muslim country for some time. Our relationship exposed me to dynamic idea exchange and common interests. I now refused to settle and wanted more but still feared commitment.

Saint and I formally married in 1994. He worked different jobs collecting unemployment because of workforce reduction, or firing; I never really knew. He stayed home, resuming work when unemployment ran out. He wanted kids and deserved them. I was childless by choice and did not want to sacrifice my children to my craziness. It was bad enough Saint bore the brunt of it several times.

After four years of Jungian-based therapy, I concluded the marriage for both our sakes. My guilt and shame were enormous. It made perfect sense to dump an abuser. It was more difficult to justify dumping a Saint. He happily remarried shortly after we divorced and has two kids.

My best friend and I attended a spiritual retreat that May. We drove to the event, discussing our lives and challenges. I remarked to her that I intended to be with a man who was intelligent, funny, well read, and who knew how to converse. Amazingly, he walked right into my life at the event. He was a multimillionaire and showed me his credentials to prove it. The psychic cost to me for this relationship was enormous. He moved out of the house he shared with his already estranged wife and into his own. Every year after September's end he seriously announced intentions to end us and return to his marriage. There were five annual endings; each gashing deeper into the other, tearing open my original childhood trauma: the near-death of Mum after she birthed my twin brothers when I was four.

The fifth and final ending left me lying in a fetal position on my floor, CONVINCED I would die that night. My breath came in short fits. Rapid heartbeats pounded in my head. I felt skin and muscle fall from my bones. I was now dust and my mind's eye saw a vacuum cleaner wearing a grim-reaper hood. I surrendered to "death by beater bar" and was sucked into the machine; before I could laugh out loud with joy, I opened one eye and looked in the lower corner of my window sill. There, shuddering against thirteen-degree temperature and windchill was a black sparrow. At daybreak, she flew away. My dust, bones, and muscles reconfigured *ME.*

Psychiatrically, I experienced complete annihilation of Self; spiritually, deep emotional trauma dismembered me and I reconstituted into a stronger version of myself: one who now saw the grim reaper for what it was: a powerless, unplugged vacuum cleaner covered with a black towel. My new Self realized truth in both versions of what I had been through. I was a robust sparrow propelled across strong hot and cold wind. I wrote the experience in my journal and discussed it in therapy. It was the end of Multimillionaire and me.

Spirit was not finished with me yet. My brother, Curt, died in 1996 from an overdose of cocaine. Curt's death left me sad and questioning my competence as a therapist, while knowing the impossibility of treating my own family members. My Uncle Micky died a year later in August. After his death everyone gathered in Aunt Minnie's kitchen: Bonnie, her two boys and, now, my only brother. My dad could not get himself to come. We remembered the funny things Uncle Micky said and did and I jokingly added this:

"I remember starting my period and Uncle Micky telling me I could be raped!"

Everyone laughed. Reflecting on my seriousness as a little girl, I was now thankful to him for being so protective of me. It was a bittersweet afternoon.

I promised to call my Aunt on Monday to see how she was doing and I followed through:

"How are you doing?"

"Who is this?"

"This is Connie, Aunt Mini!"

There was a pause on the line.

"Connie, I don't ever want to see you again. I will be much better off without you."

My chest constricted and the tile on the floor of my apartment turned cold.

"WHAT?"

"I said, I never want to see you again—stay out of my life!"

"What did I do?"

"I am going to give those handmade lap quilts you gave to Micky and I to the Good Will; don't come over here again—ever!"

She hung up and I stood there clutching the phone receiver.

I waited an hour and called Bonnie:

"What's wrong with Aunt Mini—she kicked me out of her life?"

"I don't want to see you again either. Don't call here or come around."

"Why?"

"You know why—I am hanging up."

I cried for over two hours. My hands shook and I threw up twice. I tried to figure out what I had done. Maybe Bonnie and her Mum were angry because I divorced Saint or had been seeing Multimillionaire. Maybe it was unresolved anger over Mum's death and Uncle Micky's.

I called my brother and updated him:

"I am clueless about what happened, do you know?"

Again, a long silence that filled my head with craziness and anxiety. A thought occurred to me and I shared it:

"Are they mad because I mentioned Uncle Micky telling me I could be raped since I started my period?"

More silence.

"But everyone laughed after I said it and no one was mad at me when I left!"

"Connie, you know what you said or did. Your mouth has always gotten you in trouble your whole life. Sometimes you're not responsible for what you say."

He started screaming at me for causing trouble, I screamed back at him, and he hung up.

In a weak place, I called Multimillionaire and he grilled me to tears; he insisted I must have done something for my family to act that way, good Catholic that he was.

"WE don't throw people away in my family."

I thought to myself, *What about his ex-wives and me?*

I was numb and my head filled with breakthrough negative thinking Prozac couldn't handle. I looked all night for a bus I could lay under and couldn't find it then, but realized it was the same one my family had just thrown me under.

I put on my big girl pants and went to work helping others NOT to kill themselves. I ran groups and listened to reasons why death seemed comfortable to some and then—with the members' help—prevented others from committing suicide or homicide. Group members made gains through their own efforts; I only lifted the veil to help them see—and be—whole. Some went on to become college professors, writers, social workers, and great mothers to their families!

My supervisor approached me one day:

"Connie, I want to thank you for the hard work you do here. Administration has noticed and wanted me to tell you so; In fact, Dr. Smith said he is willing to supervise you with what you are best at."

"What is that, Linda?"

"Keeping women out of the hospital—you have saved the organization thousands of dollars, if not more! You are good with everyone, helping them overcome depression. You are amazing— keep up the good work!"

I had never cut myself or attempted suicide, but I shared with women commitment fear, mood swings, and a black-and-white world view. I was as REAL as the Velveteen Rabbit: worn and tattered from loving and returning the favor; experiencing life outside the norm, and flying into the wind. I had been there, done that, and survived.

I have been married for seventeen years to a handsome, funny, smart, and adventurist man who is my equal partner in crime and an engineer. We are risk-takers who work through difficulties and celebrate our victories hiking, cycling, and motorbiking through piñon pine, juniper bushes, and cacti of the high desert. He gifts me with stability and loves that I am, "just too much."

I am a queen under a vast turquoise sky who has faltered and stumbled. Now I am standing on solid rock at the edge of the Grand Canyon along with other professional helpers and members of the Havasupai Nation. We stand together in the spring breeze. I think about the wind blowing away confusion and bringing truth, just as a large gust scatters baggage around Hilltop. I breathe in deeply, filling my lungs with air. Soon I will be surrounded by the copper walls of a giant arroyo whose rocks won't suffocate me: the beauty and pleasure I feel is unimaginable.

I breathe in again and think to myself:

Well, who said a wind horse couldn't be a helicopter?

Connie C. Cox, LCSW, is a seeker of Beauty and Pleasure who walks with the elementals and goes where spirit sends her: writer, artist, healer and facilitator of women's empowerment. As a Licensed Clinical Social Worker/Therapist/Advocate, she directs her intention toward resurrecting the disembodied feminine and restoring it to wholeness across the planet. She takes no prisoners! Aho.

Transcending
the Baby Bump in the Road

Shelley A. Rael, MS, RDN

"No matter which way we go, our lives are changed,
and we will always have this connection."
— Shelley A. Rael, MS, RDN

I n the fall of 1989 when I was nineteen, my friend Sarah and I
are hanging at her boyfriend Kevin's place before he got home
from work. At the time, I am dating someone, but it isn't serious.
Kevin's friend Ted is there and the three of us are lying on couches,
talking nonsense. That September day, with Ted as our witness,
Sarah and I make a silly "pact" that we will not get married before
we are twenty-five years old. To me, this sounds reasonable.

"Why twenty-five?" Ted asks.

I feel confident in my answer. "If I met the man I would one
day marry right now, today, I would need at least five years to get
to know him enough to marry him."

*How could someone deliver such devastating, life-altering news
so casually?*

Earlier this evening some of my sorority sisters noticed that I
was throwing up uncontrollably for the past hour or two. I had
a migraine—the kind where you are in so much pain that the
idea of taking an ice pick or ice cream scoop, popping your eye
out and digging out that part of the brain that is causing pain is
a real possibility.

I was practically immobile, only getting up to head to the toilet to vomit and return to the room in agony.

When I returned from the bathroom for what would be the last time that night, I was confronted by three sorority sisters who witnessed what I was going through and confronted me in chorus. "We are taking you to the student health center for help." I agreed.

Next thing I knew, all three of them had escorted me out the front door and I was being whisked away in the car. Safety in numbers or they just wanted to be the first to learn I was dying.

In the exam room, I explained why I was there, and was asked the inevitable question all women are asked that could explain the reason we are sick, "Could you be pregnant?"

Up until recently, the answer was always no, because it was not possible. This time it was a no, but without the "not possible" clause.

I started birth control a couple of months earlier and I didn't miss a single day. I knew pregnancy is possible in many scenarios, but no, *not pregnant.*

"Well let's do a test just to be sure," the PA said.

That jackass comes back to tell me that I am pregnant.

I don't sleep around, even though that isn't a pre-requisite for pregnancy. It was the one guy. And I was on birth control. Why hadn't it worked?

I could not walk out of the room and face another person.

Of course, I had to. I walked out and to the elevator directly across the hall focusing on the "down" button—the one thing I could see—and waited for the elevator to arrive, ignoring my escorts.

They came up behind me asking what was wrong, but I couldn't speak for fear of what would come out. When the doors opened, I walked straight in all the way to the back with three bodies following me in and three sets of eyes observing me. I turned around and looked to the ceiling, the sky, heaven.

This is not happening.

"Shelley! What is wrong?"

I heard the combination of urgency, fear and impatience. I know the second I open my mouth and say it out loud, *people will know. Know that I screwed up. And be relieved that it isn't them.*

I open my mouth and the words come out as a sob, "I am pregnant."

I need to tell the dad. I don't know why it was necessary that night, but I needed someone else to know. The other person whose life would be totally and permanently impacted by the information I learned just fifteen minutes ago.

As I head to his place not far from where I live, I am sick. Not just literally sick, but worried and sick from fear. I am about to tell another person that his life is about to head in a new direction. Someone I hadn't seen in *how long? A week or two?*

I knock on the door at the back of the house where he lives with his roommate, who should be at work now. He opens the door, and he seems a bit surprised—but happy to see me. He is holding a paperback book in his hand and the television is off. I knew him well enough to know that this wasn't his style. Luckily, no one else is there. I remember his face genuinely smiling, and even though it has not happened yet, I know that smile will fade soon. I am not sure what the reaction will be.

I sit down and at first, I cannot say anything. I start crying and then just have to blurt it out.

"I am pregnant." For the second time, I said it out loud. And then to clarify, "It is definitely yours."

He takes this news in with seemingly little reaction.

What happens next is a blur. I just want someone, anyone, to tell me that this will all work out...somehow. But this is real life and this is not how things work. Even if someone had told me I wouldn't have believed them. Still, I wanted *someone* to say *something* reassuring.

"We will figure this out," he tells me, "but I need to study for a test tomorrow."

What can I say? I am not staying here to process this with him right now. I am going back to the sorority house and I have no idea what to do.

Hours pass and I am not ready to share this news with anyone else. I pray people won't talk.

Sarah tells me that I should have an abortion.

"No, I can't," I inform her.

"Why not? What choice do you have?" she asks accusingly.

"That just isn't an option for me."

"What if he doesn't want the baby?" she asks in reference to the father. "What if he wants you to have an abortion?"

"He can want it, but I don't, so it won't happen. It isn't an option."

She cannot comprehend this. "This will ruin your life. And his. You are trapping him into this."

I knew this would come up and it will be stated behind my back, but never expected anyone would say it to my face. *Why on earth would I deliberately DO this to anyone, let alone someone I wasn't even dating anymore? Why would I do this to myself?*

The people around me had no idea what I was going through.

I am pregnant. I am having a baby. What I am I going to do? There is no answer to that question. None.

There is nothing else to do right now but go to sleep.

News travels alarmingly fast.

I am not ready to tell anyone else. How to tell my parents who are living overseas in Europe? How tell people around me? It is too early to say anything. And this isn't exciting news to share. Not in this situation.

I am twenty years old, in college, and the baby's dad just turned twenty-three, having returned to college for the spring semester after taking a break from school in the fall. And we are not together. Most people who knew us as "together" over winter break and social gatherings here and there as 1990 started, know that we aren't really together anymore.

The pregnancy is whisper-behind-my-back news: "Did you hear…?" and "I thought she was smarter than that," and the "Who is the father?" gossip.

This is not the "congratulations – when are you due?" joyous news.

This wasn't a "next step" in a relationship that was on a path to an engagement or marriage. This was a college "boyfriend." Nothing more. Or that is how I felt.

I asked those who knew to tell no one else. I am not ready to handle this myself just yet, and I don't need unsolicited advice.

Within forty-eight hours of learning my news, I am given unsolicited advice and have to deal with people knowing when I have not told them.

I realize that my life is no longer my own.

Why is my choice anyone else's business?

The only other person's whose opinion matters is silent. For now.

I wake up each day instantly remembering the secret I am carrying. Literally carrying inside me. I am pregnant. With each day, I know this is real, yet at the same time I cannot believe it.

I play the part of the Shelley I was before the news. I still go to the parties and socialize. I laugh and pretend that I don't have a care in the world. Nothing has changed—at least to the outsiders who don't know. I still have classes, which I barely attend. I miss morning classes, because I am too sick. I won't be able to go to school in the fall since the baby is due in the middle of the fall semester. *Who knows when I will be able to come back to school?*

When I socialize, I look in people's eyes wondering if they know. *Do they know?* Because of the baby I no longer drink or do things that could harm it, but I don't make a big show of it. I laugh and pretend I am the same as always. I instead of the rum and Coke in the water bottle, it was just Coke. No one notices the change. Or if they do, they say nothing. When I am sick people think I am drunk or hung over. I don't correct them. The alternative? Tell them I am pregnant, which I am not ready to do. I would never be ready to announce it. I plan to let people figure it out.

As the spring semester continues, I act like I have moved on from the previous "boyfriend," so to most people I am "available." From an outsider's perspective, there is no reason why I couldn't go out or date someone else or someone new. But when a few guys indicate perhaps we could do something more than just hang out in mixed company, I laugh it off, playing that I am just having a semester where I am free and unattached. While most people don't know it, I have other priorities even though I don't quite know how to deal with them.

Why would I continue with this lifestyle while pregnant? Consider this: I had no place to live other than the sorority house and I was terrified that I would get kicked out of the house for being pregnant.

While I did hear from the baby's dad here and there, I didn't hear much from him in the days following the news. With each passing day, I felt more and more that I was doing this on my own and I would soon need to figure out where I was going to live that summer since the sorority house closes in the summer. I wouldn't be able to continue with school anyway.

I had to tell my parents. Of course. This required an expensive, long-distance collect call. They lived overseas in Scotland, so I was able to avoid it for a week or two, but I needed to tell them before the rest of my world figured it out.

I was the oldest of two children and between the two of us, I was the "responsible one," the "dependable one." I did what was expected of me. Usually.

My senior year of high school, I wanted to spend the night at my best friend Anna's house. Not an unusual request. So, when I asked if I could spend the night at her house that coming Friday, I assumed it was a formality. But it wasn't to be. I was not allowed to spend the night at her house that weekend. Why? Because Anna's mom Beth had a boyfriend who would sometimes stay at her house and they were not married. My parents did not condone this behavior. Anna was always welcome to spend the night at our house. But the point of spending the night at her house was because she had cable and a VCR and movies to watch. We didn't.

The next day at school, Anna casually asked right before class if I was coming over on Friday, and I had to tell her no and then explain why. How do you explain to your friend that you can't spend the night because my parents didn't approve of her mother's behavior?

Now, it is time for me to confront the inevitable again. I still am not prepared to tell them. This is not some "adventure" or experience I went through that will be forgotten in a week or so. I can't sweep this one under the rug and ignore it like speeding tickets and a no-call, no-show from work. This isn't underage drinking or having fender benders. This is life changing. And I have to tell them. Everyone I know, and many I don't, are going to soon know that I "messed up." This is a big one. And this is no longer just me. *I have another human to deal with who, at the moment, is one hundred percent dependent on me.*

I stand in the low-traffic area hall in the sorority house where the most remote phone line in the house is located. In this part of the house, there are a couple of bedrooms, but one isn't being used and the occupants of the others are gone—out for the night or home for the weekend. No one is around.

Preparing for my call required calculating the time difference of eight hours, the long-distance rates that go down after 7 p.m. and again after 11 p.m., I needed my college algebra class to determine the best time to break this news. I press so many buttons to make a collect call overseas—long distance, country code, local number, the calling card number. I don't know how I got more than fifteen numbers entered in the right order.

As the phone rang across the country and across the Atlantic to another continent, I walked down the hall to the unoccupied room pulling the tangle of phone cord between the base of the phone mounted to the wall and the receiver behind me and close the door. I pace in a small circle since the cord is leashing me to the wall on the other side of the door is already stretched to full length. My heart is racing. Over the hum of a long-distance connection, I hear the foreign ring-ring of the phone at my parents' house and I'm wondering if it would be the kitchen phone or their bedroom phone they would pick up? Part of me wants no one to answer. Part of me wants to get it over with.

After a few rings, my dad answers. It doesn't matter who answers. No matter which parent I tell the reaction will be the same.

There is a bit of formality. I am sure he knew something was wrong since they hadn't heard from me in months and a call was almost always a sign that this was something serious.

"Well, I need to tell you that I am pregnant." I ripped the bandage off and just went with it.

"Okay," he sounded calm, though I am not sure what else I would have expected, and he starts asking questions in his even and steady voice.

"Do you know who the father is?"

The expression "a dagger to the heart" now makes complete sense. Apparently, this is what they thought I was up to here. I cannot hide the hurt.

"Yes!"

"Are you getting married?"

"He hasn't asked."

He hasn't. In fact, he would soon tell me that he doesn't want to marry me because he wasn't in love with me. In 1990, this was not something people were publicly doing: not getting married just because of a baby. It wouldn't be for another couple of years that television would have a single mom that the vice-president of the United State would criticize.

"When is the baby due?"

"October 21st."

The questions are reasonable since I had been the prodigal child for the last couple of years.

My dad never offers to put my mom on the phone but instead tells me that she is in the U.S. Her father, my grandfather, was dying of cancer and she was there with him and her mother. He tells me that he will call her in the morning since it was late where she was.

I later find out he called her as soon as we got off the phone.

It is done. I told my parents, at least I told my dad and now my parents knew. A weight is lifted—relief. Not that anything is changed. There is still a lot more to deal with, but this part is done and over with.

As the phone call ends, he tells me, "We love you."

I know they do.

The spring semester is just over halfway through. At the beginning of April, Easter Weekend, I am about fourteen weeks pregnant and into the second trimester.

Good news travels fast. Except this wasn't good news. I was unmarried, no boyfriend, no family nearby and soon, no place to live. Yes, that is *great* news that I am having a baby.

The shame overwhelms me. I feel like a fugitive. I have a secret that I don't want anyone to know about and I feel a constant need to mislead people as a result of this secret.

I want people to stop asking me questions about my future. I don't have answers about what I will be doing in a few weeks let alone in a few months.

As spring goes on and I get my checkups I've almost resigned that I will go through this mostly alone. At least without the baby's dad. After mostly silence for a couple of weeks following the big announcement, he starts calling on most nights after work around 9:30.

I am not sure why he is calling other than to talk. We don't talk about the things that should be discussed. It is like how we should have talked months ago: we are learning more about each other. I don't know where this is going other than he is back in my life in some way.

I am confused by this relationship. *Where are we? Is he going to continue to date other people?* We don't discuss this, because I am unsure of my current title in his life. How will he introduce me to people?

I know that marriage isn't happening. I know I am not moving in with him. Things are unresolved between us. I am having the baby, we are having the baby, but the discussion doesn't go much farther.

Part of me is hopeful that he will tell me and show me that things will be okay—not just with the baby, but between us. He doesn't. I don't ask, because I only want one answer, so I don't risk it not being the one I want.

Part of me is hurt that not only does he not suggest marriage, but explicitly says that it isn't even an option. It makes me cry, but I know that getting married for the sake of getting married is not right. The other part of me is relieved that he doesn't bring up that we get married because I would have said yes, even knowing it wasn't right.

As the spring semester ends the week of Mother's Day, a holiday that now has new meaning for me, I have to move out of the sorority house since it closes for the summer. *Where am I going to live?* My parents are still in Scotland and I am not moving in with the baby's father.

I don't have a job anymore. I *had* a cashier job that my sorority sister Jennifer, a pharmacy major, helped me get at a pharmacy. She tells me that the owner-pharmacist had hired me because he knew I "wasn't like the other cashiers who always end up pregnant and have to quit." I realized I couldn't stay at this job. Not because anyone would fire me, but because this was another place where I felt that I couldn't continue to show my face.

A few months earlier, recalling the initial shock of the positive pregnancy test and subsequent confirmation test when I started prenatal care, I was still confused by the birth control pills not working despite following instructions.

Working at the pharmacy, I knew the pharmacists there were generous. If someone had a headache or nausea while at work, they were quick to help with something stronger than an over-the-counter strength ibuprofen or Pepto-Bismol. The previous fall before working at the pharmacy, I'd had strep throat twice, requiring two rounds of antibiotics.

So, when I started to get sore throat in mid-January, I told my pharmacist-boss that I would probably have to call in sick for a couple of days. I was handed the same antibiotics that I had been given by prescription the previous fall. When I started taking these, my sore, and probable strep, throat went away. The antibiotics worked on the strep and they also worked by making my birth control less effective at just the right time, something I only realize too many months later.

I knew I was done at the pharmacy when a second cashier gleefully, yet quietly flipped the wall calendar behind our cash registers to November and pointed to a date at the end of the month, five weeks after I was due in mid-October. I share nothing with her and decide that I can no longer work here.

How could I face Jennifer, or anyone there, anymore?

As the halfway point of the pregnancy nears, summer is coming and hiding the baby bump is not going to be an option much longer.

No job, no place to live. A baby. *A boyfriend?* I still don't know. The place he lives with his roommate is a good set-up for two people, not three much less four. There isn't room for me to move in. Not that he suggested it.

I am applying to jobs every day and I cannot find one with the economy plummeting into a recession. The summer of 1990 is a tough time to be looking for a job, and now I am not only pregnant, but showing more as the summer goes on.

I get my checkups as scheduled. I am barely gaining weight. The wrenching pain that notified me I was pregnant did not end with the first trimester and doesn't just happen in the morning. I am sick throughout the pregnancy and throughout the day.

Most days I hear from the baby's father, but some days I don't. We hang out, but he also goes off with friends without inviting me along. I don't need to be with him all the time, but sometimes he takes off with his friends and their girlfriends. I know because the girlfriends ask why he didn't bring me. I am so confused, but more hurt, about our relationship right now. I want to have him as part of my life, but I don't want to be that pushy "girlfriend" forcing him into something which will only lead to pushing him farther away. It may sound strategic, but really it was fear that pushing would lead to abandonment. I needed someone, even if only part-time. I hated that I needed someone, so I pretended I didn't. Most people had no idea of the struggles I was going through. Including the baby's dad.

I end up sharing a two-bedroom apartment with a couple I knew. It starts out as a godsend but soon becomes strained. They buy a St. Bernard puppy but don't train him or take him outside enough. They don't clean up after the puppy or themselves. For no apparent reason they install a deadbolt lock on their bedroom door making me feel untrustworthy. The take all their things to their room, including the television, and rarely come out unless they need something from me. It is uncomfortable, but it is a place to live.

I give them my share of the rent for June and July. When the landlord discovers the they have a dog he tells them they have to leave. They move out taking only their possessions and leaving trash and dog shit behind.

Come August, the rent is all mine.

While I continue applying for jobs, I have to enroll in Women, Infants, and Children (WIC), the federal assistance program. I need food. I had hoped some miracle would allow me to avoid this. As part of the process, I have to sit through a nutrition class. Being my first class, I complete a quiz asking about basic nutrition information, fruits and vegetables, and grocery shopping. When the facilitator reviews my quiz, she asks if this is my last class. Confused, I tell her it is my first class. She is surprised since I got all the answers correct, which further confuses me since it was about basic nutrition information. As I sit through the rest of the class learning about the four food groups, I find out that I have to attend monthly nutrition classes before I get my vouchers. I cannot believe that someone is getting paid to teach this. *I could totally do this!*

One afternoon I come home to a notice that my electricity is cut off. I had just been wondering how things could possibly get worse, and bam. I want to sit and cry and scream at my former roommates, but this will accomplish nothing.

As I scramble to get the electricity issue resolved, I learn from the utility company that they have not been paid since May. Even though the utility company left notices, I realize they were intercepted by my now former roommates and utilities were not included in the rent I gave them.

I write a check to get the electricity back on within two hours because I need my refrigerator and stove to eat. I write a check for an amount I don't have, but knowing I have a few days before that catches up with me.

In the *next* couple of days, I learn that the rent has not been paid since May and I have to leave by the end of August if I don't have rent. By some miracle, I am at least allowed to stay until the end of the month.

I feel betrayed by my former roommates, but I am not really surprised. While part of me felt that something wasn't quite right with the whole arrangement, I had no leverage to challenge them. I couldn't pay for a place myself. In the end, I was screwed with or without them.

As the summer is winding down and the fall semester is about to begin, the baby's dad and his roommate are moving. They rent a house together with a third roommate.

While I thought maybe we would move in together, he already had committed to the other guys. I am pissed and frustrated at all of them at being so clueless to my needs—but in reality, they have no idea I am struggling. I hadn't shared the seriousness of my situation with them. While I have no place to live, I also realize I need to give up on the idea that we will be living together when the baby comes.

The baby's father and I discussed very little about the future. When I once attempted to bring up necessary conversations, such as baby names, I realized that he had no clue about what was really happening and all the preparation it took. When I found out I was pregnant, I immediately knew that I had to "grow up". This did not happen for him. I imagine that a baby growing inside someone else, something that can only be felt by the mother carrying the baby, is abstract to others, especially a twenty-three-year-old male.

He can go about his life and not give much thought of a baby coming. He doesn't have the scarlet letter of a growing belly under his chest. He can live as if nothing has changed because he isn't throwing up or doesn't have a baby pressing on his bladder and he can fit into the same clothes today that he did a few months ago.

We both know one thing for sure: we can barely support ourselves. He is a college student living paycheck to paycheck. I am applying for jobs daily that I know I will not be able to keep. I can't even go into an interview without people suspecting I am pregnant.

We agree on some things: the solution to everyone is adoption. It isn't fair to the baby. We are not in love with each other. We don't really know each other. This isn't the right time.

Over the summer strangers leave me pleading handwritten notes on my car and mail me letters telling me that they wanted to adopt my baby. The baby's father and I do not discuss adoption because these appear; it is just the route that seems to make the most sense. I never feel unsafe because of these people, but it is odd to think that in my midst of being unsure about having a baby, others are desperate to take the reins.

The baby's father and I visit an adoption agency where I answer questions about my health and pre-natal care. We do paperwork, feeling we have no other option. I am saddened, but also relieved that this baby will have a chance at a better life than we can give it right now. The possibility of a future with the three of us fades as we do this and I wonder, *what will become of us? Will this just be a memory of something that happened in 1990? We will have no reason to continue a relationship anymore.*

The baby is due October 21 and I will turn 21 three weeks before. While people celebrate that milestone birthday in many ways, I have a new concern with this milestone birthday: I will lose the health care coverage as my father's dependent because I cannot be a full-time student. No one insures a pregnant woman, bringing up yet another problem and the realization I will have to apply for additional public assistance.

I continue applying for jobs, hoping for an office job. I apply for a job as a bookkeeper. A few days later I have a phone interview and am hired over the phone to start the following Monday.

Over the next few days, my phone is cut off, the bounced check to the utility company is catching up to me, the baby's dad and his roommates move into their house on the other side of town, and I do not have rent money for next month.

I tell people that we are going with adoption.

My parents come back to the U.S., heading to Colorado Springs, about 400 miles away from me. On the way there they visit me and meet the baby's dad for the first time at a restaurant over lunch.

Later, while he is at work, my parents propose that I live with them after the baby is born. I will not have to pay rent and they will help care for the baby so I can work. I don't have to give the baby up for adoption. They are hopeful and they know that this is a difficult decision.

It's true, the baby's dad and I had not decided on adoption as a result of a long conversation; we just both knew it was necessary. There was no need for a discussion.

We had absolutely no foresight into the emotional aftermath of this decision or any other potential ones facing us.

I hesitate. I know I cannot live with my parents indefinitely, especially since I haven't lived with them in over three years and I have changed so much! I would still have to deal with the baby's dad and any resulting relationship. We would always be tied. Thirty years from now, the baby will still have happened. But us keeping the baby would necessitate an additional commitment between us.

I thought I wanted this guy, the baby's dad, but I didn't know. I felt more pain than comfort in his presence. He kept me at arm's length and offered no other clues as to what he felt about me. I had zero insight into what was going on in his mind and was terrified to ask. Yet I didn't want to make this decision without talking with him. It was my body and my decision, but we had talked about it because it did involve him. We had decided the adoption route was best for us and the baby, and we had already started the paperwork.

On a deeper level still, I am undecided. Like the people begging me to let them adopt my baby, I write a letter to the baby's father outlining my parent's offer and leave it in his car. This way he will get all the details of the proposal right away and I don't have to wait for him to get home from work in the hopes to catch him alone.

When I talk to him later in the evening he says, "So you are moving." It is a statement, not a question.

I am unsure how to respond. It is stated as if the decision is made when I really want to talk this through.

"This means we keep the baby," I clarify.

"Right." He gets it.

"That means you are part of my life forever."

I don't even know how to drive this conversation. He is talking like it is a done deal and I want to make sure he gets it: he will be a father and responsible for our child forever. *I* will be part of his life forever and we will be forever connected differently than if we go through with adoption.

No matter which way we go, our lives are changed, and we will always have this connection. But do we do something that will keep us in each other's lives forever if we keep the baby? Or do something that makes this connection a memory? But I don't say all this because I don't know how to speak up for what *I* want. *I don't know what I want*, and I don't even consider my own feelings as I weigh my parents' hope to see their grandbaby against the still unknown feelings of the baby's father. When I found out I was pregnant, I knew that my life was no longer my own. I struggled with knowing what I wanted so much that I looked to others to help me with the decisions I felt I couldn't make by myself.

After about thirty to forty-five minutes of conversation, another life-changing decision is made: we keep the baby and I move with my parents in their new place in Colorado.

I will move to Colorado with the baby later in the fall following the birth in November or December.

After speaking with the baby's father, I let my parents know the decision. They head to Colorado where they will settle into their new home and prepare for changes coming later in the year with the arrival of their grandbaby.

Kelly, a friend from the sorority, and I stayed connected throughout the spring and summer. She knew about my deadbeat roommates, my looking for work, and the confusion around the baby's dad.

When I learned that I was NOT moving in with the baby's dad, I shared with her my devastation that I was unable to keep my apartment but had no place to go.

It is in later August, with less than a week for me to come up with rent or move, when she tells me that she and her two roommates decided that I will move in with them. It is a deal: I pay one-fourth the rent, any long-distance phone calls, no additional utilities and we all share groceries. I can move in now and pay my quarter share of the rent for September.

This is one decision I don't have to think about. I agree instantly and I am relieved and grateful.

I move in with Kelly and my two new roommates, whom I meet for the first time when I arrive. They are excited a baby is coming. Their place is a three-bedroom house and I share the master bedroom with Kelly. A borrowed an Army cot is set up in the master bedroom for me, since there isn't room for another bed. It was a place to sleep in a house with good roommates and low rent. I was in a better place than I had been most of the summer.

I start my job having only been hired over the phone and given a start date. It is late August well into my third trimester. With a job, a place to live and knowledge that when I have the baby it is mine to keep, I now have some direction.

I am still sick many days and, at thirty-two weeks, have gained less than ten pounds. With each check-up they note that the baby is growing at the appropriate rate, and most of the time the minimal weight gain is not mentioned. As long as I am gaining and growing there doesn't seem to be a concern.

A new concern: *where the baby will sleep*. I have no crib or bassinet or anything baby related. I am not prepared having just found a place to live for myself.

I still see the baby's father several days through the week and weekends. He works and goes to school and we still had the same social circle of friends. I still had no idea of our relationship status long-term. We just didn't talk about it. I did want a relationship with him but didn't know how to say it. I realize I would rather have a distant relationship than no relationship.

We do things together such as go to football games and movies. At a football game I overhear him tell his friend he was going hunting for fall break, less than ten days before the baby is due. I am shocked and hurt. In response he reminds me that it is the week before the baby is due and he will be back by then. He doesn't know that a baby has its own timeline and we only guess the actual arrival date. He could be hunting while I am having a baby alone.

To me this will affect the outcome of our relationship. Even though we are keeping the baby, if he is not there when the baby is born, I don't see how this will work out. I feel that if he misses this I will move on and figure this out on my own. I say none of this. My twenty-year-old self is still too terrified to stand up, to tell him that I need him there.

Two weeks before the baby is due my roommates host a baby shower. At this event I learn from the baby's dad's mother that his parents had been aware of the adoption decision and only recently learned the latest plot twist of keeping the baby. I find out that her son doesn't open up to his own family on major events, giving me some insight that it isn't just me that he is not open with.

After the shower, I have a small used crib on loan, some gifts of clothing and a baby book.

On Sunday, the day after the baby shower, I am thirty-eight weeks pregnant. With a couple of weeks left to prepare, the baby's dad and I had planned to shop for essentials that afternoon. He would come over after playing flag football with some guys.

When he arrives that afternoon, he tells me that he had been hit in the head. Even though he isn't feeling well, we go to the store as planned. After buying a few things, he takes me home since he is just not up for doing anything.

On Monday, he tells me about his visit to the student health center. The diagnosis is a broken jaw and he is having surgery to wire his jaw shut the next day. Since he is medicated and scheduled for surgery, we agree to see each other on Tuesday evening.

At nearly midnight Monday, I cannot get comfortable or sleep even though Kelly generously has given me her bed while she sleeps on the Army cot. I recall, in the midst of Braxton Hicks contractions, that taking a warm bath helps alleviate them. While taking a midnight bath to relax, I don't even consider that this is anything more than the discomfort of the later stages of pregnancy. I am still two weeks away from my due date.

An hour later, the cool bathwater is no longer helpful. I exit the bathroom to find my roommates up. Three-fourths of the house believe I am in labor.

My back is bothering me and no matter what anyone does or how I lay down, nothing helps.

I am experiencing long bouts of pain. We think they may be contractions, but no one knows how to time them. *Are we supposed to time them from start-to-start, start-to-stop, stop-to-start?*

One of my roommates calls the hospital to report an eleven-minute contraction. Apparently an eleven-minute contraction is not labor. My roommates are told to wait until the water breaks.

They call the baby's dad, arguing with his roommate to wake him up. He had taken a painkiller to get through the twelve hours before his surgery. When they finally reach him, he informs them that when the water breaks then it is time.

I head to the bathroom while my roommates discuss what to do. Being that I am much more comfortable in the bathroom, they make phone calls and decisions on my behalf, while asking me for updates through the door. I am now bleeding and somewhat panicked. They tell me to come out, but I refuse.

"My water hasn't broken, so we have time!" I say.

They break the lock on the bathroom door easily. As they drag me out of the bathroom, they inform me that we were going to the hospital. I am surprised to see the baby's dad in my room since

I thought he wouldn't drive. I overhear phone calls to our parents that we are hospital-bound while my roommates are dressing me.

I find myself across the back seat of a car with the baby's dad holding my hand and telling me to breathe.

At 3:35 a.m., we arrive at the hospital.

Entering the hospital, I am brought to a standstill every few steps. I am annoyed that the baby's dad was on painkillers due to his broken jaw. *Can he empathize with my pain? Is he even feeling pain?* He looks so calm while I cannot stand up and can barely speak, despite my desire to comment about the baby coming before his hunting trip.

A wheelchair arrives and while sitting isn't comfortable it is better than being doubled over in a hospital hallway.

I soon find myself on a bed, undressed from the waist down while I am asked a series of questions: What is your name? Date of birth? Blood type? How many weeks are you? I just think they are trying to distract me because the baby is nearly here.

I later learned the reason for the interrogation: they had no idea who I was or my medical history. My roommates were downstairs checking me in, but in that moment, they did not know anything about me.

Following directions, I push once and once again. There are no questions about the pain among the litany of questions and chaos around me. There is no time for anything but directing me through what turn out to be the final steps of the delivery within minutes of my arrival.

When I deliver our baby boy, I feel the baby's dad's tears on my face. My medical chart arrives soon after.

I briefly hold my newborn baby before he is handed off to his father while I undergo post-partum repair. It takes over fifty stitches to repair the results of a less-than-four-hour labor and delivery. As I am getting sewn back together, the baby's father wants to know a name. *Now* he wants to discuss names.

We named our son, Antonio, shortly after he was born in those early hours of Tuesday at a healthy seven pounds, six ounces with his father present. Just two days later and he would have missed it because of a hunting trip.

A few hours later, the baby's grandparents meet their grandson and take their son to his oral surgery appointment.

While we had not slept since waking up Monday morning, Tuesday is a full day with visitors, paperwork and medical visits. So much had changed, literally overnight.

Shortly after he awakes from his surgery, the baby's dad is back at our side, jaw was wired shut for the next six weeks.

Because we are not married, I cannot put the baby's dad's name on the birth certificate without additional paperwork. In fact, during the delivery and the hospital stay, the baby's father legally had no say in anything related to our son. On Wednesday, moments after I was officially discharged, we learn that the paperwork to declare that baby's dad as the father, accepting paternity, could have been done while we were still admitted in the hospital. Since we are already discharged, we had to return to the hospital later.

The next day we return to the hospital and the baby's dad pays ten dollars to declare his paternity of our son. A formality of the exchange of cash, a signature, and a stamp of a notary and he is legally the father of our son.

That evening we drive the hour to his parents' house so I can stay with his mother while he went hunting for two days.

In the next few weeks we decide when I will move with my parents. Since I cannot work while caring for a newborn, I continue to live with my roommates until the move. The baby's father and I do not discuss living together.

The week of Thanksgiving marks six weeks of challenges following our son's birth. Along with that milestone, the wires come off from the now mostly healed broken jaw. In the throes of post-partum recovery, I am able to drive again (I was not supposed to be operating a vehicle until then).

The baby's dad and I also make the decision that the week after Christmas is when the baby and I would move to Colorado Springs.

Thanksgiving and Christmas are spent with the baby's dad's family.

Just before the baby is twelve-weeks old, I moved. Family and friends feel this is the end of things. Friends are saddened at the loss of the baby they have known since before he was born. The baby's paternal grandparents think I am leaving, and they will never see us again despite being five-hours away.

The relationship status between the baby's father and me is still in question. He tells me to date other people, but I won't. I have an infant! And I don't really want to date.

I write him letters daily (we are in the early '90s, before email becomes a thing). He calls long-distance daily (yup, no cell phones yet either). We talk and learn more about each other with 400 miles between us than when we were in the same room. We grow closer despite having more physical distance between us.

Over the next seven months we see each other four times. He comes to visit us, or we meet halfway between our cities for a weekend together.

As agreed, my parents help take care of the baby and I search for work. I finally get a minimum wage job working evenings and weekends. It is challenging to live with my parents, having a new baby and no outlet of friends or a partner to share the stresses of the day. I have little privacy. Even though the baby and I have our own room even phone calls are taken in the extension in the kitchen or my parent's bedroom.

In late spring of 1991, the baby's dad suggests we move back to Albuquerque later that summer so we can move in together. It makes sense to share expenses and childcare responsibilities. However, with the conservative upbringing we both had, our parents are disappointed in this decision. *Did it really still matter that we weren't married?* We already had a baby outside of marriage. Apparently adding cohabitation to the list was a continuation of disappointment in our choices. We knew we needed to figure out our relationship and if it was anything other than co-parenting. At this time, this is still outside of social norms.

Later that summer we move and start to figure out what we are doing as a couple, as parents, and as two people who need to finish college. With luck of timing, I return to my employer from the previous year right as my replacement prepares to leave. We find an apartment and move in over Labor Day weekend when our son is eleven months old.

I am working full time for minimum wage and no benefits and the baby's father is going to school full time and working part time. We manage part-time day care and between work school schedules spend more time with our son individually but not much time together.

Our expectations when moving in together were very different. He comes and goes, meeting up with people for pickup basketball, hanging out after work, and going bike riding on weekends. This is his lifestyle and he doesn't think much of sharing this information until he is walking out the door, if at all. He doesn't check in with me. We aren't *married*, after all.

This causes problems in our relationship. Since he was the one who asked me to move in with him, I was expecting a partnership in parenting and a developing relationship between us. He wasn't quite there. As I am navigating my early twenties as a mom, he is a single guy in his mid-twenties still living day-to-day on his own agenda.

I don't make plans with my friends very often, mostly because we have different priorities. When we go out with our friends as a couple, we either take our toddler with us or get a babysitter. But mostly we couldn't afford a babysitter and the people trusted with his care were usually the same people we would go out with.

The baby's father would make plans according to his own agenda; I wouldn't make plans in case he wanted to do something with me. I would become resentful of my own actions along with his. My life revolved around our son and what his dad wanted to do.

One Saturday as he informs me that he is heading out to meet a buddy to go mountain biking, I throw out the possibility that I may have had previous plans. He replies that if I wanted to go out, hang out, and do things with my friends, then I just need to "ask him to babysit." That's when I inform him that his role in our son's life is a father not a babysitter. For me, this was one of the many turning points in our relationship. I remember watching him realize that he had to take on the role he agreed to, and I also remember feeling that I finally found my voice by relaying that "babysitter" was not a role he could choose. He was a parent and equal partner.

Over the next couple of years, we push through with the many stresses that come with being a young family: tight finances, competing interests, and getting to know each other in a way that should have happened on a different timeline. It is not easy and many times I wonder whether our relationship will continue.

Shortly before the two-year anniversary of us moving in together, the baby's father graduates from college and is preparing to enter into the workforce full time. We had agreed that after he got his degree and was in the workforce with a steady job, I would return to school and get my degree. Not sure what I want to get my degree in, I start evening classes at the community college to complete core classes.

Then I remember my experience in WIC a few years earlier, being taught about nutrition and things that I thought everyone knew. Who knew that "nutrition" was a college major and I could become a registered dietitian with this degree?! Not only did I find this interesting, but it was something I really want to do: *teach others about nutrition.*

As I learn about the requirements for this degree, I discover that it is a science degree and requires graduate work. The path ahead seems daunting, especially having to start from the beginning, but I am focused, and this is something I really want to do. While I was still unsure of myself, having my son made me realize that if I applied myself to something I really wanted, that I could do this. I now had a plan.

Through this, a lot of seeming barriers crept up. Science was not my strongest subject, yet I had chosen to pursue a science degree. The graduate work, including a competitive internship, would mean more time in school. Once I made the decision to do it, I was determined I *could* do it. Even though I didn't yet have the benefit of hindsight, I had made it through one of the most challenging times of my life. Being single, pregnant, and keeping a baby without the benefit of knowing whether anything in my future would "work out" I wasn't fully connected to this recent history. But when it came to school and getting my degree, something in my mind told me that this was doable.

Even though my now-boyfriend had graduated from college, there was still uncertainty on what route he would take with his work and career. We were at a place in our relationship where this became a joint decision. Despite many opportunities, he chose to work full time for the company he had been with for the past six years.

With our lives heading in a positive direction, marriage was brought up more by our friends than between us. I hated when people asked, "When are you getting married?" I hated when I got excited by "teases" of a ring and the subsequent disappointment that made me stop anticipating it. I never gave an ultimatum, since I would not gamble with the possibility of him walking away.

In early September of 1993, two years after we had moved in together, I *think* we get engaged. It isn't formal with a ring or bended knee. I am not even presented as a question. I happen to make on off-handed remark about "when we get married" and, without any expectation of a response, he tells me to "pick a date."

Confused, I am not ready to question whether it is a "real" proposal.

The next morning when he comes home from work, he asks me if I told our son that we are getting married. Our son was not yet three-years-old, so this news is no different than asking if he wanted to watch a movie or take a bath. He didn't know that the way we lived was anything other than normal. But this did confirm the "engagement" was real. There was no proposal in the traditional sense and no ring, but he is now telling people that we are getting married—even if it is our three-year-old.

For so long we didn't know where we would end up and if it would be together or separate. We knew that "happily ever after" was for fairy tales. Even though our parents are still together, having both celebrated over fifty years of marriage, we knew the realities as well.

When we met in college four years prior to our "engagement," we were having fun. We were on parallel paths, never considering if we would be in each other's orbit long-term.

When we met, I was still on a self-destructive path of excess in areas that are best left to moderation or even abstinence. School was not a priority. He knew a college degree would happen eventually, but then, what job or career would result?

When we look back at 1990, we agree that we were both wandering. We have no idea where we would have ended up had we not had the baby bump in the road, but we are both doubtful it would have been together.

Today we realize that God had other ideas for us.

Little did I know that that Ted, the one person who witnessed the silly pact between Sarah and me, would be the person with whom I would have the roller-coaster ride, get engaged to four years later, and marry eight months after that, a few months prior to my twenty-fifth birthday. He was the catalyst of tears, kisses, ups and downs, adventure, and life-altering moments. The father of my baby would be the person I would eventually fall in love with.

Our son was three-and-a-half when Ted and I said, "I do" in front of people who never thought we would "make it."

As kids we heard, first comes love, then marriage, then the baby carriage.

We rearranged it. First came the baby, then love, then marriage. When we did get married, it was the right time.

And through all of this, I found my passion, got a degree, and pursued a career in nutrition. If it wasn't for the unexpected baby that led to the WIC experience, there is no way to know if I would have found this profession on my own.

When our son was ten years old, he saw me finish the final milestone of my formal education when I received my Master of Science in Nutrition.

Nutrition is my passion and I love sharing my knowledge about nutrition and eating well and how it affects our health. Now I used my voice to help people navigate the myriad of nutrition myths and misinformation, helping them on a path to health and wellness through food.

Today, Ted and I acknowledge that the difficulties of the massive shift that happened in 1990 and the next few years saved us from something—from ourselves, from the wandering, from the lack of direction.

Happily, ever after? It is still in progress, but things look promising.

We have celebrated many milestones in the thirty years since we met.

The person who is referred to as my "baby's father" is my life partner.

Yes, my college boyfriend whom I later married and continue to raise our son with.

The one who supported me through school and told me that I could succeed in my profession even when I had doubts.

And while in the early stages of our non-traditional relationship, when I was unsure of his support, he is the one who knew that one day things would work out as they were supposed to.

Deep down, I knew it too.

A registered dietitian nutritionist for over twenty years, Shelley Rael, MS, RDN, loves that her profession is her passion in which she helps people change their mindset about food, eliminating rules and judgment while supporting a lifestyle in which people are healthier and enjoy life. She is an author, professional speaker, does media appearances, and offers programs to help people lose weight, be healthier, and reach their personal wellness goals. Shelley is living the life in Albuquerque and is on a mission to enjoy life with her husband. She is a mother, grandmother, and has three rescue dogs. Find more about Shelley at her website, ShelleyRael.com.

Is It All
Black and White?

Lori Cheramie

"Every part of my body, mind, and soul was asking me
to slow down, but I was not accepting of this message."
—Lori Cheramie

I
t was a Thursday afternoon and I sat with the doctor after an intense ultrasound. I remember the look on her face, with deep, sad eyes and a serious grin that prefaced life-altering news. Having "the conversation" with young women about such a decision must have been as heartbreaking for her as it was for me. She talked about the many fibroids in my uterus, the suspicious ovarian tumor, and the long history of my endometriosis. The tumor needed to be removed and we would schedule surgery that next week.

Processing this information seemed easy and worst-case scenario, I would still have one ovary. To any other thirty-four-year-old, this news may have stopped time. We are often conditioned to believe a woman's life path is to be a mother. It is a vision most of us are fully immersed in from the time we are toddlers, dreaming of that day we too would be a mom. However, I just did not slow down enough to even process the trajectory this may take on my pre-planned life. I put surgery in my day planner like any other meeting.

The day before surgery my doctor called and said, "Lori, I hate to do this, but I have the flu and I can't perform your surgery. I have asked another doctor to cover for me." She advised me that it was best not to wait, and I was in good hands.

As I woke post-surgery, I saw this crazy image of a man in scrubs with a fishing vest. I thought I was dreaming and would later learn that Dr. Jacobson had an interesting way of accessorizing his daily scrubs with his passion of fishing. He spoke very technically, and I remember the expression on my parents' face of "get to the point."

"We could not save the ovary and it was removed."

I did not want to feel that pain or really acknowledge what this meant. I took care of the problem and it was time to move on. This had become my rhythm of life, take care of it and move on, no matter what that meant for my body and heart.

Nine months later it was like Groundhog Day and I was having the same conversation, but this decision would be much greater. A full hysterectomy was next and whatever was going on in my body kept creating tumors with no indication this would stop. I had not stopped to consider my health and how my busy, chaotic lifestyle with a jet-setting career might be impacting my inner world of *presence*. It was a pattern from my earliest years to be a front runner and push myself to perfection. The need to prove myself was buried deep within. I'd spent a lot of time avoiding a deeper connection to myself and this is where it had landed me. How far back did this pattern go?

It was late August of 1977 and my first day of kindergarten. I was wearing my blue plaid Catholic school uniform with my huge backpack almost pulling my tiny frame back toward home. In my mind, however, I was standing taller than the day before me, fully ready for this new challenge. The obligatory first-day-of-school photo with my parents was off-putting to me; this milestone was serious, and I was ready to take on the world. After the four of us kids piled into the car, I waved at our beloved neighbor, Mrs. Francis, who was watching the excitement, and the acceleration through life began.

School was easier for me than many others as I thrived off the structure and organization that it created. Good grades and an abundance of extracurricular activities filled the years. I vividly remember the feeling of disappointing others arising within me at this young age yet didn't fully recognize how this would shape my choices for the long haul. I felt the internal battle of standing in my own truth versus doing what others wanted.

I was exposed to so many strong role models during my structured Catholic school years, I was destined to be a leader. It was in second grade that I was chosen to be in the Christmas pageant as Mary. I was so excited and even a little nervous to carry that role. Would it be foreshadowing in my life to be a mother or serve as a role model for women?

In high school, my friends were abundant and strong. Wanting to make a splash in my new school, I felt ready to meet new friends, new experiences, and get a fresh start. Within two weeks of school there would be an election for class president. I did not know enough people to make an impact but desperately wanted to take a chance. I had to get creative and make an impression. It was the beginning of the art of storytelling.

My mom was always up for a challenge too. She found me a red and white polka dot dress, mouse ears, gloves, black nose and the entire outfit to be Minnie Mouse. I was going to take my schoolmates on a journey through the magic kingdom of what school would be like with Lori Cheramie as Class President. Costumes were never mentioned as a prerequisite; rather it was supposed to just be a typical "please vote for me" speech. I was so scared when my turn came that I wanted to wake up from what I thought was a bad dream. But quitting was not an option, so I moved ahead, used some positive self-talk, and smiled my way through that speech.

A victory would follow and Student Council continued to be my strength. It challenged me to meet new people, learn public speaking at a young age, and stretch beyond my limits. One of my closest friends I met through Student Council was Ashley. I adored everything about her but most of all her wit and how popular she was with her beautiful sandy brown hair, strong posture, and warm smile. We got into trouble together, traveled together, and I always felt like her little sister. As she was leaving for college there was a disagreement that involved trust and questioned both of our integrity. It was so strong it tore us apart and I remember the pain as if I had lost a limb. I ignored those emotions and accepted we were no longer friends. Besides she was off to college and I still had my senior year.

When I began college, I again wanted to challenge myself and not follow the same path as others. It felt like my circle of friends were all joining a select group of sororities. This was uninteresting and I longed to be a part of something different. I convinced myself I should just join a different sorority to meet new people and get a fresh start. This also meant I could avoid my old friend Ashley, as she was a part of a sorority of all fellow New Orleanians. I shifted that emotion of resentment by creating a shield of armor around my heart that would last for decades, resulting in a pattern in which I would later suffer the consequences. The sorority life, while exciting, was truly not for me. It hardened me to a single focused competitive woman with little awareness of being present and more focused on taking instead of giving. This person I had become in college was the overachiever on steroids—I was ready to be an adult, make money, and bury emotion. It was like checking a box on a well-designed to-do list. Next…check the box for college.

With a fast four-year pace through college I was starting my career at twenty-one as an eager advertising sales executive. My career started like everything else I had entrained my body to do, succeed and overachieve. Life was great and my personal life was following along as it should with my college boyfriend to soon be my husband. If I planned it all perfectly, I could have 2.5 kids before I was thirty and maybe order that white picket fence. Was life really this simple, this black and white?

It was 1996 and I got a phone call that my dear friend Ashley from high school, from whom I was estranged for years, was diagnosed with cancer. Her prognosis was not good. My mind flooded with the anger that I had stuffed down inside for years. I prayed for her, and remembering her young face, hoped for the best but was too caught up in my own world. I did nothing else. I was frozen in my own shell so much so that I never even attempted to visit her. I let it slip through my hands and within a short time she had passed away. I never made the time to say goodbye or, more importantly, say I was sorry. I recall vividly this being the beginning and decline of hiding emotional pain. This life lesson of death and how quickly things change was one of the hardest I encountered. However, I packed up those emotions and stored them away. I still wasn't getting it. Feelings rushed at my insides; *how could I not make peace with her before her death? How could I be so selfish?* A sensation of drowning and not being able to get any air kept me awake for days and years even when I tried to ignore that voice in my head. Life is not that simple, and I should fasten the seat belt because courage was needed ahead. The lessons keep coming but sometimes we are not ready to hear them.

As a young female, working for a Fortune 50 company in the 1990s was still a challenge. The need to prove myself competing against the predominantly white male executives was required. Selling Yellow Pages ads in 1994 quite frankly was easy, who could imagine a world without the *Yellow Pages*? I loved helping businesses, gaining their trust, and I also loved the commission that came with each sale. Each day ended with a calculation of what I sold, how much I earned, and added it to my tally for the week.

I was part of an inside sales team who were mostly women with a few men just "earning their stripes" to become an outside sales rep. Outside sales jobs were reserved for men and the occasional single woman who would choose not to have a family because they traveled. Launching my career held a powerful memory that shaped my future in business. At the time, the premier *Yellow Pages* ad size was the back cover of the directory costing thousands of monthly dollars. That coveted space was riddled with personal injury attorneys. I had just returned from sales training and learned about this premier ad space but was still feeling like an amateur. I was assigned a sales market in Farmerville, Louisiana, a small town of about 5,000 and "everyone knows me" was the objection

I heard on every sales call. It was a late Friday afternoon and I just called on the local bank that decided to cancel all of their paid advertising. This was the worst-case scenario and I was terrified to tell my sales manager. I became a warrior and was going to just figure it out. I had few accounts left to call on and up next was Auger Timber company. What in the world would they need advertising for? I was a city kid born and raised in New Orleans and likely saw very few timber trucks. I did some self-talk and reminded myself, "What do I have to lose?" That moment was another valuable lesson I take with me tenfold through life. If you want something you must ask. You may not always get what you ask for, but you have to ask.

Auger Timber had a "bold listing" which was the smallest paid advertising. I was a few minutes in my sales pitch and the office manager at Auger Timber was so kind as she said, "Thanks, honey, we are all set and can keep everything the same." Here was my moment as I was up to bat. *"Don't swing and miss, Lori"* was what I was thinking. I dug deep in my marketing brain and "branding" popped in my head. My voice cracked slightly and I said, "There is just one thing I would like to recommend to you: the back cover is now available and based on what you told me about your credibility in town, I think it would be a great opportunity to brand Auger Timber." I remember a pause and she said, "What did you say?" with a little chuckle. My inner voice of doubt kicked in and thought, *"How stupid could I be, I knew they were not interested"* but I had to answer. I dug deep in my core and said it again. She said, "Wow, we never knew that was an option and we would love it!"

I did it! I sold the best piece of advertising available and I could hardly contain my excitement! I was a problem solver and perhaps young in years, but I was not afraid of a challenge.

Few women walked the career path I envisioned at my company and the ones who did seemed to be single or divorced with no kids. They were able to travel, relocate, and keep the pace of the men, with the exception of the 6:00 a.m. arrival to work, which was accomplished mostly by men who seemed to wear a badge of honor if their car was in the parking lot first. As a female, there was also the clothes, the makeup, and the hair! The dreaded hair to position perfectly in place and with my unruly black mane was a true exercise in torture to get ready for work. I was never going to be there at 6:00 a.m. but I can promise you that I was almost always last to leave. A few promotions later and years of rave reviews I was sure to get to the top. I was aware of the "boys club" environment, joined them for happy hour and regretfully now, even played along with what I knew was unprofessional banter. I made mistakes but learned to develop the art of taking responsibility within reason. I worked Saturdays, late nights, holidays, and did whatever it took to keep the pace and prove myself. I was in one of the largest sales divisions in an upper management role typically reserved for the tenured men.

I was unstoppable until that December day when a woman ran a red light and hit me square in the driver's door. I have little memory of the accident but recall the rocking of my head back and forth and each time it went left it would crack a little more of the window. I looked up to two terrified faces asking, "Are you ok, are you ok?" I was speechless. I couldn't even find air to speak. I was in shock. My world came to a stop. I went to the hospital with cuts and bruises accompanied by whiplash that would remain for years. I was working three hours from home when the accident happened so my husband had to travel to pick me up as my car was totaled. Every part of my body, mind, and soul was asking me to slow down, but I was not accepting of this message.

The next day I grabbed my laptop and moved swiftly through the office door like it was any other day. My boss asked, "Why are you here?"

"I have to be here, I have so much to do," I said.

The reality of work being non-negotiable and a force within me was beginning to become a great divide. Life at home was not perfect; it was not bad, but it was more non-existent. It was a place of ease with two people growing at a much different pace and a vision not aligned. My world stopped for a reason and needed redirection. But again, I wasn't willing to hear it.

The physical limitations from the car accident were tough to endure through the long work hours. My neurosurgeon expressed his opinion that I was lucky the damage was not more severe. There was lots of soft tissue damage and a constant shoulder-neck pain that was at times debilitating. Several months of physical therapy followed, which was more a task like punching a clock. I was going through the motions. The reality of creating more physical damage as I raced through therapy was not even a thought in my mind. Work was unmanageable and I was unable to express my fear of how I was going to get it all done. I felt conflicted and torn and needed a better purpose. The walls around me were falling and if I changed the scenery it may all work again. That was the solution, I was a problem solver, so I began the search for a job with purpose.

I became the Vice President of the American Heart Association for Louisiana. Vice President sounded like a big title and it felt bigger than me, but I was ready to step into those shoes. Meanwhile I had to face the reality of my marriage. How could I confront the obvious that may have forever gone unsaid? Simply put, we had outgrown each other. The surmounting pressure of work, the strains of different future goals resulted in a drift apart. As a result, we lived as roommates and this is not what I envisioned about marriage. The courage to move through saying the words of "divorce" were painful, embarrassing, and I needed to detach. The new house we had built, the shared group of friends, and the routine of life was changing rapidly. The day it all hit me was when we sold our house and I was moving out. My body shrunk along the wall of my empty master bedroom and I let the tears flow with only the witness of my dog, Cenla, and my two cats. It was going to be me and the pets as my shield to block the world of seeing my own fear.

The pain of divorce is undeniably one of the greatest time-stopping shades of grief I had yet to experience. I knew it was right for my future, but it was not without compassion and great sorrow did I exist in that moment. My new job was my outlet and the support of my dear sister, who happened to live in town with me at that time. She was motherly, caring, and concerned. She checked in on me during one of the busiest times of her life. Her strength carried us both until I could stand on my own again. I dived into work and I was in familiar ground with new friends (coworkers), a new environment, and a new task ahead. I was becoming really good at this reinventing myself and starting over. I'd always fall back into default of keeping my pace instead of feeling my feelings. This was success, just keep moving and the hard stuff won't catch you. Three weeks into the new job, 9/11 happened serving as such a monumental moment in time for all, time would stop for the world outside just as it did for me when that car hit me. Chaos is the nature of the beast until the trauma is so large that one cannot outrun it. While the impact to me personally is not even comparable of those who loved and lost; it still played a role in my immediate future. As a VP of fundraising for the AHA, I led a team with lofty monetary goals as one of the nation's largest non-profit organizations. It was challenging to lead a team through this and suddenly living my passion didn't feel like it was a fit. Everything in my life felt like the wrong size clothing and it just didn't fit. Fourteen months later I received a call from an old boss. He offered me a job to come back to my former company in a newly created role. It was back in marketing, which was my passion. It created a space for me to have structure but also creativity. I was going to enter a new market and a chance to move to a new city with a fresh start. I have been here before, it was a new space, new people, new challenge, and a time to rewrite the story! It blinded the physical pain I was still experiencing from the car accident after years of just learning to deal with the pain. It was my space and I knew I would thrive.

The adventure of the new job was great but the fear of being alone was in the back of my mind. Dating was awkward and being alone was a pouring salt onto old wounds I'd have to feel when forced into that silence.

I would quickly be involved in a serious relationship with little time for myself. He would be everything my first husband was not. It was exciting and so very unknown. How could this love be different and why was it new to me? I had some resistance from friends and family on this new romance, however I was not really good at listening to advice. The reasons I fell in love all seemed to focus around vision, money, success, and career. We were aligned in hard work and being the best at anything including work, hobbies, and, for him, as a dad. His two sons would be with us every other weekend. Daily life was fast paced as we both worked long hours in the same industry allowing post work talk to be effortless. We would later elope to a storybook wedding in Napa Valley. Our entire relationship was the highest of highs and the lowest of lows. His kids were so kind and welcoming to me as a "stepmom," but that title was hard for me as it felt cold and shallow. And, it was what I became.

It was a whirlwind romance of good versus evil and one I was not equipped to handle. I made so many mistakes of not being present. My health was beginning to unravel led by my heart unraveling. I was no longer first in his life rather third or maybe even fourth behind kids, work, hobbies, etc. I wanted to blame this all on him, but life has taught me so much since then and I have moved past this anger and resentment. Work was thriving and our common thread. We buried our heads in work, keeping us blind to so many mistakes we were making, and I knew early in this marriage that something felt wrong. Many arguments were left with sleepless nights, exhausting workdays, and lack of self-care. I was scared, confused, and began to retract within. At thirty-three years old I no longer recognized myself.

My friends were limited since my world was my husband and his family. My pets became my best friends. They were the best listeners as many nights I would sit on the floor of the closet in tears and recite, "This is it; we are stuck here, and we need to learn to make the best of it." In our first year of marriage things were in bad shape and we needed counseling. The words we would say to each other left scars so deep that even after healing they would always be present. The pain of each argument was like a knife cutting deeper through the layers to my heart until one day it would pierce so strong it would pierce through it. The pieces of us were

left on the floor. *Who would clean it up?* Being an overachiever
was not any less in my arguing. He quickly learned what would
stop me: the D-word. He threw out the divorce word so easily it
reflected no real value on our marriage. But what did that mean
to me? As the word would resonate it was a pit in my stomach. I
would envision the shame and pain of telling others I had been
divorced "twice"! *What's wrong with me? Am I loveable? Am I able
to love? Which was it?* A fear of being a two-time divorcée was
keeping me stuck in place like drowning in quicksand. I needed
a distraction.

Some immediate health concerns that had to be handled were
now again at the forefront. As a young adult I had learned that
I had endometriosis. It was aggressive and it became almost too
routine. I would do laparoscopic surgery multiple times to get
back to a place of manageable pain. I began adding prescription
medicine like it was a new skincare product. Just keep numbing
the pain and being reactive. This was the new me. The deep pain
in my shoulder, as a result of my car accident, was a knot and it
would radiate through my heart. I was now on anti-inflammatory
medicine four-to-six times a day. My endometriosis was becoming
worse and had a medical chart the size of a thesaurus. My physical
body was like a house of cards and rather than repairs, it was easier
to just mask the discomfort and add on more layers.

I could not keep up this pattern of multiple surgeries to sup-
press the endometriosis with the knowledge it would continue to
come back. Lupron shots to force early menopause was the last
option at age thirty-four. When I was not working, I was in bed
with pulsing headaches. The ability to multitask was not possible
and my health needed my full attention, but I was not ready to
give it. My new family around me was becoming more and more
distant, soon they would be invisible, and I would too if I didn't
wake up. I am not sure I ever really understood being a stepmom.
I loved these beautiful children that were in my life but my ability
to acknowledge and accept that role was a challenge. I wanted
the best for them and to empower them with the core values my
parents provided; however, I always felt I was inadequate or out
of place. My husband was very protective of our roles and it was

clear these were not my kids. I wanted to make this picture work so badly, but it never seemed to connect.

It was now 2006 and I was being faced with the same decision but much more final than the partial hysterectomy as reflected upon at the start of this journey. Real fears of the C-word arose, as I saw my dear friends Ashley and a few others have cancer at a young age. I accepted this information as there was no reason to even think about it; my husband did not want more kids and it felt as if it was meant to be this way. I never processed these emotions, the sadness, and grief. This black and white life I envisioned for many years confined in that Catholic school structure was suddenly a mirage. I quickly woke up from the daze and thought "no time for this." I was ready to move on.

My mom surely was saddened, and I knew there must have been sorrow in this decision, but she wrapped me in love and support and was there to get me through yet another surgery. The reality of giving birth to my own child was now gone with little reflection.

Throughout the same year I began to experience extreme fatigue, unexplained skin rashes, unexplained bruises all over my body and a feeling of overall sadness. I would go home for lunch breaks from work and literally collapse of exhaustion and nap. This was not my body, something was wrong. Through the series of doctor visits in looking for an autoimmune condition, I was given two antidepressants. My migraines increased and the constant sinus problems were treated with a merry-go-round of antibiotics. I was on six medications, and I carried a pill pack that reminded me of what my elderly grandmother would carry. Being in my mid-thirties this was beyond depressing; it was a dark hole in the ground, and I was burying myself in it every day. Through all of this, I was not paying attention to my declining marriage. The thread of hope was torn to pieces. I did not understand it because I felt different than my first marriage it felt like love and passion, but was it just because I was starting to connect with myself and allow myself to feel through my heart as I masked all the other feelings? I needed answers but my health would dominate my thoughts and I was in it alone. I journeyed through a roller coaster of possible illnesses. It was during this time that rapidly doing my own research began. I needed to figure this out because the health-care today was becoming so specialized and the only connection was me the patient. Seven medicines daily were now just part of my story. Moving through such strong pain throughout my body was like turning to a new chapter of my new story. I had opened the gates and now all the pain was there but the opportunity for healing was coming to the forefront. It was time to handle the chapter of my neck pain.

It's 2007 and six years post my car accident. I was being treated again for the neck pain. After two short visits with a new neuro-surgeon he concluded it was my shoulder. I was sent to a highly regarded orthopedic surgeon who determined the scapula was damaged during the accident and causing referred pain to the neck. My feeling of relief was immeasurable, I was a problem solver so yes, *let's fix it.* The surgery was scheduled, and I would get help from my mom for what would be an intense twelve-week recovery.

Things were still bad at home, but never would I imagine the next year would unravel like a spinning top out of control. I was out of surgery and moved to a room before discharge. As with any surgery someone must be with you and there to drive you home. My husband had brought me so never had I imagined what I would find out. I was in severe pain and I needed something to drink desperately I grabbed a soaking cloth next to me and sucked the water out. *Where was he?* I needed help.

My doctor happened to walk by and saw the tears stream down my face. He came in handed me some water and asked where my husband was. I replied a shameful "I don't know." You could see his expression of disbelief as if I had been mistaken. It felt like hours, but I believe it was twenty minutes and my husband would arrive. This was the wake-up call, my reality of importance to him was becoming nonexistent. *Where was he? What was so important he had to leave?*

"Just go through the motions" is what I kept telling myself....

My thoughts began to unravel on where to focus my attention as my health needed to be my full-time job. I had a growing active full-time career, and I would be forced to face another full-time job of repairing a dead marriage. I had to be a positive role model, I had to be a leader in the community. I had to be too much. The merry-go-round of life was like shifting gears on a car. *What would I handle today?* Work, family, health, but never in sync and not together but rather in silos.

Something had to go, and my marriage was already one foot out the door; we just didn't know how to clean up the mess. I would have to face it regardless of the consequences. I asked so many questions that I often heard "I don't need a detective, I need a wife." We were planning a trip in December to see my sister and her family and the day before our flight he announced he would not be going. The reality of having to tell my own family something was wrong hit me like a softball in my stomach. People were about to see the chaos behind the perfect curtain of my life. There was no discussion as his face was lifeless and he was firm in his decision. I made the call to my sister and filled it with the best excuses, work, kids, etc. I am not sure she ever believed me, but she went along with it. My trip was overshadowed with worry, fear, and sadness. As I returned home my anger had taken over and this was it: I was ready for the fight of my life. I had to address the elephant in the room. We were not aligned, and I knew he was keeping something from me, and we needed to address it. The argument was bitter and filled with rage. He was not ready to handle his surmounting issues. He didn't want to take ownership to these issues, and they were not aligned with my core values. He said it loud and clear, "I am done, it is over."

The finality of those words felt like the last words of any book; there was no more to read or imagine.

It was over.

My heart felt empty, lost, and numb. I would collapse in fear. Fear of the world I had to face.

The holidays were approaching, and this could not be worse timing, especially with kids. He was calling the shots, we were to get through the holidays, file for divorce after New Year's, and put the house for sale shortly after. I was like a walking zombie taking orders and pushing ahead. The call to my parents was a breaking moment, or should have been, but I was too numb to feel the full extent and it was filled with my own sadness that I had disappointed them again. Their youngest daughter was getting divorced again. My projections on them was completely inaccurate, they empathized and showed no sign of shame. They wrapped me in support and love ready to be the parachute I needed so desperately. They were indeed my greatest lifeline. The holidays came and went and I have very little memory of that time. The brain is an amazing force that can protect the heart and shield the most painful of times forever.

We filed for divorce and communication became only what was necessary. The house was for sale, and I was no longer invited to be around on weekends with kids. I was to remove myself from the equation. He did not care where I went or where I was, but I was not to be home. *Why didn't I have the courage to stand in my presence and take control?* I did not want my marriage to end, I had not done anything wrong, I was allowing myself to be a victim. Each day at work was an empty stare at the computer as I gazed out the window for hours. My diet was coffee, diet coke, and occasional crackers. My sour stomach could not tolerate anything except the bottle of Pepto I would drink like a soda. I was becoming lost within myself, no longer that strong sassy little five-year-old ready for kindergarten. I was scared, weak, and collapsing.

During my second marriage I had not made many friends. I often sat alone at the kid's events. I was a fish out of water, the corporate executive with no kids of my own and had nothing in common with the other parents. It was at a baseball game that I had met a friend who would become the second lifeline that I needed. Stephanie is as gorgeous on the outside as she is inside. Her long black hair and soulful eyes exemplified her kindness. She was one of my only friends. While our relationship for the most part was surface, my intuitive side knew I could trust her and she would understand. One day at lunch together I blurted out "I'm getting divorced" and she listened with no judgment and created a bond to last a lifetime. We hardly knew each other, but in this moment, time stopped and the getting real was like ripping a band aid off a wound to find that the healing was just beginning. It gave me the courage to take that one step forward. I had said it aloud in the community I lived. I was a leader, a chamber board member, community volunteer, and I was strong. I could do this. My heart started pumping blood once again and for the first time in a while, I could feel it.

Baby steps could not be more literal at this time in my life. The courage to get out of bed, work, eat, communicate with others, or just keep moving forward was like steps through concrete. I began counseling twice weekly as I could not focus long enough to do anything. I needed it to just get basic things in life done. My soon-to-be ex-husband could see my decline. Perhaps to make the situation civil he asked to talk through things. I believe this was his closure and while it was not mine at the time it was certainly the catalyst for the closure. I sat in what was our house, looked around at every picture of me that had been removed and I felt like a stranger in my own home. He grabbed my hands and I stared deep in his powerful blue eyes; I felt his breath on my skin as he apologized for the pain he had caused. My heart raced, tears began to flow, and I had no idea the impact of what he was about to say would have on my life. His anticipation and quivering lip indicated something strong was coming. As his eyes gazed down at his feet, he looked up directly in my eyes and said, "The truth is, Lori, I never loved you."

After those words, there was more of an explanation and as I can only surmise one of infatuation, but it did not matter. My heart closed like a door with an open window and the pressure sucked it shut. I felt it skip a beat and my head was spinning. I have no idea what happened after that moment but later that day I was on the floor of my living room drinking wine around 1:00 p.m. I wanted to hide. I wanted to be invisible and fade away. How could I be so stupid to make this mistake. I needed help that could only come from within. My body was limp and as I had felt all too real my health issues, it was my soul and heart that were broken.

My counselor was a miracle worker, she brought me back to that fierce five-year-old and it became all about me. It was my self-love that would win this battle. I needed all the shades of courage each day, courage to wake up, courage to go to work, courage to start over. Why was this so scary, reinventing myself was so easy for me in work, play and life. I had done it a million times but never with matters of my heart. My heart had cracked open and in came flooding the rivers of life feeling every wave, rock, limb, and path set before me. I was feeling me for the first time since I was a girl. People often use the expression "leap before they look" and this was me. My counselor had studied me so well she was bringing that inner child back to light. I knew I had to surround myself with positive friends to lift each other up and have fun! The friends I made post my divorce will forever hold a sacred place in my heart. We were a diverse group of men and women all recently divorced that had found each other. We would be a shoulder to cry on, a person to meet for dinner, and someone to just laugh through the painful days of repair. My new normal of talking divorce was getting easier, but my courage to find myself again was weak. I needed a "leap before I look moment" and I needed to feel courage to understand it again. One of those crazy after work happy hours with friends we entertained the idea of skydiving! Three of us were in, the date was set, and it was probably the most pivotal "leap before you look" times in my life. It was the feeling of courage I needed again, I needed it to move forward. Saturday morning arrived and I got a call from one of the others planning to skydive and he said, "I can't do it, I had a bad dream and I just can't do it." This caused me some concern, but I quickly realized it was *his* dream and not *my* story so I must move ahead. My friend Mark and I drove out to the landing strip and stood on the ground while we learned the many intricacies of skydiving. I felt my feet on the ground and wanted to keep them there, but this courage thing was too big, and I needed to grab on. It was time and we were instructed to sign the disclaimer. I was doing this, and I barely stopped to breathe or read any implications. It was time. The door opened, the wind raced in with the force of a hurricane and the noise was deafening. All the instructions I had learned were gone from my memory and I was thinking, *I hope that was not important.* We begin to motion back and forth in preparation of the roll out and he says we will go on three....1....2 and just like that we went on 2!

The feeling was so different than I anticipated; it was a feeling of being pushed up by the force of the wind below my horizontal body. It was within seconds the chute would open with a tug upward so strong it felt as if my arms could be ripped off. I caught my breath as the chute opened and was able to focus my eyes. It was time to enjoy the view. *Perspective* was all I could think during this time. How different the ground looked at what was now about 6,000 feet. Minutes later we were only feet from the ground; I could see myself being alive and all of my fear released in the air around me. It was a burst of freedom as my feet hit the ground.

Being a two-time divorced woman in my mid-thirties was embarrassing. I was so ashamed to ever talk of this past. Externally I was getting better at convincing others I was just fine, but my head and heart still needed a lot of work. My new life in a new home was falling into place. My health was fair primarily due to the many prescriptions holding it all together. I felt like those were now the pillars or foundation of my being. Preventative migraine prescription, anti-inflammatories, antidepressants, hormones, and these were all the Band-Aids covering the wounded inside. The shift of proactive healthcare versus this reactive approach was intriguing but I was just not sure how to get there. Slowly I got more focused on my diet, fitness, and this was mostly driven for aesthetic reasons of being single again. However, the cause and effect as it relates to feeling better was becoming even more obvious. In my spare time I began to read more and more about preventive wellness and the role of removing toxins in our life. This newfound obsession was the beginning of a lifelong journey to self-care as critical healthcare. My immediate improvement in health was still slow. It was the summer of 2008 and I was experiencing more unexpected turns with abdominal pain. I would face another surgery soon and it was for appendicitis. *How can such a young relatively healthy woman have so many unexplained surgeries and ailments?* In my black and white world, it was simply unacceptable. I was not letting this interrupt my positive view ahead and I could feel glimpses of a happy me on the horizon. It had been so long since I felt anything but sad and scared. The future was looking brighter.

It was a Monday night and I got a call from my good friend Mark asking if I was up for a post work cocktail. Later that night I remember looking over my shoulder as I heard someone tell Mark hello. My eyes caught the look of a handsome man with his NYC cap and his deep brown eyes. I knew everyone in town, or at least I felt like I knew who the most eligible bachelors were, and this was not someone I recognized. His striking looks certainly had my attention. He approached us and Mark introduced me to his friend Keith.

We joined Keith at his table and we had a great night talking about work, hobbies, travel, and I was clearly smitten. The end of the night came, and he suggested we meet again for dinner. Soon after Keith and I went to dinner on our first date and it was perfect. He was strong in who he was and that was a place I longed to be again. After a few weeks of staying in touch and dating he would recognize some insecurities in me that would force some setbacks early in our relationship. *Did I say too much or scare him away? Was it too much drama?* Self-doubt on the dating scene was my worst enemy and it was hard to admit, but I was not ready for a relationship I needed one with myself first. It was painful to feel rejection from him and I began to think my future was grim on finding a real partner in life. After all I had already failed twice. *It must be me.* My physical health, like diet and fitness, was the easy part and it was coming together nicely. But what was longing for attention was my mind and soul connection.

My inner soul had always longed for more: to be different, to live differently. The dance of a traditional life versus unknown of adventure was ongoing in my head. The next six months was filled with a back-and-forth game with Keith. We would get close, then he would push away. I was so confused and hurt, and in love. I finally got the courage to stand in my power and ask him what he thought about taking our relationship to the next level. I was scared of the answer and wondered, *should I just live in avoidance?* The reality of the situation was pretty clear: Keith felt I was not ready. He saw in me right away what took years for me to uncover. I was not ready. I needed to come into my own world to truly be present in a relationship. I needed to experience life on my own and no hiding behind a man, career, or anything else. The journey was beginning slowly. The pain of a broken heart was different this time, it was becoming more about me and not what had happened to me. Finally, I was willing to face the truth; the truth of who I had become and how I had become her. I would heal my heart in time. The next several months were some of the most exciting times for me. My finances were getting back in order, I was active in the community and I was back in my groove of leadership. I longed to still be with Keith.

A few months passed and being in this small town occasionally Keith and I would be at the same location. Always friendly and eager to see each other, the timing was still not right. We both continued to date other people and my journey of self-care began to evolve. My priority to create a life of independence and self-love was unfolding.

It was 2009 and Keith and I had an encounter. Shortly after, he reached out and wanted to go out again. My heart impulsively said "Yes!" but my head wanted to withdraw and protect myself for fear of rejection. However, I felt stronger now and wanted to take the risk. I agreed and that night we planned a ski vacation with friends. It was there that everything changed and on the return flight home he held my hand tightly without saying any words and I knew it was the symbol we would be together on this journey through life.

Keith and I were now exclusively dating, and things were becoming very comfortable. Our morals, our background, our vision of success was in alignment. Both of us had aggressive corporate jobs and we began to realize this small Louisiana town was just a stop on the path of new opportunity. Keith challenged me, celebrated me, and was so honest in all aspects of his life.

The pain of deception in my previous marriage was definitely a roadblock early on and something I had to learn to better understand. Healthy love was not like any other love. The wounds of my broken heart with my recent ex-husband were deep scars that do not just disappear. Keith was teaching me the journey to become whole again.

Life is a balancing act and as we all experience many parts of the equation some can be completely off balance while others are simply perfect. It is also easy to ignore or avoid parts that may be lacking while others may be going so well. It's truly finding that inner scale to learn to nourish and respect the aspects of all that can result in the greater foundation. I was in love, love like never before. My life felt like vacation and each day with Keith was a gift. We were eager to find hobbies, travel, and adventure that would challenge us both. Work would take us from Shreveport, Louisiana, to Memphis, Tennessee. This was an exciting new journey, a new life and together with my love. Moving is hard, it is stressful, exciting, and easy to take for granted. Work for the first time was challenging. It was not challenging in the sense of difficulty, rather it was changing in culture and opportunity. I needed to make a change and it would need to be soon. The reality of dedicating your life to one company was the norm back then; however, it was clear that landscape was gone. The amounting stress of work was beginning to impact my life and the scale was becoming unbalanced again. Soon after our move to Memphis, I was approached to change jobs, it would be a lateral in pay, and slight shift down in title but at this point that was of no concern to me. The big corporate dreams were gone. Love and adventure for life were my passion and work had been replaced to a distant second or third.

I jumped into my new role filled with excel spreadsheets, a mountain of analytics, and increasingly unhappy customers. The hours at work were becoming either a battle with customers or within my own company. My diet and fitness were falling apart as I had no time to plan, meal prep, or get to the gym. My body was starting to feel it again, it was aching and getting sick often. Keith was quick to recognize this downward spiral of my health and was not going to let it overtake me as it did in my last marriage.

He was my energy and balance. I was looking for a better way to cope with work but could not find the clarity. It was like being lost in a corn maze without finding the exit. I looked terrible and I felt terrible.

The doctor visits started again, and it was here I would learn that my preventive migraine meds were actually the cause of kidney issues. The light bulb was brighter than ever now and if one Band-Aid medication was causing another illness to be bandaged then something needed to change. I was determined to find a solution to come off all these meds. But how, wasn't that scary. We are programmed to think these meds are the only way to keep going. I respect and appreciate that prescription meds have a purpose but there had to be a better way. The focus was becoming clearer and a more preventive approach called out to me. I knew food could do it but what else was there?

My cousin had been down a similar path of wellness and I was intrigued by her journey. I began to learn more about allergies, inflammation as it relates to our food, and heavy metal toxins from environmental exposure. I have always been a good student, and it was exciting to learn more about this healthier path. I completed a few blood tests on metal toxicity, my food sensitivities and began adopting a new diet and lifestyle. The shift in focus allowed me to detach from the stress of work and learn to manage it rather than embody it. Call it a coincidence or perfect storm, but around this same time I received an email from my dear friend Stephanie. She was asking my opinion on a business opportunity with a live clean mission. It was a business to promote clean label products and the timing was perfect as I had become more focused on preventive nutrition and what I put in my body but simply never really thought about what I put on and around me. I was eager to learn more of these products and how it could become a business opportunity that coupled with helping others and a chance to make a difference. It was a "leap before you look" moment but my intuition told me it was right. Things progressed slowly at first as my full-time job was occupying most of my time, but my passion and heart were more complete in this new opportunity. It was then in August of 2015 that Keith had a great business opportunity to move to Boston. Boston seemed like Mars to us southern kids. How would we handle the snow, the culture, what would life be like? My corporate job was not something that I could easily maintain. This caused some stress, fear, and soul searching. Another "leap then look" chance was here!

I was excited, scared, and nervous. I had decided to take my passion business full time! *What did it mean to be an entrepreneur?* I had twenty plus years of one industry that had become effortless, but also lifeless in some form, and now I was one of those, an entrepreneur. We moved to Boston and the new adventure began!

The relief of my corporate job being gone was so undeniable. It was impacting my headaches, my energy, and my overall mindset. At this point we were all about evolving with our overall health and living clean! I was feeling better than ever and the decision to remove meds one by one became much easier as I was beginning to see signs of my kidney issues clearing with the removal of the migraine medication. My inflammation improved enough to eliminate the anti-inflammatories and the headache triggers were being revealed including stress, diet, or weather, almost all of which could be controlled. It was empowering having this knowledge and it was something I wanted more of each day.

As we arrived in Metrowest Boston we had no idea how different day-to-day life would be for us. The seasons brought a vibrancy like no other and a zest to be present each day not knowing if this would be our forever home. That lesson would become even more painfully obvious with the sudden death of Keith's father shortly after we moved. I held his hand on those gray days, letting his heartbeat reside right next to me against the cold air of Boston. We were a pair now; nothing would change that. We were thousands of miles away but fortunately Keith had time to make a few last visits. To watch the person you love the most experience the pain of death of a parent is heart wrenching. I felt helpless, I needed to be the strong one. My new life as an entrepreneur was easy to put on hold. Finally, I was getting it: life was about so much more than work, it was about being there when it mattered most. *Had I come all this way just to figure this out?*

We moved, we had life circumstances, and it just felt uncomfortable. What would the future hold? Questions of doubt rose in my mind. *If I was really going to be good at this, being an entrepreneur, was I measuring success all wrong?* I needed to dig deep in my journey. I began a routine of all the things I always wanted to do but couldn't because of my old structure of an eight-to-five job. I incorporated a variety of daily exercises and took my time as I balanced my day. It was fun taking time to do laundry, grocery shop, and even clean the house. These were all things that were "chores" in my past life. The newness of this would soon fade as I wasn't challenging myself enough. I was a community leader and now I felt more timid than ever in this new crowd of New England. *Was it their educational level? Was I not good enough? Did they like Southerners?* I was shrinking in my confidence and began to feel the pressure of success. I needed that courage again, the one I had when I jumped out of the plane, and I needed it more than ever. I began joining networking groups and jumping in. I had a business that was truly part time. I loved the products I offered, and sharing was authentic, but I would minimize the opportunity.

The weekends were filled with travel to explore New England. It was then becoming more and more clear that my fears were still keeping me from my full courage to be successful. Perhaps it was old definitions of success holding me back?

Given the opportunity of being an entrepreneur, I am living my passion for health and wellness. I am being me. I don't believe in accidents in life and my inside scale, while it had been balanced by chance before, is balanced by purpose now. I now know that all pieces of the pie are essential, and important to nourish. My soul is now nourished—through my true love with Keith, through my spirituality, and mostly through loving myself. To top it off, I now really appreciate each encounter; I understand that how I impact that person or place is invaluable and helps to make the world a better place.

I wish I could pinpoint a day, place, or time that the revelation hit me. It just wasn't a simple *aha*, but a series of events. The afternoon pick-ups at the CSA for farm-fresh vegetables, apple picking on a Friday afternoon, afternoon walks through the amazing landscape, not having to calculate vacation days, the removal of seven meds to one, etc. *I had my life back...* in the moment I began to wake up and enjoy the beauty of the sky.... in the feeling of holding Keith's hand as we walked our dog, Penny, through the street without a timetable or deadline to meet.

It is the feeling of presence.

It is not black and white, but it is success for me.

Lori Cheramie is a natural leader who created the entrepreneurial life of her dreams. She serves as a consistent top leader with MŌDERE as she passionately shares their "live clean" mission. Lori is an experienced corporate executive who led sales teams and marketing through over twenty years at a Fortune 50 leading technology company. Her experience from her decades of corporate leadership and now a developed entrepreneurial career allows her to experience time freedom as a true servant leader. Lori is originally from New Orleans and currently lives outside of Boston, with her fiancé Keith. Her passion each day is do better than the previous by helping others use their voice and make a difference.

Connect with her by email: lori@myhealthymindbody.com.

Now I Know...

Rusanne Jourdan

"God wastes nothing and it's only in reflection that
we see a glimpse of what's at work in our life."
—Rusanne Jourdan

It was 1966 in Baton Rouge, Louisiana, and I was two and a
half years old. I lived in a simple, small three-bedroom house
on Cloud Drive with my baby sister and my mother. I can still
remember the layout of my room and the humble home in which
my early years passed before me.

Numerous times my mind has returned to a particular night,
wondering *why did it happen? Who came to see me that night in my
childhood bedroom? What, if anything, was the message?* It doesn't
haunt me because it is so full of beauty and peace. Now I know it
was simply a piece of the quilt that makes up the entire tapestry
of my life's journey and purpose.

It was like any other night except this night I had a special
visitor. I awoke and sat straight up in bed as the glowing light
filled all the space in my room.

"Mommy, Mommy come and see! There's a lady in my room.
It's the Blessed Mother and she's in a blue dress. It's beautiful,
Mommy. Come and see!" I was so excited to show her this beautiful lady that lit up my room with the most brilliant presence of
blue I had ever seen.

I ran out of my room to get my mother. Mom came from her
room, clasped my hand in hers, and walked me back to my bedroom to tuck me back in bed, thinking I had had a dream. The lady

in blue was gone. I told my mother that she was at the foot of my twin bed. Her dress was light blue with a long train of incandescent material that glowed and lit up the whole room with a calming and relaxed light. Her grace-filled presence saturated the space. I can still feel and see her now, a radiant blue light beam. I remained in my little bed, calm and still, the darkness now surrounding me. It was as if she simply came to say hello and check on me.

I often think about this visit and question what it meant. *Why didn't she say anything? What was the reason for her coming and more importantly why to me?* I would often pray to God for answers to many questions I have about this visitation. It would be much later on in life that I received some clarification around the beautiful lady in blue who visited me that night.

I'm the eldest of two girls and have two half-sisters. I was born and raised in Baton Rouge, but I knew in my heart I would not always live in my hometown. My life was going to be unlike anything I knew there. I desperately wanted something different and exciting. I was fearless and wanted to explore all possibilities.

My sister Karen is two years younger. When Mom came home with my sis, I sat on the chair with my arms held high, "Give her to me! Give her to me!" I said. "She's mine, she's mine, my baby doll." To this day, we are very close. Most people who met us growing up thought we were friends rather than sisters because of this closeness we shared.

My mother and father divorced when I was two years old. *Was this around the time the lady in blue visited?* I'm not sure, but the questions always presented themselves.

Like, *"Why did Dad leave? Didn't he love me? What would make him leave and not even come see me?"* I'd see other little girls with their daddies and my heart would physically hurt. Whether it would be a father twirling his little girl around and around in a circle or propping his daughter on his big, broad shoulders to run around with, giggling, laughing and enjoying time together. I found myself frozen, dazing, desiring it was my father. He was absent. That feeling of absence, remains and touches inner parts of my being.

As a young girl I was extremely inquisitive. Mom didn't answer my questions in detail, which is understandable now. But then I eventually stopped asking questions and vowed, "This is never gonna happen to me! I will never get married and never have children. This is not what I want! And no man will ever get close enough to hurt me!" Very early on I built tall brick walls around my heart. This way no one would get close enough to hurt me again. I would be in control of who entered and exited my heart. Only maturity brought the knowledge that it would be knowing and trusting my God to bring the peace I so desired.

I did have my maternal grandparents, who were loving and caring. They showed so much love to me. As my biggest fans, they supported me, financially and emotionally, throughout my childhood and young adult years; this was also a way they supported my mother, who was raising two young girls on her own. The possibility of a loving marriage bubbled as a spring of hope inside of my empty walls. I have beautiful memories of the time spent at their house. My grandfather, Russell, who I'm named after, was the most jolly, funny and sweetest man. He adored my mom and called her Tidbit. Mom was a very good dancer and bowler, two activities she and Papa did often together. I have vivid memories of them cranking up the music and dancing the jitterbug in the living room. Joy and laughter permeated the air; it was possibly the only picture of pure joy I had witnessed between a man and a woman.

My grandmother, Mimi, was in always in the kitchen, whipping up some yummy Italian food. They both had Sicilian backgrounds. Every weekend we gathered at their house for Sunday lunch. There was enough food for twenty people, even though we were only a party of around eight. All of our favorite dishes were prepared. Such tender love was brought to life by hands that made our food. Spaghetti and meatballs, stuffed artichokes, casseroles, potato salad, stuffed bell peppers, green salad, ham or roast, and garlic bread. Then for dessert: fruit salad with sliced coconut, pecan pie (my fave), lemon pie, the list went on. And this was every Sunday! Love and creative expression came in the form of food. I wonder now how Mimi had the energy and stamina to do it. I think she loved it because it brought the family together, for better or worse. Although her drive and personality drove many mad, she had a sincere desire to keep *la famiglia* together.

There was a certain chaos that accompanied our home on these Sundays. At lunch there would be three televisions going with three different sporting events because the men had bets on the games with bookies. During halftime and after the game, a buzzing and ringing accompanied our conversations—or debates. An outsider would describe them as knock-down, drag-'em-out arguments.

The "discussions" were about anything, and especially the subjects most people said to stay away from. Nothing was off limits and everyone had a strong opinion, whether it be about politics, religion or current events. Really any subject would do for all of us to voice our opinion. Early on I learned to jump in there and fight to put my opinion forward. It was not unusual to scream and holler, and often not give anyone the opportunity to finish a sentence. Blood pressure escalated, feelings were hurt, and cussing occurred each time. Then we gathered to eat again, take home leftovers for lunch the next day, kiss and hug, and do it all over the following Sunday. This went on for years. A dance of family and collision of expression wrapping its many lessons around my young woman self.

My grandfather was a role model for me in many ways.

When my sis and I slept over with Papa, as we called him I recall him getting up early and making us breakfast, then taking us to school. "San, Karen, get up and have breakfast! You're gonna be late for school!" I'd hear him holler out. We'd wake to a table full of food: eggs, bacon, toast, pancakes and orange juice.

"Papa, this is too much food!"

"It's ok," he'd say. "Eat what you want."

Then he'd get us into his car. With the radio on full blast, he sang and danced in his seat the whole way to school. We laughed until our tummies hurt watching his belly jiggle up and down as he performed his moves while driving. God only knows how we didn't end up in a ditch! He probably knew Carrie, his wife, my grandmother, would have killed him! It was not unlike her to run around chasing him through the house—with a knife—teasing she was going to get him, or with a peach, offering to serve it up with the skin still on as he got the bad kind of goose bumps from the fuzzy exterior of the fruit. It remained comical entertainment for us all. We would roar with laughter as they put on their performance. To this day, I think of these times when I see or eat a peach.

Mimi was a unique character. You either strongly disliked her or you loved her. I loved her with my whole heart. And she loved me! She'd tell people, "I love all my grandchildren, but there is something special about Rusanne." I realized even at an early age that this wasn't "the right thing to say" (especially out loud) and I would tell her so, but no one told Mimi what to do.

She was the boss. And I was her sidekick. Her shadow. I admired her. I wanted to do what she did: help people! She and mom weren't the closest and this was difficult on my mother, especially when I'd get mad at her or not like something she did; I'd put my little arm on my hip and announce, "That's it! I'm going to live with my grandmother!" Once, Mom offered to help me pack my things and explained that if I went I'd be staying and not returning home. I then decided to stay at home.

But there was no denying Mimi's unconditional love. It forged a bond like I had never experienced. She loved me for who I was and I was craving that! I loved watching Mimi. She was self-educated and one of my most vivid memories is of her sitting on the sofa next to a lit lamp with a yellow legal pad and pen, writing. Always writing. Her trademark was the eyeglasses she wore. They were encrusted with rhinestones that sparkled in the light and matched her bright, sometimes blinding, personality. I never saw anything or anyone intimidate her or swerve her off the road she was traveling, always on a mission to help people. I wonder now looking back how much of her service was an attempt to fill something empty inside of her.

She would always be at work, whether as the State Director for Mentally Disabled, preparation for a speech at the Rotary Club or another organization, or planning where she would next be involved in assisting those who were disadvantaged or in need in some way. One time I sat at the Louisiana House of Representatives at an open session where she was advocating for funding and positive changes for the mentally retarded (as they called people with special needs at that time). She delivered that speech with gusto and confidence to a room full of predominantly men. She had courage beyond belief and a conviction that was unstoppable. She roared like a lion protecting the young. I knew then I wanted to have power the way she did, I wanted to have a voice and use it, especially for those who did not have a voice.

She was always writing a thank you note, or a request for something— even of the President of the United States or the Governor of Louisiana. It didn't matter who they were. She feared no one. But it seemed to me that they were afraid of her. When we'd go places, I'd notice people would clear out of the path. I later realized it was because no one got out of her sight without committing to something she wanted as means of support for a cause—if she caught them, they were going to have to reach in their pocketbook and write a check. Both of my grandparents were stout people, but it wasn't her size that made people get out of her way. It was her drive, her passion, and her personality. She knew what she wanted and she would get it. I now know she was a workaholic and it's where she got her identity, a pattern I would repeat.

What I didn't know then about the time I spent watching my grandmother in action was it would be my training ground for the work I would do with children… including my own child. God wastes nothing and it's only in reflection that we see a glimpse of what's at work in our life.

I had two strong women role models in my life, my grandmother and my mother; and as different as they were, they both helped mold me into the woman I've become. In fact, a lot of women in the South are strong, opinionated, and vocal—and this is seen either as an asset or a liability, especially to men.

In the Deep South, it was a lot about "looking the part"; after all, how in the world are you going to amount to anything and especially find a man that's gonna look after you?! Things I often heard said to me were: "Rusanne, go put some lipstick on, and have you done your hair?" "You're not leaving the house like THAT, are you?" "I'm not sure that hairstyle is becoming and for goodness sake, girl, you forget you have a back of your head! It looks like a rat's nest is living back there!"

So how you looked and presented yourself was critical. And to find a man to provide for you was of the utmost importance. What he did for a living, or what was he studying to become, was a common question. He needed to have position and money, or he wasn't a potential candidate. And God forbid if he was a different color or had opinions different from the status quo of the family. Consequently, one either pleased others or rebelled.

I rebelled.

I had a high school sweetheart and at fifteen years old he had the nerve to talk to Mom about us getting married. "Are you crazy boy? Don't you even think that's gonna happen!"

I was then sent off to confession at the Catholic Church for any indiscretions, especially if it involved boys and sex.

I can't remember anyone my mother or grandmother liked, except a much older man who was wealthy and prominent in Louisiana. He was three decades older than me, and it was like a fairytale. I was twenty years old and he was in his mid fifties. He was married yet there were talks of us having a future together, even a child. He expressed desiring a little girl with my eyes. He exposed me to a life that was full of beautiful, yet very worldly things. It was nothing to hop on a private jet to Vegas or his private ranch to ride horses and watch old movies.

In hindsight, I am sure the relationship was accepted by my family because of what he could offer financially. I learned early to "turn the charm on" to get what I wanted, or what I believed I wanted that would bring me "happiness." The question was— underneath all these family dynamics, loud voices and cluttered cultural norms of the South—*what did I want?* I knew very little and was interested only in me and what I wanted... and I desperately searched for something that would fill the vast emptiness in my heart I believed a man or nice, worldly things could fill.

When I turned twenty in 1984 and I represented Louisiana in the Miss USA beauty pageant. It was through this experience that I met many new people, including the older man I began secretly seeing. It was as if I had been thrown in a movie, "looking and living the part." All of a sudden life was different, exciting and full of travel and opportunities that would present choices I never dreamed of.

In fact, as life would have it, the man I was secretly seeing was instrumental in me traveling to Hawaii for summer school, where I would meet my future husband and father of my four boys. The relationship with the older gentleman would eventually end, and I'd step toward a new horizon in search of the next big adventure.

It was 1987. My sis and I loved to hang out and go to different restaurants. We'd each take turns choosing a restaurant to go to each month. It was my turn. We both loved Maine lobster so I picked this great restaurant on Florida Blvd. called Joey's. We and our waiter had mutual friends, so I asked him what he was doing that summer. He said going back to Hawaii for summer school, and mentioned that it was a great way to go to Hawaii for three months. "Just take one course and you can hang with locals and have a great time!"

I looked at Karen and said, "We are going! Start packing your bags, we are going!" From the time I was a young girl, I had a burning desire to go to Hawaii. When I was six or seven, I would dress up in my hula skirt, perform the hula and sing, "Tiny Bubbles," a song by Don Ho. *Had a seed been planted knowing I would meet my future husband there? Was the story already written? Why did I desire so much to go to Hawaii?* Almost twenty years later I would travel to Hawaii and in fact meet my future husband.

One thing I now know is every choice and decision leads you to a destination— some good, some you may question, but they certainly lead you somewhere.

I traveled to over twenty cities in Mexico as Miss Louisiana USA 1984. I toured several Mexican cities to promote Au Petit Jean Shoes with Miss Universe, Miss USA, and Miss Mexico. I stayed back for a few weeks because of a cute Mexican guy I met and when I ran out of cash (of course, he had none), I called Mom asking her to wire money. "Are you crazy, Rusanne? Get your ass on a plane now and come home!" I now know I was desperate for the love of a man and would go just about anywhere to get it!

That empty space inside from missing my father was always there, but I wasn't in a place to realize it. I just kept pushing forward, running faster to fill it up. Now I know I missed my earthly father but it was my heavenly Father I was ignoring as well. I didn't need anyone, let alone God.

The next big adventure: Haiti. February, 1984. I was twenty years old. It was Carnival time in Port-au-Prince. Miss Southern University and myself, representing my state as Miss Louisiana, were invited to take part in the festivities. The weather was hot, the food was hotter, and the people rolled out the red carpet wherever we went. We were treated like we were famous. They loved beauty queens.

My chaperone got sick at the last minute and Mom got to travel with me. We arrived and little local boys came to our hotel room every day offering to get us a Coca Cola or a candy bar; they'd run with bare feet in the dirt to get us anything we wanted. We'd give them change and there they were, waiting each evening wanting to get us stuff and of course put some change in their pockets. Beautiful people. We were treated like royalty, getting picked up for the hairdresser and makeup to be done daily. Then Carnival time came. I had never seen anything like it. There were literally millions of people in the street. I was placed at the top of an eighteen-wheeler with music blaring, a caravan progressing through the streets, and people dancing, eating and drinking. It was quite similar to the Mardi Gras in New Orleans, except louder and bigger and I was the only Caucasian in sight! When it came to the last night of the Carnival, the mayor of Port-au-Prince brought all of us out to dinner.

The president of the country, Jean-Claude Duvalier, came into the restaurant. He was known as "Baby Doc," as his father had preceded him, Francois "Papa Doc" Duvalier. There were no elections during either regime and both presidents used force to keep the populace subservient. Haiti was the poorest country in the Western Hemisphere, with widespread problems of starvation and unemployment. It was my first experience to see such poverty and discrepancy in the social and economical levels of a community. But I loved the country. I loved the people and I loved the excitement and exhilaration of being in a foreign land. This feeling and the desire to feel it again would drive many of my future decisions.

On the President's arm was one of the most gorgeous women I had ever seen, with jet-black hair slicked back from her chiseled face wearing a camouflage hat. She was the First Lady and walked in with a flow of importance I had never witnessed. There were at least eight soldiers armed with machine guns surrounding their table, protecting the leaders of the country. I felt the significance of the potential danger if someone made an attempt to move too fast or come too close. I felt the heat of the armory pointed to my back.

This particular night my mom wasn't feeling well and decided to stay at the hotel just a few kilometers away from the restaurant. She had designed and beaded the most beautiful gown for me to take on this trip. The mayor asked the delegates in our party to walk outside to dance, as it was the last night of the Carnival and there were two eighteen-wheelers in the street outside the restaurant having a battle of the bands, tunes flying back and forth in the hot, humid evening. I could feel the music beating in my chest. I could feel the excitement in the air and could smell the alcohol and the sweat. Many people were intoxicated and the atmosphere felt hallucinogenic as it drew me in to the crowd. The elation of the people was tangible. I had forgotten about the lady in blue. I was becoming something of the world and it fed my emptiness in a way that kept me wanting more. Life, I thought, was exciting and had endless potential to fulfill me.

We made a circle and began dancing and laughing. I wore a long, white, skin-hugging evening gown with the garnet necklace the mayor had presented to me earlier that evening. We held hands and moved to the beat of the music, first to the left then in the opposite direction with laughter and joy. Then suddenly guns shots were fired. Immediately the bodyguards swept us up and directed us with abrupt and serious commands to follow them. I was told later it was a drunken man in the streets firing off bullets to signify the end of the festive event. I never found out any details but we were quickly moved into the restaurant, asked to get down on the floor and crawl through to the kitchen, and jump into a waiting, running car to take us back to the hotel. The President and First Lady were escorted out quickly as well. All I could think about when I was doing the army crawl through the kitchen restaurant was how Mom was going to kill me if I wrecked that gown she had worked so hard on.

Before our scheduled leave from Haiti, I begged my mother for one thing: some people we met during our stay had invited me to stay with them for a few weeks. They spoke of all the adventures we could have, including watching voodoo ceremonies from atop a mountain. Meeting and hanging out with locals was something I desired to do. At twenty-one, I thought I could make my own decisions. My mother thought differently and refused to allow me to stay. I argued and fought until I got physically sick on the plane going home because I didn't get to stay. Now I know she was protecting me. So was God.

A short time after we left Haiti, citizens started protesting against Duvalier's government and there were protests, deaths, and unrest. I believe "Baby Doc" and his gorgeous first lady fled from Haiti to Europe.

After a fulfilling and exciting year in 1984, it was time to consider the reality of what I was going to do with my life.

So after owning and running a women's cosmetic company and a women's shoe company with my Mom in 1984 through 1987 I decided to go back to LSU to get my degree. I graduated in

Political Science in December 1989. I had aspirations of attending LSU Law School. I wanted to do something that helped people and make a difference in others lives. My inner voice was in the back of my mind reminding me, *I could somehow do something to make a positive impact.*

In the summer of 1987, my sis Karen and I attended the University of Hawaii at Manoa. I met my future husband one night when we were celebrating completing final exams. We partied, shared some laughs, and went out a few times. I wasn't in love, but there was an attraction. Maybe it was his exotic, Middle Eastern skin and big dark eyes, or his playfulness when we traveled around the island, having dinner or going out on a boat. He loved to have fun and would plan things with no expense spared. He was shy, with very boyish ways that seemed innocent and safe.

The night before he left, he and his mate gave us a T-shirt with Australia on it. I thought it was Austria in Europe. Little did I know then this country would become my home. We wrote a couple of letters back and forth and lost contact for two and a half years. As fate would have it my future husband's best friend met a girl from Baton Rouge, Louisiana. This led to him getting my details and I later worked with this same gal when we lived some of our married life in Baton Rouge.

After graduation from LSU in December 1989, I spent Christmas in Louisiana then boarded a plane to Melbourne, Australia. My life was getting ready to take a major turn. Just like the plane taking off, I too was flying right through my life. But back to that question, *what did I really want?* I'm not sure I even gave that a thought. I liked everything fast and exciting! No thought of consequences. And no one was going to tell me how to live my life!

Marriage proposal made and accepted. Mom encouraged me to think through it. She believed things were moving too fast. She told me to get engaged if I must but to come home and think it over. Did I ever listen to Mom or for that matter any authority in my life? I was twenty-six years old and believed I could make decisions for myself. Did I ever really think I couldn't?

My grandparents flew into town. They loved the city. I have photos of Papa in the city of Melbourne standing on Russell Street.

He was the hit of the party and I was *not* getting married without him giving me away! It was a beautiful wedding with over 300 people I didn't know. I didn't even understand the majority of what was said in Arabic during the ceremony at the little Greek Orthodox Church my husband had been christened in. We would later christen our third son, Jordan, in that very church.

We married in February 1990. My family left to return to the States and it hit me! *What the hell have I done?* I believed I was doing the right thing. I loved him, but on my honeymoon I would think of family and friends and the life I left behind. It was all I knew. This was different. In the midst of my other adventures I could hop on a plane and return home, sometimes with my mom dragging me by the hair, but this time it was different. I was in another country with a husband I really didn't know in a family I didn't know. And all were in a culture I didn't know speaking a language I didn't understand.

I had urges to return to my tribe and what I knew. At night the tears burned down my cheeks and left a stained highway of grief. The family was in the restaurant business. My husband worked seven days a week so if I wanted to see him and every other member of his family, I would have to go there.

Here I sat in one of the most beautiful countries in the world. Like a mini New York, the city of Melbourne offered it all: fabulous restaurants, beautiful clothes, and cosmopolitan living with the hustle and bustle of city life. From the outside all was gorgeous and exciting. On the inside my heart was ripping apart. Where was the lady in blue? I had been too distracted to connect to her. I was too distracted to connect to the me inside of me.

I sat at the family restaurant with a glass of wine looking the part. It was all about looking the part. That little scene act had started early and I had it down pat, the happy wife from America who had just moved there. She had fallen in love with a handsome, well-off Australian after a whirlwind romance—all of a few weeks! The waiter would ask, "Would you like another drink?"

"Sure," I'd say with a big smile on my face.

In the meantime, my husband had an entourage to cater to rather than giving me any attention. I felt alone in a foreign land.

I felt I didn't belong. I wanted to run to the airport and board a plane. *What was I thinking?* I hardly knew this man and he and his family lived very differently. I didn't know where to turn and had no one to turn to. My heart was heavy. I would carry it to and from that restaurant daily and it grew heavier each day. But the moment anyone saw me, in particular, the regular patrons at the restaurant, I'd turn it on to look the part. I learned quickly to put on the academy award performances. But there were no rewards, only the day-to-day acting as if all was ok. It was exhausting, slowly weaving lines of brokenness into my heart and bone. How long would I keep this up?

All I had ever wanted was to be happily married and there was no way I could be honest with anyone, especially my mom, and admit I was homesick and unhappy. *Suck it up. Look the part. Things will get better.* For better or worse I had made a decision and I was not going to fail.

Eventually I did find work and friends I loved and I adjusted. But my heart still wanted to return home, not necessarily to go somewhere but to get out of where I was. The family was not "my people" and I saw things I didn't like and my gut was saying "RUN!! Either with him or by yourself, but RUN!!!"

We were considering starting a family and I wanted to be nearer to my mom and sister. In 1992 we decided to move back to Louisiana and our first two sons were born there. Life was good, but it was his turn to have his heart heavy to return to his homeland. So I cut a deal. I said I would return to Australia with conditions.

Seven years later we were returning to Australia with two young boys aged five and three years old. I'm not sure how my mom and sister handled it. Mom continues to say it's like mourning the living and it wrecked us emotionally to be so far, especially taking her grandchildren so far from her. I have a tendency to not remember all the details. I imagine I have gotten really good at it to protect myself. If you can't remember it then it can't hurt you, right?

We boarded the plane with two small children to move across the water. We sold everything except personal belongings. We were starting over yet again. I did find Australia conducive to raising a family and I had grown tired of working a corporate job sixty to seventy hours a week and traveling interstate. I wanted to be a mom to my children. My husband had a business venture he learned about from New Orleans and we had high hopes of a bright future. We smelled opportunity and we were excited. The conditions were discussed on the plane and we were in agreement with our goals and a vision. There would be no involvement from his family. We had learned our lessons. This was about building a future for our family. It was the first time I felt like we were a team and ready to take on the world and build a beautiful future.

The years 1999 to 2005 were busy! We'd landed in a new city to make our home in, Gold Coast, Queensland: spectacular beaches, theme parks, sunshine... beautiful one day, perfect the next. We'd purchased our first Australian home, kids were settled in school, a third boy was born in 2002. Life was good. Business was lucrative. On the outside our life was picture perfect. Another boy was born in 2005. Even though I tried so very hard for a daughter we had four, healthy, beautiful boys! Life seemed complete and happy....

Then the house of cards came tumbling down. Promises were broken. Lies were spoken. Friends and family were involved in the global business and there was a lot of money made, yet I had no information or access. I was kept at home, the gal who wanted for nothing. Except all I wanted was my family restored. What continued for all those benefitting from the business were parties in Vegas, overseas trips to Germany, Dubai, New Zealand, and the US with an entourage and women to entertain, and boats and fast cars purchased, while I stayed home raising my boys.

The relationship could not be repaired and I left the marriage in August 2009. It was as if I could see the blue sky again and I knew I would come back to life, for I felt dead. I believed the inner whisper I heard; I was being told it was time to make a change and to not be afraid. The lady in blue didn't show her presence, but with a faint voice she was coming through to me. Now I know God was always with me, loving and protecting me through it all.

But this was brief and the real storm would hit once the decisions were made.

What followed in a short time was hell on earth for me. Loss upon loss. I was in the battle of my life and there were times I didn't want to live. I didn't want to fight anymore. I craved simplicity and harmony. I felt as if a train had swiped me sideways and I didn't know how I would ever recover. There was emotional, mental, and physical stress. There was financial hardship. Spiritually, I was dry and dead like a weathered limb barely hanging off a tree. The lady in blue had died. I had completely forgotten about her and about that little girl that lived inside of me. How would I make it?

And to add to all heartache my youngest son was not well. Something wasn't right and I had no idea what to do, how to help him or what the outcome of things for him, or me, would be.

My fourth son, Christian, was born in July, 2005. He was the most beautiful, placid, loving child. My mom and sis flew to Australia to be at the birth. My best friend came from Melbourne. She was my lifesaver when I lived in Melbourne all those years ago and became like a sister. I will forever be grateful to her and her family for making me feel loved and part of their tribe. Other girlfriends that lived locally were there at the hospital too. It was a real sisterhood coming together at the birth of my son.

My doctor came to visit Christian and me the next morning at the hospital and jokingly said he had never delivered during a Tupperware party before. I think he was too scared to clear the room. It wouldn't have worked any way. There was a unity of sisterhood in that delivery room when he arrived. I loved being pregnant and childbirth was a beautiful experience for me. The pain left me so quickly, replaced with elation and love for the new creation I was blessed to carry and hold.

I focused on being a Mom to my four sons. I loved being pregnant, I loved giving birth, and I adored them all. They were all so different but all who saw them said they were clones with beautifully tanned complexions, light blue-green eyes. Really sweet young men. My heart was full when I was with them. My heart was broken when their father and I couldn't reconcile our differences. The glue that attempted to hold us together felt more like slivers of glass that slowly cut my heart into pieces.

What never died was the heartbeat of each child, whether they were with me physically or not. My soul and bones were dried up; only my body was alive, sometimes I thought only barely. But God's grace and His reckless and abundant love were there, always there. I still hadn't looked to Him. He was chasing me down but again I was running faster.

The event that stopped me in my tracks happened in mid-2006.

Christian was about thirteen months old. I had him on the changing table singing a lullaby, as I often did.

"I love you,
yes, I do,
sweetest little boy
I ever knew.
Sweet as sugar,
sweet as pie,
you're the apple of my eye!"

This was a song my grandfather often sang to us as kids. All the boys loved it, Christian too. Then one day I noticed he was not responding—not just disinterested in my singing, which does leave a lot to be desired, but he would not look at me or respond in any way. My heart shattered in a million pieces. Deep down in the pit of my soul, I knew something was not right. I shared this concern with a few people close to me and they assured me that it was nothing to be concerned about, that he was just a laid-back baby. When people held him, they described him as a little koala, docile and quiet. He would just snuggle in. My mother's intuition told me differently. Many thought I was overreacting, but I knew something was not right.

He had hit all the milestones on time or even early. But as the days progressed I saw my little man spiraling backwards. He lost all language. He wouldn't look at me. He couldn't talk to me. He didn't respond to his name. Yet he would bolt from the yard to the TV if he heard his favorite show come on. I was lost as well. I didn't know what to do or where to go. I felt like I was on a boat in the middle of nowhere completely alone and there was nothing and no one in sight. A mother is supposed to be there and take care of their child. I felt I was failing as a mother and most importantly I was failing my son.

How does one survive when all one knows is taken away? A ship with no tether floating at sea, how does one get back home to make life right?

Anyone who knew me well would often hear me say, "How blessed am I, four beautiful and healthy boys!" How does a mother cope when her baby needs her and needs healing, and she feels helpless and incapable of providing support and care? Mothers are supposed to fix things. When a little one falls and scrapes their knee, Mommy picks them up, cradles them, and says, "It'll be ok, Mommy's here. All is going to be ok." She cleans the cut, places a Band-Aid on it, and tells her child all will be well as she kisses the wound. Mothers make it all better.

This was not a scrapped knee. Mommy couldn't do anything to fix this or make it better. For the first time in my life, I felt out of control. Some things simply cannot be "fixed". Some journeys we have to swim through like a dark, scary swamp to get to the other side. It was a scary, lonely, isolating, terrifying path that seemed to lead to hell and back. I was more than happy to take his place but I could not. It was a path we would have to take together, not knowing where it would lead.

Another drastic turn took place on that December 13, 2007 and life, as I knew it changed forever. I didn't ask for the fork in the road but there was only one way to go and my legs could hardly put one foot in front of the other. How does a mother feel and function when all she wants to do is help her child and all there seems to be presented is a series of dead ends?

His father and I slowly got in the car on that sunny Queensland day to take the one hour drive to a specialist I had found after twelve months of appointments and disappointments. No one had been able to help me. I had high hopes this woman could help me and Christian. I would have sold my soul for answers. It was like being in a maze with an entrance but no way out; I would wander through the maze each day, sometimes wanting to run away and not look back. But it was my love and determination to help my son that kept me going. And God was there every step I took but I was still unaware.

As we drove to the appointment, I kept thinking about how Christmas was approaching and it should have been a day where we were all at the beach or swimming in our pool. The kids were on holiday and this was usually a time of fun, laughter, and relaxation. I hadn't laughed in a very long time. I felt we weren't even a family anymore. I felt I wasn't even capable of being a mother to my older three boys. I felt like a zombie simply getting through each day, sometimes each hour, sometimes each minute, trying to hold it together for the family. The marriage was slowing falling apart and I felt isolated and alone without the emotional support I so desperately needed. It would be another two years before I knew I had to leave and begin my life on my own with my sons.

"What did I do to deserve this? How could you do this, God? You are a loving God!? I've never done anything to intentionally hurt anyone in my life. How could you put me, my son and my family through this? I hate you!"

I didn't know what to do. I felt I couldn't breathe. I was barely existing, certainly not living. My life was falling apart and I did not want to live. I wanted to turn the hands of time back to when I could change things. But this was not possible. It was interesting that I still turned to God, angry and upset with Him for at that time I blamed Him. Now I know it was not Him that caused any of the devastation, sickness or heartache for God is only good. And as my heart cried out and turned to Him, He began to slowly open my eyes to truths I had never known before. I was slowly being resuscitated back.

There were no words spoken as Christian's father drove us to the appointment. We pulled into the medical center parking lot and all I wanted to do was grab my baby and run, run as fast as I could. It was the most difficult day of my life. Every time I thought of what we were facing, my eyes welled up like a river and the pain in my heart was equal to someone ripping my skin off.

We had been to one appointment with this doctor the week before and she had asked tons of questions as my little guy walked the perimeter of the room like a solider afraid to enter the center of the room where we sat. I felt just as afraid as he looked. He didn't speak. He didn't make eye contact. He didn't play with the toys offered to him. I prayed for someone to shake me awake from this nightmare so I could find out it was just a big joke. Why did she make us wait an excruciating week before giving us the formal diagnosis?

Then suddenly there it was—out in the open—like a fog-horn, deafening and loud screaming in my ears...

"Your son has autism," she said. "I think that after you really take a look at this you will realize he was born this way. He will most likely never speak, never be able to live on his own, and will need to be institutionalized. And I hope you will be ok because I had to give this same news to another mother a couple of weeks ago and she went home and attempted suicide."

What?! I can't believe this is happening. What did she just say? For the first time in my life I was speechless. The world stopped. The room was spinning and I couldn't hear anything else after that. I could not speak. I didn't know whether to hug her or slap her. I only heard Christian's dad speak up for me and say, "You don't know this woman but she'll be back and our son will speak to you one day."   That never happened. I never saw her again, but Christian did speak.

We slowly walked back to get in the car for the ride home. It was only an hour away but time was warped. It felt like I was crawling and when I made any progress someone would grab me and pull me back. I still could not speak. His father did not speak. The silence was so loud! *Autism, autism, autism* kept ringing in my mind. This would be the case for several months with it being the first word I thought of when I woke and the last word I thought before passing out each night.

Day and night, I'd catch myself holding my breath. I needed and desperately desired my husband to hold me and say, *"Honey, it will be ok. I know it's not what we would have asked for or expected, but we will get through this together. I am here for you."* Such words were never whispered or spoken. Instead, there was total shock and silence. I don't even think I cried, not in the car on the way home, and not often in the months after. Tears were being stored up for sadness that awaited on several fronts further down the road in the long journey that lie ahead.

Halfway home something had risen up inside of me. As I sat next to Christian, tucked in his baby seat, completely oblivious to the sentence we were just given, I had looked in his big, blue piercing eyes and vowed to him, "I will never leave you. I will die protecting you and I will find a way to help you in every way I can. Mommy is here and I will never leave you."

It was soul to soul and with this secretly spoken, our journey began.

The journey to healing and growth for Christian... and me... and those other wonderful people God brought into our lives. I now know it was God who spoke to me so I could speak to my son with the love and conviction that could only come from Him.

Not eating or sleeping much, I was depressed and obsessed with trying to find out how to help my son. This Christmas was going to be different. It took every thread of energy just to go and buy gifts and put them under the tree for the boys. Christian's oblivion even to the gifts spiraled me into a deeper depression. I was drowning; my family was broken and Christian was not improving. I never attempted taking my life but I did think about it—often! This was no way to live and I wanted no part of it.

I researched. I read. I hired people to help me. I got up in the middle of the night to speak with people in England and the US. At one time I thought I'd sell up and move to the US. Then I'd change my mind. I was spiraling out of control. Christian was on every diet I learned about and every therapy imaginable. I thought, "If this is what life is going to be, I'm checking out!" I desired to stop living if this was what life was going to be. But I could not leave my children without a mother. So I mentally swayed between feeling depressed and despondent and wanting to jump off a high cliff and then regrouping and going into Mother Warrior mode! I was going crazy and I'm sure driving everyone close to me equally mad, as they watched me try to navigate.

Then a God-given friend spoke Scripture to me. Earlier, when Mom had encouraged me to get back to church and find the spiritual support I needed, I told her, "Guess what? That will never happen! I don't want God in my life. He is not helping me. Who needs a God that would allow this in our lives?"

The friend spoke Jeremiah 29:11 (GNB): *"I alone know the plans I have for you, plans to bring you prosperity and not disaster, plans to bring about the future you hope for. Then you will call to me. You will come and pray to me, and I will answer you. You will seek me, and you will find me because you will seek me with all your heart."*

And he added, "Russ, when Christian finishes his time here on Earth he will be with God in heaven and there will be no autism. He will be complete and whole as we all will be. And you will be with him." My heart stopped and then I knew. God had not caused this. He is love and He loves me and He loves Christian as He loves all of His children. And that was the beginning of my love story with our Creator.

It was not as if things changed drastically or overnight but I began to change. My heart was softening to the love of Christ. I began studying and spending time in God's Word and this is when the healing began; for me, for my son, and for my family. I could not fix my marriage, because that takes two people working at it, but I could take control over my own part, my motherhood, and my relationship to myself and my world.

The Word and God's personal message just for me had begun sinking into my heart and awakening my soul to hope. Now I knew I had to go to the Source of all life and have some conversation, but rather than speak, it was time to listen. It is in the stillness and quietness that God speaks. I was too busy trying to do things myself and had to slow down. I instinctively knew that God had the answers, I didn't. Yes, the professionals had tactics and strategies to get Christian to his potential but God had the wisdom and guidance to touch a place that needed to be touched and healed within myself. As I healed, Christian healed. My family healed. We are still healing.

It was as if I was lost and depleted, a dry well in the desert. The hunger and thirst for God's Word was overwhelming. I couldn't get enough. I was being resuscitated one day at a time. I sought, He led. I surrendered, He carried. I cried, He comforted. I prayed, He heard. I screamed at Him, He listened. I ran, He chased. I realized He was always there, never leaving me. Retrospection is so powerful. It's often only when we can go back into the scenes and experiences of our lives can we see the supernatural occurrences. He never left me. He was always there. It was I who ran away. I couldn't change things. I could never have a father when he was absent during my childhood; I couldn't repair my marriage. The relationships with males in my life had caused my life to form the way it had, but I could seek a new way and stay in commitment to healing myself and my children.

At my lowest point of my life, I felt I had to start writing some things down. And in my studies of Pastoral Care and Counseling, I was learning the benefits of journaling… and it was a way I prayed and spoke to God. I was home a lot taking care of Christian and my other boys, trying to rebuild my life. Although it was challenging, having to stay close to home probably saved my life. Because I was home, I had a massive amount of time to unravel all the pain, walk through it with my Savior, and allow the healing of my heart to begin. This adventure was of a very different kind than those I had sought in the past. Now I know it was part of the plan and it was God's protection as well as provision.

First, I would get the boys to bed. Next, drink red wine, lots of it, and journal into the wee hours of the morning. Then I'd walk, many times stumble, into the walls of that beautiful house, which I'd taken my 401K from the US out to put the deposit on. It looked very probable I was going to lose the house, but I would climb into bed, only to repeat this routine night after night after night. My pen and paper kept me company; my journal was my friend that I could talk to. It didn't talk back from the pages yet I felt God speaking to me through the dialogue that was written. I wrote prayers, I wrote music, I wrote poems, I wrote desires, I wrote my visions and my dreams, I wrote about my heartache and loss and pain.

But one night I was sitting at the family home at that same spot at the octagon-shaped wooden table underneath our octagonal veranda. That table had catered so many celebrations—taking the two younger boys home after their birth, kids birthday parties, girls' nights around a meal, family and friends dinners, announcements of births and deaths, heavy and confronting conversation, and happy and celebratory chats.

I looked out to the pool where my boys had swam so many times with their mates and out to the adjacent park with trees, where we'd hung piñatas for kids at our parties to whack and fight over the lollies that fell to the ground. And I simply wrote, "I BELIEVE I AM FINALLY FINDING MY VOICE" .... and down shot a white feather onto the page that lie before me. It took my breath away!

WOW! My heart skipped a beat. *Where did this come from?* I looked up and smiled, then quickly shut the journal and ran inside the house to get tape to stick it on the page. I kept thinking no one would believe me! And then I giggled with God for sending me a personal message. I didn't know exactly what it meant yet but I was learning to wait and trust. He would tell me in His time. His little girl could be so impatient. The light, the essence of the lady in blue that visited me all those years back was still there. I didn't see her this time, but this magic brought the feelings up from the inside. She was alive and I was alive.

Other times when I was journaling I would take a break and turn some music on and dance in the park next door, under the moon with my hands spread out twirling. This time a father was twirling me around in a circle but it was my Heavenly Father. I had worked on forgiveness, radical forgiveness. I forgave so I'd be set free and allowed to continue out of that wilderness of un-for-giveness into the path of light my Father had designed just for me.

I love to dance, usually with someone, but it was only me and my God under His stars and His moon in the night air.

Is it a coincidence that I wrote I was finally finding my voice and nine years later I would be part of the Voices Movement led by the vision of a woman I would be introduced to by a gorgeous girl I worked with twenty-six years ago? Is it a coincidence that I danced under the moonlight with my Creator asking him to heal my mind, my thoughts, my soul, and I'm at this very moment sitting at a retreat in a house nestled in the red mountains of Sedona, Arizona? And this house is built and stands on Moondance Lane.

Is it a coincidence that Christian was diagnosed on December 13, 2007, and December 13, 2009, I found myself in a little Uniting Church giving my life to Christ?

I had come to the end of myself and knew I had to surrender to His plan. There was nothing to fix but there was a life to live. There was no more looking the part; I only had to look to Him. He loved me just as I was and just as I am.

Is it a coincidence that my studies took me on a road to becoming a School Chaplain, supporting young people mentally, emotionally and spiritually? God knows so much better what is for our good. I can't help but be wowed by the fact that it's even not just any school. It's the exact school I so desperately wanted Christian to attend, a mainstream school, because if I'm honest with myself I was ashamed about any of the alternatives. I wanted... I wanted... I then had to realize and do what was best for my son. So five years later, I am also serving my son's school, which is next door, with the Chaplaincy Service and paperwork was signed on December 13, 2018.

I reflect on some of the experiences I've had as my spiritual eyes and spiritual ears have been awakened. The only audible voice I have ever heard was a women's voice and it was an early morning in 2009 when my physical eyes had just opened. She said, "You really should be writing this down." I was not scared or freaked out. I may have even giggled on the inside again at the beauty of my connection with the lady in blue. I knew I had to keep writing even though I didn't know why. Sometimes we just have to get going one step at a time, not worried about the destination.

I had always had a desire in my heart to write a book. The moment I connected with Chloe Rachel Gallaway about the book now in your hands, my heart knew this would be it. Learning not to jump too fast and seek peace and guidance with God, I asked her to give me a couple of weeks to pray and make a decision. I had learned from past experience that if it was something God wanted me to do, He would swing the doors open and if it was something that wasn't right for any reason doors would be shut. That was my prayer. That was what my soul was communicating.

Three days later I was at a Bible study and the facilitator asked if anyone wanted prayer. I said, "Me, please, I have a big decision to make and I'd like some clarity." My answer spoken through her was, "Rusanne, I see your testimony. It will be through words on paper. I see paragraphs."

Nearly a year later, I see them too and have experienced a new awakening of finding my voice and honoring my story.

Now I know… my God is on the path with me.

Mother of four beautiful boys (Brandon, Austin, Jordan, and Christian), school chaplain, author and advocate, Rusanne Jourdan has many passions: to study, teach, and share the Love and Gospel Message of Jesus. Born in the Deep South, USA, she has made her home in Australia for the last twenty-two years. She loves writing, studying, reading and traveling. Rusanne has a heart for people and has a strong desire to advocate for the disadvantaged and young people with additional needs. She believes our purpose is to give others encouragement and hope, especially when life's challenges present themselves. Rusanne, or "Rusty" as the Aussies have come to know her, desires this message of love and hope to reach the hearts and souls of women and caregivers, for our journey is unique but also similar. She may be reached via email at *rusanne.voices@gmail.com.*

My Dance of Life

Joan Teagle Brumage, LCSW

"We must let go of the life we have planned, so as
to accept the one that is waiting for us."
—Joseph Campbell

The greatest moments of our lives are spent as a child
Children see life as life should truly be seen
A child's world is made of stories, playgrounds, imaginary
friends and enchanted forests. Children love unconditionally
And give wholeheartedly to the world. They, like no other,
See the real meaning of life. The fire that lives within them
warms our hearts, and brightens our world.
If we could always live our lives the way a child does, would
not our hearts be forever tender, and our soul eternally fresh?
  —Karen Brumage

Each time I read this poem by my youngest daughter, Karen, I
fantasize about how my childhood might have been different.
Born three weeks after the bombing of Pearl Harbor, I remember
so many nights waking up in painful agony, screaming for help
when a viral infection, bronchitis, leg cramps or sharp back pain
interrupted my sleep. Hearing mom and dad's "We're coming,
Joanie!" as they ran up the attic stairs to my newly renovated 1930s
bungalow bedroom was reassuring. I hoped they could "fix it" this
time. Calmly talking to me, they each held an arm, slowly walking
me back and forth "to get that charley horse out of my leg," often

releasing the cramps. Coughing from bronchial congestion slowed down once mom massaged stinky Vicks menthol jelly on my chest before softly laying an oven-warmed towel on top. I do remember Mom asking me why I had covers up to my neck on a warm humid summer evening. *"I don't know"* was my usual answer. I just knew my body hurt and I was afraid of pain. Not once do I ever remember either parent exchanging a lighter cotton nightgown for the long-sleeved flannel one clinging to my sweaty six-year-old body.

My upstate New York blue collar grandparents and mom and dad joined America's WW II focus: sacrificing and rationing food, sugar, and butter to pay the servicemen and women in our military overseas. Grandpa Bill owned a hardware store and plumbing business, while also serving as Scotia's Fire Chief. My grandmother, Nana, was a Block Captain. They proudly displayed a red, white and blue placard with two blue stars, representing my two uncles serving. Although my younger brother and best buddy Dick and I didn't understand the meaning of war. We did, however, love listening to our Navy's war planes flying overhead during air raid drills. I remember many evenings taking baths, in our white claw foot tub, when air raid sirens turned our laughter into squeals. Mom and Dad created a game out of mandated darkness during drills. They turned off all lights, tightly closed the cream-colored drapes with blue sashes and lit tapered candles that stood straight in our china candlesticks. Dad would whisper, "Listen kids, the planes are flying overhead to keep us safe from the enemy." Hot chocolate with marshmallows topped off these happy occasions that, unknown to us, were traumatizing to those children whose homes in Europe were bombed by the enemy.

Days of fun and frolic with neighborhood kids numbed out memories of my body's discomfort. Dick and I used every opportunity to spend free time with Nana and Grandpa Bill. Their house was also two blocks from our Mohawk elementary school, and our local candy and ice cream parlor. Nana often surprised us by standing outside of Stewart's Ice Cream parlor, waiting to treat us to our ice cream of choice. Dick often chose a strawberry cone while I always selected an ice cream sandwich. When the three of us walked into her sunny kitchen, a plate of chocolate chip cookies or Rice Krispies Treats greeted us.

Dick and I would rather stay with Mom's family than make the occasional visit to our father's parents, Grandma Lula and Grandpa Fred, where we were expected to be "seen and not heard." My godmother, Aunt Dorothy, often joined us for Sunday dinner of German specialties.

Summer vacations were pure joy for Dick and me. We cherished the time we spent at Nana and Grandpa's two-bedroom camp with a wrap-around porch overlooking Ballston Lake. For fifteen years, we were called "the town kids" by our lake friends who embraced us into their circle of life. Days of boating, canoeing, swimming, and fooling around on farmland, lying in fields of tall golden grass as we caught and released butterflies with their vibrant blue, orange and yellow colors filled our carefree days. Nana did not have a chore list for me as Mom did.

Grandpa Bill's annual Fourth of July birthday brought aunts, uncles and cousins for a wonderful day of celebration at the lake. Swimming and diving off our boathouse roof, fishing in Grandpa Bill's (Gramps as my cousins called him) rowboat, was his way of spending time with us. After catching a bullhead, Grandpa said, "Joanie, take this nail and hammer it through the fish's head." To my surprise, I wasn't squeamish, rather enjoying skinning it and taking its head for a souvenir. While we played in the lake and avoided helping in the kitchen, my uncles took turns washing their cars. This annual summer event united sixteen family members for one day.

Fourth of July menus never changed: table grace, followed by a parade of pot roast, fried chicken, mashed potatoes and gravy, Nana's freshly made applesauce, potato salad, coleslaw, and fresh green beans. Eleven of us sat under the hanging Tiffany lamp, the men talking about the store and women changing topics. My cousins, brothers, and I drew four straws as to who would sit at a nearby card table, decorated with Nana's embroidered table cloth. The boys shared their secrets, while I sat there silent, looking up into the eyes of the largest, embalmed deer head I had ever seen. I was the only girl in the family after my cousin, Ann, died from

Leukemia when I was five. I was expected to help the women clear the dark oak table for dessert while the boys helped Grandpa Bill crank the handle of his ice cream freezer to make his farm-fresh peach ice cream. Before the fireworks began over the lake, we would light sparklers then gather to sing "Happy Birthday" to our grandfather. Chocolate cake with white icing, and homemade, fresh peach ice cream completed our day. It was the one time no one got mad at anyone—the perfect finale to a perfect family holiday celebration. The large stone fireplace inside camp kept us warm on rainy summer nights.

When Dick and I turned seven and nine, respectively, life changed for us. Our father received a promotion and accepted a corporate job with International General Electric in New York City. We moved into a modern 1950 two-story brick house in Eastchester. Instead of neighborhood hopscotch competitions or bike races up and down Sanders Avenue, Dick and I played cowboys and Indians in our basement and rode our bikes on the nearby golf course. There were no kids our age and the one girl I met tried to kiss me and showed me her father's porn. I didn't tell my parents; I just stopped playing with her. One year later, brother Robbie, our childhood mascot, was born. My parents changed their focus from family to fun and frolic with friends by joining the neighborhood cocktail circuit. When it was their turn to entertain, Dad wanted me to help him make Manhattans in his stainless steel cocktail shaker. He frequently teetered and tottered when he stepped off the last step of his daily commute from Grand Central Station. Mom would shake her head back and forth: *Oh no, he's coming from the bar car.* As our family enabler, she would try to fix everything. Each time it happened, he said it would be the last time. I never thought he really tried. I wanted to disappear out of range of her accusing him and his slurred denials.

Though often I pushed disturbing memories away at times, they— persistently—returned. I recall sitting quietly in the backseat corner of our 1942 Chevy as a memory surfaced: we were sitting at Nana's kitchen table waiting for Mom when he opened a bottle of yellow beer and took a few sips. "Would you like to taste it Joanie?" he asked.

"Sure, I guess," my curious voice whispered.

He poured it into a floral Kraft cheese glass and I took a few sips. I liked it. After two more sips, he took it and poured the rest into his glass. "Mom just pulled into the driveway," he said. "This is our secret, Joanie—mom wouldn't like it."

Magical memories of our family gatherings slowly dissolved due to the 150 mile distance from both families. There was another reason. As dad's drinking increased, so did his angry outbursts, inappropriate sexual comments, and dirty jokes. Slowly, over time, family members made excuses to not drive the three hours for a weekend visit. Mom said, *"It has become a family issue." She didn't know what to do about my father's drinking.* We missed our cousins and contrived ways to go to the lake in the summer. I now believe unknowingly, Dick, Rob, and I existed in isolated glass chambers, capable of watching and listening yet, often defenseless to rescue one another from dad's verbal attacks. My brothers and I each experienced a different relationship with our father. Dick was his *Scapegoat*, often being blamed for something or criticized for a chore he completed. Helpless, I watched him walk away with his head down, gritting his teeth in spoken anger, eyes glistening with tears, staring straight ahead. The *Hero* daughter, I often closed myself off in my room. I used to think I stayed on his good side. I'm not sure Dad knew how to relate to his youngest son. Robbie was the *Lost Child* who silently stayed in the background. Mom, Dick, and I protected him by diverting dad's attention. We loved our little brother who was always following us around the neighborhood. We had one another's back and still do.

My religious beliefs were solid to my core during my teenage years. As a conforming, dependent child raised in the Lutheran Church, the religion of dad's German family, I truly loved and believed Jesus Christ was the Son of God. We said grace at our table nightly and *The Lord's Prayer* at bedtime. I was beyond excited to be confirmed so I could take Communion, believing it would make me closer to God. I selected the white dress all girls wore to show purity at our Confirmation. I *believed* I was a pure, loved child of God.

To achieve Confirmation, we had to memorize each commandment and the articles of faith in *Luther's Small Catechism*. The Fourth Commandment told me, "*Honor Your Father and Your Mother*" and I honored my elders, believing they spoke the truth. I felt excited to grow up, hoping to go to a junior college. My parents always told my brothers and me, "You can do anything you put your mind to. If you have an idea, run with it!"

Dad could be like two persons in one as his drinking and family conflict increased. On a New York winter night as mom and I were doing dishes, I asked her why she put up with his angry outbursts. "This is not what I wanted, Joanie, it is what I had to accept. He only hit me once when I was pregnant with you. I told him I would leave if he ever did it again."

The crazy realization that took me years to comprehend was how alcohol could switch my father to his dark side as he verbally and emotionally attacked my brothers at the dinner table. Somewhere in the midst of this, I wanted to find a courageous voice.

Did he have a bad day I wondered, as he would pick on Dick, shaming him until my brother's pain and red face rage was near total eruption? I shall always remember the last night he raged at them in front of me at the table. Now thirteen, I could not tolerate his outbursts. After he referred to Robbie as a mamma's boy I stood up, slammed the wooden mahogany chair into the table, turned to him and screamed, "Don't you ever talk to my brothers like that again!"

Mom's mouth dropped open when he raged at me, "Shut up, bitch!"

I immediately ran up the living room staircase as I listened to mom -yell, "Enough, Bob." Something was happening to me, inside my teen age body, and I was not sure what to think. Turning left to walk into my bedroom, I spotted my pink bedroom sheets in a pile on the floor, soaked in spots. Mom, thinking I had wet my bed, told me to wash them earlier that day. I did not follow her instructions. I remember suddenly screaming downstairs at him, "I'm thirteen and can get pregnant, you know!" Running to the bathroom, I turned on the shower, took off my clothes and sobbed, dropping to my knees as the warm water cleansed my shaking body.

This event is an example of a repressed memory. Until I found my voice, I had no memory of this slice of personal history that had become my norm when I was stressed—*taking a shower, allowing water to drown out the sounds of my sobs.*

Since I had skipped first and third grades, I was graduating high school at age seventeen. From my sophomore to senior year, I was part of a group of four girlfriends, all of us class officers. As treasurer, I learned a little bit about setting up balance sheets with my fifty-cents-an-hour babysitting money. Since I had to buy most of my clothes, I also was a checker at our local A&P, a gig that paid seventy-five cents an hour. I accounted for every dollar in envelopes I kept in the top left drawer of my light-brown maple dresser. Mom drove me to the bank every two weeks to deposit my earnings. I had accumulated $190 when I noticed the $31 I planned to deposit the next day was missing. Immediately, I knew where it was. Flying down the staircase where Mom and Dad sat watching *The Lone Ranger,* I yelled into the air, "*Who took my $31 babysitting money out of my wallet?*"

Silence... then... "Dammit, Joanie, I was going to tell you," Dad said. "I needed it and will pay you back when I get paid next week."

Mom glared at him. "Bob, why in heaven's name would you do that and not ask her?"

Then I lost it. "This is not the first time I thought money was missing from my dresser drawer. I have to pay for everything around here. *I'm tired of this!*" I yelled, then ran back to my room.

Robbie, now six years old, followed me into my bedroom, closed the door and climbed into my lap, whispering, "Please don't cry, Joanie, it will be alright," as he wiped my tears with his tee-shirt. Then a knock and Dick walked in, closed the door and joined our huddle on my gray and white bedspread. The three of us held each other for a very long time.

Sitting there, we heard the word DIVORCE escape my mother's lips. We looked at one another. I wondered if her secret affair, that my brothers knew nothing about, was about to be revealed. It was a secret kiss I stumbled upon one night after their Masonic meeting. Dad was a Patron and Mom a Matron. Confronting her at our dining room table in an empty house, I gave into her tearful, "Please don't tell anyone, not even your father, Joanie." Not only did I not want to be her secret keeper; I refused to be a Rainbow Girl, as part of that entire bad taste in my mouth I wanted nothing to do with the Masonic organization.

Divorce!!! Not a common word for marriage breakups in the 1950s. Although I often heard my aunts, uncles, and grandparents fight or walk out of a room, no one in either family had ever divorced. Yet my mother and father were breaking their marriage vows. Dad's drinking and their flirting with others caused great rumors among their peers. Dad was also going to work overseas for his company, another reason divorce seemed like their best option.

As angry as I got at my parents, I never thought of them divorcing. Wasn't it shameful? I was a confused daughter. *Yes they had problems; yet, what about all our happy years as a family? Wasn't that enough to stay together? Didn't Jesus condemn adultery and mistreatment of others in the Bible? Why didn't they work harder at their marriage?*

They decided to speak with our Pastor who counseled them for a few months to no avail. I worried about my youngest brother. I knew I would be okay since I would graduate soon and hoped to attend a junior college. Dick planned to enlist in the Air Force after graduation, while Robbie was ten years younger. How would he and Mom live if our parents divorced?

And then an unexpected bombshell: my parents had not saved anything for my continuing education. I was shocked, angry and, for the first time, afraid for my future. Knowing my saved $300 would not help, I was thrilled and grateful when Aunt Dorothy offered to finance $800 for my only option, Katherine Gibbs Secretarial School training in New York City. Mom and Dad agreed to pay my monthly commuter train ticket, plus $100 for expenses. With a dress code of business attire, high heels, hat and gloves,

I learned the art of shorthand, fast typing and became a valued administrative assistant.

Accepting a position in the Jell-O Division of General Foods, I continued to live at home until their nasty divorce was finalized. *Of one thing I was certain: with God's help, I would find a man who loves and cares about me and I would love and care for him. "I will never, ever get a divorce," I said to God in my nightly prayers. I truly believed this promise to myself.*

When our house sold in 1961, Dad returned from Korea to help Mom and Rob settle into a new one-bedroom apartment. Dick (aka now Rick) joined the Air Force. The stripping away of happy memories bled into my family picture album. I knew it was time for me to move on and give myself permission to put myself and my life first.

My colleague from General Foods, Susan, and I decided to move to New York City. We rented a one-bedroom apartment for $150 a month. Anything and everything was at our fingertips in what is now called The Big Apple. Sharing our love for cooking, we entertained, went to plays, museums, Radio City Music Hall Christmas Shows, and my love of all genres of music, and ballet escalated. Living a life free of chores, babysitting, and penny pinching was freedom I had never known in my nineteen years. I was free to make my own choices: what to eat, wear, when to go to a party or just be alone. *Why did I have to know what I wanted after years of being told what I needed? Was this the dance of life? Would my boyfriend of four years, Joe, continue to dance with me?*

After nineteen years of responsibilities to others, I decided I wanted no obligations to anyone. Before I could tell him I wanted to break up, I received a telegram from Dad. He was coming to New York on business and wanted to take me to his favorite restaurant, The Garden, and to an off Broadway show. I had never been to a show with my father. Thinking it would be like the night Grandpa Bill took me to dinner months earlier, I thought of it as a date with my Dad. Having inherited my skill of sewing from Nana and Mom, I decided to make a red scalloped-hem crepe dress.

The night of the occasion, Dad picked me up in a taxi, which took us to the restaurant. I still have the paper placemat and

Playbill program from that night. At dinner, I asked him which show we would see. Placing his hand on my right knee, he whispered, "A burlesque show starring Ann Corio—she is good Joanie. Uses fans so you don't see her naked." I told him I did not want to see a stripper. Here we go again with his sex talk, I thought.

Prior to intermission I felt nauseated. "Dad, I want to leave, my back hurts and I feel queasy."

"Okay Joan, I don't want you to take a taxi by yourself," he said.

"Why not, Dad, I do it all the time?" I said, yet I agreed to come to his room to receive a gift he brought for me from Pusan, Korea. Years later, Susan recalled that when I returned from that evening, I walked straight to my bedroom, told her I wasn't feeling well, and was going to take a shower. When she heard me crying, she ran and opened the bathroom door, helping me from the shower to bed, where I passed out.

A few days later, I called Joe, asking him to meet me on the corner of 48th and Lexington Avenue after work. It was a habit we often timed to just bump into each other. He was excited to see me. Instead of embracing, my sense of urgency pushed me to tell him I was ending our relationship. Seeing the shock and hurt on his face when I told him we were through still lingers within. I abruptly turned around and hastily walked the twelve blocks to my apartment. Once inside, I collapsed into a heap of sobs. *What had I just done to the first man who I now believe truly loved me? Why was I wanting to suddenly erase all men from my life? Why did I always feel so trapped and afraid?* It never occurred to me that my father's visit may have influenced my decision. Maybe marriage wasn't for me.

My health continued to nosedive. Tremendous back pain radiated down my legs. I could hardly step into the bus to work, a thirteen-block walk on a pleasant day. When the pain became unbearable, I ended up in New York Hospital, shortly after my twenty-first birthday. After many tests, the head physician told me I might have the beginning of ankylosing spondylitis or arthritis of the spine. *"We won't know yet, Miss Teagle. The spine is likened to a tree trunk that doesn't show much. A lot is changing inside, causing your pain. Until the tree branches bud and bloom, we can't test to see what is happening. Your pain is real. I suggest you wear a back brace under your garments. We will discharge you in one week."*

Being inpatient at the age of twenty-one was wonderful. Nurses gave wonderful backrubs and nurturing massages twice a day. And, I didn't have to cook my meals. At that point, I was glad there was no man in my life.

One afternoon, Mom visited me announcing that she and Dad (who was still home from his job with IGE in Korea) met with my doctor that morning. "Joanie, Dad asked the doctor if you were a virgin and he said no you were not."

Stunned, I said, "Mom, I have never had intercourse with Joe who is the only boyfriend I've ever had. We fooled around. The doctor is wrong!"

At that moment, I was shocked and angry. "Why the hell is he asking the doctor that question?" I screamed. "It's none of his business."

"I don't know, Joanie," she whispered, shaking her head.

I dumped my anger on Dad during his visit that evening after work, the night before he was to return to Korea. Immediately, I told him how angry I was he asked the doctor if I was a virgin and then switched gears, reiterating our different ideas on diversity. "You are still a bigot, Dad…do you remember when you didn't want my class friends of different races or religions to our home for my graduation party? Mom and I fought you on that," I said. "I was surprised you were okay that night. Maybe it's because you knew you'd be in big trouble if you caused a problem. And, why do you tell me I'm naïve, and I lack confidence, and the one I hate most… keep your legs crossed? That's crude, Dad!"

Quickly lifting his six-foot frame out of the visitor's chair, he kissed my forehead, saying, *"Joanie, please take care of yourself. I love you. I'll see you next year"* and he walked out of my hospital room.

Two days later, I was released from the hospital. Slowly, the inflammation in my body retreated, and I continued my career goals working for major corporations in Rockefeller Center. I dated a few men; one even proposed after three months during a carriage ride through Central Park. Not interested! For the first time ever, I felt calm and at peace by myself or with friends and had no back pain or illness. Although I noticed I was drinking more, and even passed out on top of a bed of winter coats at a party, I liked being single and not responsible to anyone but myself.

All of our past will come to catch up to us someday. My journey was just beginning when I met Jim Brumage at a party in my apartment building on February 14, 1963. His flirtatious smile greeted everyone at the door. Intermittently, he returned to my side to flash that grin, warming my heart. Naïvely, I believed it was only for me. Our courtship was quick. I had never felt as close to any man and believed he was loving, kind, and attentive. When he told me his college girlfriend had broken their engagement, I immediately wanted to make sure he knew he was loved and cared for. It never occurred to me that I was worthy of that for myself. When Jim proposed three months later, I accepted.

My *Protector-Advocate* role continued to become the story of our life. Mom and Dad wanted us to wait six months to be sure. When I shared their request, he said: "I'm not sure I'll be around then, Joan." Afraid he would leave me, I gave in. We were married on a rainy Saturday afternoon, November 23, 1963, the day after President Kennedy's assassination. Our country's grief didn't contaminate our joy. Continuing to excel as an administrative assistant to the comptroller of Exxon, earning $125 per week, I was happy when we realized our total annual income in 1963 was $11,000. We loved our life.

Growing up in the 1940s and '50s, I believed my life's greatest adventure, each time I dressed my bride and baby dolls, would be to become a wife and mother who would love, nurture, and care for her children. Thrilled to learn my morning nausea was not the flu, I gave birth to Laura in 1965. *I'm going to be an attentive mommy,* I promised, gazing into her beautiful blue eyes. Supporting Jim's desire to climb the corporate ladder began when he accepted a job with a friend's company in Michigan; my role as a wife and mother was new and often challenging. Our final move west to Colorado Springs in 1972 was exciting. Our three precious daughters, Laura, Lynne, and Karen, graced our lives with joy, love, and gratitude. Karen followed her sisters wherever and whenever she could, just like Rob followed Dick and me. In return, she let them play dress up, carry her around, and smother her with love. As a happy stay-at-home mom, my only goal was to continue my mom's Betty Crocker-style household: cook, can garden fresh jams and vegetables, and keep up with cleaning and laundry. Playing with our daughters was my joy.

On weekends, Jim and I took the girls wilderness tent camping near Cripple Creek gold country. While I was a Junior Girl Scout leader, Jim helped them as Bluebirds. In later years, he coached their softball teams, taught the skills of running track, racing, marathon training, and healthy eating habits. When financially possible, we accommodated their desire to take piano, dance, and skiing lessons on the slopes of The Broadmoor Hotel under the snowy wings of Pikes Peak. One year we had enough money for them to learn horseback riding. Living in the west, far from family, our three daughters were our pride and joy. Camping, sports, and fun family events occupied our first fifteen years as a family of five. Our neighborhood was filled with boys and girls who joined the girls in biking the streets and climbing Austin Bluffs. Our regular attendance and heavy involvement in the Lutheran Church was our spiritual anchor for life. Although we wanted to remain in Colorado Springs, Jim's $500 a month unemployment check barely covered the $300 mortgage payment and utilities. Fearing bankruptcy, I asked Dad for a $1,500 loan. Here I was borrowing money from the father who had stolen from me. Strange! I abandoned my nine-year stay-at-home commitment when Jim and I agreed I needed to find a job. Little did I know I would never return to that special time in my daughters' lives.

Utilizing my secretarial skills, I worked for the El Paso County Soil and Conservation Service, followed by one year with a cattle rancher as his Payroll Secretary. Jim decided to become an insurance agent, accelerating to the status of CLU (Chartered Life Underwriter). I started Twigs N Twists, a wholesale jewelry business, with a friend for extra income. Enjoying stringing jewelry and consigning southwest Native American artists' jewelry, we began a home-party sales business. When my business partner resigned,

I expanded by representing two jewelry lines. Jim's business grew and provided our family with welcomed financial stability. We both agreed I was travelling too much and the girls, who hated going to after school day care, needed me at home. I ended my business travels to Vail, Aspen, and other retail customers and sold my business, focusing only on The Gift Express, a small boutique I opened to carry gifts, jewelry, and accessories. Feeling financially able to move closer to the downtown, we bought a Victorian home in downtown area of Colorado Springs. This enabled the girls to walk to their elementary and high school two blocks from the store. Family and business life was busy and satisfying.

Just when life seemed to be coming back together, my autoimmune issues returned. Increased back pain and surgery for acute endometriosis placed my body into early menopause at thirty-seven. Still, I kept going. Our marriage suffered. Depressed and angry, I often wondered if we had anything in common anymore. Jim stayed away and ran races every weekend. He avoided conflicts with me by spending more time with sports friends. We navigated through our marital conflicts by attending Marriage Encounter and took a codependency workshop. Because I was also drinking boxed white wine nightly and over-drinking on business trips, I quietly, without telling anyone, went to Alcoholics Anonymous thinking I might be an alcoholic. I shall always be grateful to a member who suggested I attend an ACOA (Adult Children of Alcoholics) Twelve-Step Meeting instead. "Joan," he commented, "from what you say about your father's drinking, you may not be the alcoholic. Maybe he is!"

I took his advice and went the next evening. After hearing the Problem and The Solution, I knew my father was the alcoholic and my drinking was to numb out pain. *What pain?* I asked myself. I learned I had a "family of choice," a term that annoyed my now teen-aged daughters. *"We are your family, Mom, not those people you call friends and family,"* they said.

Trying to make sense of the mixed messages I received as a child, ACOA Twelve-Step meetings became my anchor in life. Being able to talk freely gave me a greater understanding of my alcoholic father, co-alcoholic mother (who drank to keep up), and how helpless my brothers and I were as children. There were genuine expressions of warmth such as a smile, a friendly look, and an occasional comforting hug. However, were my parents attuned and responsive to each of my brothers and me? Were they caring towards one another? The realization sunk in deeper and deeper that the boys' and my needs were often neglected. To me, conditional love is painful and can be abusive. I began to wonder if I, too, was a parent who perpetrated conditional love to my daughters.

I felt afraid. Our marriage was on shaky ground. My trust in Jim had waned as I witnessed his flirting, which triggered a past event that years ago nearly separated us. Increased criticisms of my "not healthy cooking" and weight gain deflated my confidence. *Worn down and too tired to care, I let it wash over me like wastewater that drains into a contaminated sewer.*

There are seeds that, although they have been sown, take years to germinate.

September 2, 1982, represents the day an emotional earthquake slowly permeated our world. Returning home from running errands, I was greeted by a tearful Laura standing next to her pale-faced father. "Joan, your dad suffered a heart attack during his cataract surgery and could not be revived. He died. I'm so sorry." Laura caught me as I slumped into a kitchen chair.

His strange words to me in a phone call the night before, echoed in my mind: "*Joanie, I want to tell you that I am truly very sorry for the pain I have caused you in the past.*"

"For what, Dad?" I angrily chided. "*Your drunken rages on the phone and me sobbing and defending myself when you said I was a bitch, just like my mother?*"

"*There were other things when you were a child—other times I hurt you. You were always so sensitive. You are a wonderful wife and mother.*"

Challenging his statement, I'd said, "*I don't know what you're talking about, Dad.*"

*To which he'd said, "It is simple: if I don't make it, remember I
love you, Yobie." After hanging up the phone, I laughingly shared his
apology with Jim.*

He hadn't called me his Korean nickname for years. Weeks
later I learned he had called each of my brothers with the same
message of apology. "Did he plan his death?" we asked one another.

My dad and our daughters' Pop-Pop...dead? I sobbed, grieving
and remembering happy times: when he threw me into the lake
to learn how to swim, then jumping in to teach me how to float,
when I came up for air; his nickname for me, Chatterbox, because
I always had something to say; when he taught me how to ride
my two wheeler; the day he walked alongside me to sell flower
seed packets door to door in 1948; the time he helped me recite
the Ten Commandments so I could be confirmed with his entire
family present. His biggest joy, though, was telling me how proud
he was of his granddaughters and their nickname, Pop-Pop, for
him. No more of his special barbequed chicken dinners. Pop-Pop
was DEAD at the age of sixty-six.

*Unbeknownst to me then, this numbing shock of dad's death
would become the golden nugget that would eventually crack open my
minefield of memories.* For the next four years my mind, body, and
spirit began to slowly implode with pain like it did when I was
young. Diagnosed Crohn's disease, Ankylosing Spondylitis, ongoing dental pain and surgeries, as well as autoimmune issues that
rendered me crippled and immobilized, raged within my tissues.
No amount of swimming, massage, or medications relieved the
pain. As pain ravaged my thinning body, and Jim and I struggled,
I often was not a loving mother. I yelled at my daughters, drank
boxed wine, often used the "F" word, and attempted to run my
store with mood swings that drove my employees to quit. Truth
be told, I was losing interest in everything about my life. "*What
is wrong with me?*" I would journal and scream into the silence
of our Victorian home. "*What happened to little Joanie? Where is
she?*" I sobbed.

Jim was more involved with his running friends. In spite of
marriage counseling, we continued to co-exist until Jim decided
to move out. He wanted his freedom and I didn't know what I

wanted. It was very difficult for our children to comprehend and understand. After separating for seventeen months, we reconciled and renewed our marriage vows to the delight of our family and close friends. At the same time, our beautiful home sold and I joined Jim in his new condominium.

Our balloon of happiness continued to slowly soar. Life was good, until it began to crumble like shale breaking free from its petrified foundations.

There are wounds that never show or bleed from the body; yet, they can ravage the soul.

While taking a shower on a Sunday afternoon in April 1989, my brain released a snapshot memory of my four-year-old self riding in the backseat of Grandpa Fred's tan rumble seat Ford. I sometimes rode with him while he delivered hearing aids to his customers. Before driving home, we stopped at a local ice cream parlor for a vanilla cone, walking to a nearby park to sit on his blanket and enjoy our treat. Suddenly my joy turned to angst. Antiquated nausea and dizziness overcame me. Heaving vomit and feeling faint, I stepped out of the shower, collapsing onto our bed. I passed out and remember waking to Jim shaking me: "Joan, what happened? The shower was on and there is vomit everywhere." I told him about my memory that *grandpa had touched me down there.*

"No wonder you have never liked vanilla ice cream, Joan. It makes sense now!" He held me not knowing what to do or say.

After my brain released this memory to my body, I prayed, asking God why was this happening to me and was there more to learn? Is this why I always felt nauseous and had to have the window open when riding in the back seat? When I shared this vision with Mom, she said: "*You were five when you sat on your bedroom stairs and told me you did not want to go with Grandpa Fred for ice cream, and I told him. You told him no. You had control then, Joanie.*" Her words calmed me a little.

I made an appointment with my therapist of several years, Leslie, who validated my strengths in saying "no more ice cream cone trips with Grandpa Fred." Still, I was confused. *Why didn't this help me feel better?*

One month later, I was hospitalized for extreme back pain and a possible MS diagnosis. Anorexic, I had no desire to eat. My marriage was unraveling. I had no energy for anyone or anything. When Leslie surprised me with a visit, I remember whispering, *"Leslie, if that window were open I'd jump out. I don't want to die, I just want the pain in my body to stop."*

Within the core of each of us is the child we once were. This child constitutes the foundation of what we have become, who we are, and what we will be. (Neuroscientist, Dr. Rhawn Joseph)

To boost my mental and emotional functioning, I joined an outpatient therapy group led by Leslie and her colleague, Susan, who months later, taught us dominant (my right hand) and non-dominant (my left hand) hand writing as a way to communicate with any inner child part of Joan. I will always remember my first visual encounter. When I closed my eyes and couldn't see anything, Leslie whispered, take a deep breath, Joan and invite her to visit us today.

At first, I saw nothing…then I saw the shadow of a small face peeking out behind a huge boulder in the woods. She was young with a small blue bow in her blonde hair. She looked like me as a child. She turned away when our eyes met.

"Ask her any question," Leslie whispered.

What is your name? I wrote.

My name is Joanie. I'm scared you will go away again.

"What is she talking about?" I asked. I still did not understand. It felt strange to me. It was difficult to stay present to the experience. I wanted to pull away. With my therapist's guidance and encouragement I began to communicate with this little Joanie.

Dominant right hand: *Why are you afraid I will go away again?*

Non-dominant left hand: *You go away when I get hurt and scared. I am always alone.*

Dominant right hand: *How old are you?*

<u>Non-dominant left hand</u>: *I am six years old!*

I remember feeling shocked at learning there was a six-year-old inside my body. I was speechless; yet, finally a *calm I had never known* came over me.

"Leslie, am I making this up?" I cried.

"No Joan, for the first time, you have met your six-year-old self. She was hiding because she didn't believe you would listen to her. Maybe she is afraid you will leave her behind again," Leslie said.

"Leslie, I will NEVER leave her behind again!" I shouted. "I do believe her. My body knows she is telling the truth! Are there other inner child parts inside me?"

"Time will tell, Joan," she said. "This is what self-nurturing is all about. When you carry and hold your teddy bear, you are nurturing the dissociated child part who is six. If there are more children, they will speak out in their time."

Layers of frozen memories block my mind, marking time until allowed to safely thaw.

The timeline of my journey to find my voice spans a period of three to five years. It begins with my first of three inpatient hospitalizations at Cedar Springs Psychiatric Hospital, Colorado Springs, Colorado. Celebrating July 4th, 1989, by listening to the 1812 Overture, lying on the grass at Memorial Park, I told Jim and my best friend, Terry, that I had been faking feeling better when in reality, I wanted to die. I could not get my snapshot memory of Grandpa Fred out of my mind.

Jim called Leslie and my psychiatrist, Dr. Caster. A few days later I was admitted to the inpatient unit. The morning after my first admission, I met with Leslie and Dr. Caster, who labeled my memory as a "flashback," *a sudden and disturbing vivid memory of an event in the past, possibly as the result of psychological trauma.* They explained, *"Joan, you have worked so hard these few years to seek your truth. You are still in pain and state you are very tired. We really want to help you find those answers. While you are here, we hope you will attend groups, rest, write in your journal that you enjoy, and trust your body. You have no responsibilities here. (Wow!*

I thought, I don't have to cook, clean, or make any decisions.) Joan, *you have lost over twenty pounds and are anorexic. We will monitor your food intake daily.*

Confused and so tired, like a leaf that had fallen too many times from the tree, I was ready for the hard work of life to stop. *"Is this endless pain what life is all about? If it is, I want to die,"* I admitted.

Hollow and numb inside, I felt safe and secure for the first time in a long time. *Maybe I'll never want to leave—Jim and the girls would be better off without me.* Feeling compelled to communicate with my six-year-old inner child, I journaled:

Dominant Right Hand: *Joanie, what is it like for you to be here with me?*

Non-dominant Left Hand: *As long as you are with me, I'm okay. I do miss being with your daughters.*

Dominant Right Hand: What do you think of my telling my hospital group about you?

Non-dominant Left Hand: *They will think you are crazy because they can't see me.*

Dominant Right Hand: *That's okay. I am learning to trust myself and speak my truth. No matter what others say or think. Was more information buried somewhere inside of me? The same place my childhood was buried?*

I still remember his salty gray hair, black horned-rimmed glasses, and blue plaid shirt over a torn-at-the-neck white T-shirt. His tall frame was cushioned in scuzzy tan slippers. *What a kind-looking man,* I thought.

He stared at the floor and then up at each face in our therapy group, which was starting late. Two new admits, we heard at breakfast. *Was he one of them?* I wondered. *Maybe he is sad or depressed like me.*

"Does anyone have a light?" he asked quietly.

"You can't smoke until the break," someone told him.

My usually mute roommate whispered in my ear, "Joan, what the fuck, who is this old man? I mean he is really old."

The old man whispered, "Heard that, missy."

"Overnight admit, I guess," I commented.

As our circle grew, new members introduced themselves by first name. Many new faces! A young woman with scars of grievances crossing back and forth on her right arm. Next to her a woman tried to speak; nothing emerged from her mouth. A young man hummed to himself. Then came Nurse Carol's greeting, "Good morning."

Finally, I thought. *She is late.*

Our daily routine was off this morning.

"Our topic this morning is trust," she said.

Slowly the group's responses came:

"I trust anyone who doesn't hurt me," my roommate declared.

"I trust no one," the bandaged young woman blurted in a loud whisper.

"I thought I could trust my wife," one new man tearfully stated.

"I don't trust myself," I said. "My name is Joan, and some days I want to die and don't know why."

"My name is George!" the old man announced. "Joan," he said, "that's my granddaughter's name. We call her Joanie... only I can't see her right now. I'm not sure why I'm here. I guess I'm depressed, or so the doctor thinks. I have a problem and they tell me I need help. I guess I can't be trusted anymore...I hurt something I love. My family kicked me out. They don't trust me now."

There was a sadness on his face but his lips smiled. The way he said his granddaughter's name, Joanie, felt weird. My Grandfather Fred called me Joanie. Suddenly my body stiffened, I felt icky and wanted to vomit like I did in the shower weeks earlier. Familiar heat invaded my body and quickly passed.

"What did you do to her?" the young man to my right asked.

"They say I molested her—Joanie—my granddaughter. She's five years old. I didn't mean to hurt her. I thought she liked it. She always stopped crying."   Suddenly, my roommate stood up and ran out to the patio stating, "I need a smoke."

Nausea overcame me. As the room began to swirl around me, I struggled to speak. Nothing came out until that deep place inside my body exploded with a fury: "Her name is Joanie?" I screamed

"That's my name…your family says you molested her? DAMN YOU, DON'T YOU KNOW? HOW IN HELL DON'T YOU KNOW?"

I yelled into his face. "My grandfather molested me, only he's dead now, like you should be, and I can't lock him up with you!" I lunged, grabbing his arm. Nurse Carol and a staff member pulled me back.

Again, he repeated his mantra: "I didn't mean to hurt her."

With the shocking confession of sexual abuse by this grandfatherly man I had felt sorry for, the room started spinning wildly in my head. *I had to get away.* Standing up straight and tall, I turned and ran to my room, screaming, "You bastard! I felt sorry for you then you say you hurt your granddaughter!"

My triggered memory of that helpless six-year-old me screamed out in pain. In a blind rage, I hit my forehead against the pale blue wall, harder and harder. Seeing staff running towards me, I pulled the shade off the wall lamp, threw it on the floor, and destroyed it with my feet. After pulling the sheets and blanket off my bed, I collapsed. *"Grandpa Fred took me for ice cream; he touched me down there. Is that why Grandma Lula yelled at him to leave the bedroom when he would take a nap with me in his home? Why can't I remember?"*

Suddenly, I pictured his face then it changed to my father's smile. My mind was confused. *Dad didn't molest me. Grandpa did, or did Dad? Or was it both of them?* Familiar, uncontrollable vomit hit the floor. I sank my sobbing, anorexic body on the bed, curled up, and rolled side to side like I did as a little girl. Hugging my gray teddy bear with its hidden dark eyes and white nose, I succumbed to that soothing familiar blue darkness, Nurse Carol at my side.

Awaking hours later, I was told I had been placed on a twenty-four-hour watch for any self-harm behaviors. *How could a memory such as being molested by my grandfather relax my body and empty my mind? Why did I see Dad's face?* I had no appetite for dinner. All I wanted to do was to sleep and forget. I asked for a sleeping pill, drank a cup of chamomile tea, and curled up clutching my teddy bear.

Waking early the next morning, I noticed a piece of mail on my nightstand. It was a letter from my daughter Laura: *"I'm writing to you there, Mom, because I know you are safe. My sisters and I don't know who you are any more, and I'm scared, Mom."* Her handwritten expression of her fears and her anger at me, felt like brutal honesty that beat at my heart. I remembered the many times we argued and the time I slapped her across the face when she was in high school. I now believed that not only was I a bad wife who did not understand her husband, but also a rotten mother. No amount of group validations helped. All I focused on was my roommate's comment: "Sounds as if your daughter isn't sure she can trust you, Joan, to be the mom she knew."

"Hell, I don't even know that mom anymore!" I cried. *"Why would anyone trust a crazy mother like me?"* Continuously folding and unfolding her words until lights out, I finally put it under my pillow. I couldn't read it again. As I dozed off, I remember comforting myself, *"That's okay, she didn't mean it."* Deep inside though, I knew she was right.

During morning group we were given an option to stay at the hospital for the day or go to Fly Cave, a shallow underground cave in the mountains nearby. It was a warm July day in Colorado Springs. Three members wanted to stay behind while three of us said, "When do we leave?" Scared about the unknown, yet curious about caving, I remembered my love for exploring as a child at the lake.

After crawling on our adult bellies over a damp dirt trail, we settled into one of nature's unlit circular chamber rooms. We each were given a flashlight, a small water jug, a sandwich, and an apple for our backpack. Quietly we gathered to take deep breaths, relax, and eat lunch before checking in. Peacefully leaning my back against the dirt wall, I loved the smell. After all I was a Capricorn, an earth sign. In the nurturing comfort of total darkness, I remember wondering: *Is this what it's like to be dead in the ground? That is where Grandpa Fred is now,* I happily thought.

Following lunch and a ten-minute rest in quiet solitude, Nurse Carol and our male guide/therapist started group discussion, illuminated only by their flashlights. Instructed to only turn on and shine our flashlight when we wanted to share, I was relieved. I had nothing to discuss and enjoyed listening to other group members sharing in the cool, dark silence. Suddenly, without warning, the person across from me lit up. *Only it wasn't anyone in my group. Gasping, I saw my father's face as he shined his small flashlight on my face. My father standing at the foot of my bed in the dark holding a "rubber." A fully repressed memory took over. "Dad, NO!" I screamed as I rolled my body to one side, curling up like the twelve-year-old child I believed and felt that I was at that moment.*

Arms flailing, I swung my flashlight, hitting the person next to me. The chamber room starting swirling with that familiar nausea. Nurse Carol crawled to my side, calmly taking my hand, saying, "Shine your light on Joan's and my face, everyone."

Immediately, I was back in the cave. "Joan, you are safe with us, take deep breaths in and out. Remember, you are with your group in Fly Cave."

I briefly described the vision of my father in his shorts holding a rubber and I thought it was real. "It is not a flashback but an *abreaction*, Joan," Nurse Carol explained. "Your brain and body have released a repressed memory that your body believes is happening now. Perhaps your body feels safe here. Your brain will not forget what you just experienced. When we return to the unit, we will talk more. OK, Joan?"

In that instant, my body, mind and spirit had a knowingness. My father had sexually abused me. How and when I could not recall.

Immediately, that familiar temporary peace after remembering new information about my childhood captured my body. Taking a huge deep breath, I lowered my shoulders (a technique I learned in group). My head swirled like snowflakes, with bits and pieces of memories of the past. Leaning my back against the comforts of the dirt wall, I was barely able to listen to others share their thoughts. We then crawled our way out of the cave into the warm July sunshine.

Depleted and drained of all energy, I slept in the backseat of the van all the way back to the hospital. What a day it had been. *"How could I have not remembered this?"* I muttered. *"My God, Dad, what did you do to me as a young child?"* Unable to articulate to anyone, I walked to my room and lay down on the bed, cuddling my teddy bear before drifting into the familiar dark blue for consolation.

During the next few days I remembered: *long showers as a teen covering my tearful sobs... and the loneliness. So many nights I cried into my pillow feeling less than and not knowing why.*

Meeting with Dr. Caster and Leslie the next day, I learned that the intrusive image of my father who I believed to actually be across from me was called *spontaneous abreaction* (in psychiatry it is a term where a person is triggered into the belief that a past trauma is, or is going to be, reenacted). The darkness of Fly Cave, my angry thoughts about Dad, and spontaneous flashlights triggered me into a dissociative state. In that moment, my body 100 percent believed he was across from me.

Later, during a journaling exercise I remembered attempting suicide when I was twelve. I looped Dad's belt around my neck and tied the other end to the bar in my closet. Hearing Robbie's three-year-old voice calling, "Where are you, Joanie?" I sat down and the belt broke. When he laughed, I knew he did not understand.

Another memory returned, of swimming at the lake and becoming entangled in tall weed grasses. A familiar internal voice whispered, "Let go and stop fighting, Joanie. It will feel good and you will be free."

Defiantly, I screamed for help. My two uncles jumped in Gramp's boat and rowed to my rescue, cutting weeds and freeing my legs. *I would not die in that wonderful lake I loved.*

After sharing these memories with my afternoon group, our therapists taught us about shame and how our self-talk can send us into "shame spirals." I learned that a healthy shame statement is: "I did a bad thing and I am still a good person who is worthy," while a toxic shame statement polarized self-beliefs that distance me from others: "I did a bad thing and I am a bad person."

Two days later I met with Leslie and Dr. Caster, who proclaimed that I had done amazing work during my six-week stay. My physical health was improving, and I had little body pain. I was anxious and ready to discharge, and they agreed with the understanding I could return if life became unmanageable. That afternoon, Jim called and asked me to take a walk in the park to "discuss *us.*"

After years of counseling, we agreed we were still struggling. He asked for a commitment to our marriage or he wanted to move on. Still emotionally numb, I could only commit to living one day at a time. I knew he was dating. I was conflicted, feeling numb and betrayed; yet, how could I expect him to wait? I agreed to a divorce. He wanted to file first! This decision caused our daughters a great deal of strife and emotional pain. They lovingly tried to support their mom and dad, while at the same time comfort one another from a distance. I was happy they were moving on in their lives. Laura, settled in California, while Lynne, a Navy officer, was beginning medical school on the East Coast. Karen and I became roommates until she finished her Bachelor of Nursing at University of Colorado, Colorado Springs. Guilt and shame often overcame me as I witnessed her grief and loneliness. She missed her sisters. It was a struggle for my daughters to accept that our family life had truly changed forever. The Brady Bunch, a name given our family by their peers, was no more.

As memories of my father's incestuous attacks slowed down, my physical and emotional strength increased. I was now single and committed to become a solo traveler on a healing journey to seek my truth. A reoccurring thought began to infiltrate my consciousness: would a college accept a middle-aged woman in her forties? I knew one fact for sure: after ten years, I wanted to close The Gift Express.

My train to somewhere sped up when two more brief hospital admissions provided proof that although life often appears to be returning to normal, our relapse triggers randomly deliver their crushing blows.

Second Hospital Admission, December 5, 1989 – December 9, 1989, Excited for my first Christmas in my new condo, I was decorating my tree when, I heard a knock on my door. Slowly walking to the door, I flipped on the porch light, and looked out the peephole. There they were: my father and his father -wearing his familiar brown fedora hat. The air left my body as I sank to the wooden hallway floor, double locking the door as I fell. *What's happening to me and why are they out there?* Tingling with chills and fear, I crawled a few feet away into my kitchen. Unsure if I was alive or dead, I picked up my car key and dug it into my left wrist. *No blood!* I then picked up a kitchen knife and drew a deep line on my skin. Blood dripped to the floor. *I am alive!* Frightened, I wrapped a dishtowel around my cut and looked out the peephole again. They were gone.

Running to my bed, I crawled under the covers as I had as a child. The phone rang; it was Lynne. When I told her of my vision she requested Terry's phone number. She called Terry, who picked me up and took me to the hospital, sucking my thumb and holding my gray teddy bear with its hidden eyes.

HALLUCINATION OR REALITY?

During the three days that followed, memories crystallized into a major incestuous event perpetrated by my father in July of 1958, my junior year of high school. Mom and my brothers were spending the summer at the lake so that she could work in Grandpa Bill's hardware store. Since I had failed geometry, New York State Regents Board mandated I stay behind for summer school. For thirty years, my personal memory of that summer was that Dad drove me to the lake three days after retaking and achieving a barely passing grade of Circle 65 on their final exam. Once at the lake, I stayed to myself reading romance magazines, such as "My True Story," that I hid under my pillow. I never wondered why I related to teen girls in many sensual stories. Once Nana asked me, "Joan, why do you read that trash?" as she walked through the porch.

MY TRUE STORY REVEALED

Now a sixteen-year-old, five-foot-eleven, slender teen, I was conscious of my height and felt like a freak. Anything I could do to minimize my height was my goal, except when I was in the privacy of my own home. After cleaning the house, I realized I had a few hours before my shift at the A&P Supermarket. I blew up our family's twelve-inch-deep by five-foot round plastic swimming pool, filling it with water from our hose. Dressed in my navy blue one piece bathing suit, my thirty-six-inch-long legs embraced green grass while my body cooled and relaxed in the pool. Hearing a sound coming from my bedroom window, I looked up and saw Dad staring at me. Feeling uncomfortable, I ignored him and turned up the radio. Returning from work early, due to a slow night, I encountered my father drinking scotch and water in the dim light of our living room. I ran upstairs to change before making my dinner. He stood up to follow me when I came downstairs. The look on his face frightened me. "What are you doing, Dad?" I asked.

Afraid, I ran into the dining room and crawled under our walnut dinner table. I screamed, "Get away from me!" before he pulled my body out from under the table. Before he could pick me up, and finally throw me over his right shoulder, I rapidly pulled out his twelve-inch machete, slicing his left arm. (To this day, I don't remember how or when or where I took and hid his weapon. Or, why a neighbor never heard my screams on a hot summer night.)

In the hospital, I came to realize that cutting my left wrist was my brain's way to allow cellular memories to release from my body—it was confused, believing that I was really cutting my father's left arm with his machete. During this admission I learned all my life *I had taken on the shame of my abusers by accepting and self-inflicting their shame on myself. How many secrets did I keep out of loyalty when I was a child?*

"NO MORE!" I screamed over and over again during a group exercise that freed my shame. I screamed at my father and later my grandfather (as I threw a box across the room): "Dad, I give you back your shame. IT IS NO LONGER MINE! Grandpa Fred, I give you back your shame. IT IS NO LONGER MINE!" Then I pummeled their imaginary bodies to a pulp with a rubber club.

This healing exercise introduced me to life's harmony. As if a block of ice had been lifted from my heart, my breathing became different. I could take a deep breath, release it and lower my shoulders. Instead of focusing on my victimhood, I could finally look to my future. I was outside the box of life, breaking the constraints placed generations earlier. I was discharged three days later.

Although our divorce was finalized, Jim and I committed to never repeat my parents' animosity, especially Dad's to Mom. Our decision to co-parent was difficult for me when he remarried. Focusing on healing my past, I now realize that many angels surrounded me as I prepared to close my business. My landlord, after verifying my hospitalizations with my providers, released me from my lease. Several store vendors dismissed my balances or settled on a small percentage, thus not disrupting my credit rating. I cleared my debt. Happy and feeling on top of the world, I continued to attend Twelve-Step Meetings. Another survivor of incest and I started the first Survivors of Incest Twelve-Step Group in Colorado Springs. Our meetings were full. Now, I could honestly say without shame, "I am a Survivor of incest who is learning how to thrive."

Third Inpatient Admission to Cedar Springs, March 6, 1991 – March 9, 1991, The Way of Healing The Broken.
This admission brought clarity about the night dad took me to the burlesque show.

Intake Staff Assessment: Major Depressive Episode and Alteration in Mood Related to New Memory of Father's Abuse. Patient is very emotionally shut down; has had many dissociative episodes after a telephone conversation with her mother. When she arrived sucking her thumb, she wrote her name illegibly. We had to wait until she entered her adult state. Said she was "trying to reestablish a personal connection with mom."

Goal for Admission: To stabilize mood and acquire coping mechanisms/self-nurturing skills to deal with her depression.
My head was clear when I awoke the next morning. After signing the necessary admission papers, I met with Leslie.
"I am sure my dissociative trigger was Mom's phone call yesterday," I said. "When she said I've missed you Joanie, I felt like

a child again." (It had been a year since I hung up on her, angry that she always made excuses for herself and didn't want to hear the truth about my father's abuse).

"I don't know what I would do if you hung up on me, Joan," she said.

I told her again how angry and hurt I was at her for not believing my memories. She asked me to remind her of the memory with his machete. "I cut his left arm when he pulled me by the hair," I recounted as she interrupted me.

"Joan, I remember now! He told me he cut his arm cleaning the machete. It didn't make much sense to me, because it was a large cut in the center of his left arm. Oh my God, he did hurt you! Joan, I am so sorry I didn't believe you."

She was crying. I felt empty inside. "Mom!" I yelled. "You once told me he raped you when you were eighteen. Why wouldn't he do the same to his daughter?" Look what it took for my mother to believe me.

So many times he was a nice, loving daddy. No longer would I continuously ignore myself to fulfill the needs of others. The gag that silenced my voice for forty-eight years disappeared. Now, my mommy believed my story. *I was believed!* Several hours later my brain delivered its answer. The night he took me to the burlesque show thirty years earlier, he most likely drugged and raped me after stopping at his hotel for the nightcap I didn't want. I was twenty-one when this final repressed sexual assault sank me into a bottomless abyss witnessed by my roommate. For the next three decades, this spiritual massacre would infiltrate my cellular body, spewing its carnage into my mind, body, and spirit.

My Promise to Myself: Remembering my parents encouraging "you can do anything you put your mind to," I've never considered myself 100 percent fearful or fearless. Somehow even in the darkest times, I had hopes for something better. This is why I am a survivor of Dad's sinkholes of incestuous sex addiction that led him to abuse me, his own child. *Is there more to remember?* If so, I know I can handle it now. No longer will I allow the felt blotters of my life to be fertilized with the semen of my alcoholic deceased father and unlawful touch from his father. I will turn my streets of sorrow into lanes of joy. I will help others find their true voice and heal their soul. I am determined to find and use my voice.

There was no faith in my mustard seed.
When my years of abuse forced me to bushwhack a new trail in life, the Rocky Mountains and all her bounty and beauty became my Higher Power. Disillusioned, I broke all ties with the God I once believed in. My faith in Christ evaporated, replaced by anger and feelings of betrayal. No loving God would allow a father to abuse his children one day and be nice at Christmas and birthdays. Imagine a God who would let a man submerge his sins under a cloak of apology the night before his death. It didn't make sense to my black and white thinking. Meeting Pema Chödrön at a Buddhist gathering was a blessing. When she approached me, placing her hands on my arms, she said, "You will find peace, my child." *How did she know?* I pondered. We are our own healers. My healing journey continued to change and grow.

In between my second and third hospital admission, I applied to Pikes Peak Community/University of Southern Colorado Bachelor's in Social Work Program. I was accepted and graduated in 1995. Advised by professors and Dr. Caster that if I truly wanted the strength to find my voice as a Licensed Clinical Social Worker specializing in Mental Health, I needed to earn my Master's in Clinical Social Work. I applied and was accepted at New Mexico Highlands University School of Social Work, Mental Health focus, in Las Vegas, New Mexico, then moved to an apartment near campus. After graduating with an awarded 4.2 GPA in (1996), I returned to my previous internship as a paid Clinical–Social Worker/ Drug and Alcohol Counselor in Colorado Springs El Paso Health Department. In 1999, I accepted an offer to join the Family Advocacy Team as a Treatment Manager at Holloman Air Force Base, Alamogordo, New Mexico.

Living in the high desert of my beloved New Mexico, I began a new life of working with active duty military families to include a two-year contract with the Army in Germany. After five years of service on site to our wonderful military families, I returned to New Mexico in 2003, opening my own private practice. I broadened my services as a psychotherapist to include civilian and military men, women and children ages five to ninety-five. Until this writing, I never revealed my story, except to disclose that I am an Adult Child of an Alcoholic Father. This disclosure opened many doorways of trust between my clients and myself.

FINDING LOVE AT FIFTY-FIVE

Prior to beginning graduate school, I journaled my desire to meet a cowboy who loved his grandchildren and drove a truck. That December I met John, a man in a blue denim shirt with a red bandana in his right hip jean pocket, in the rare book section of an antique store. I commented that my Grandpa Bill had given me the same *Horizon* book collection he was reading. A week later we met again in a café. He was supervising the University's library building addition. We began an affair that awoke the cores of our being. After a few months, he admitted I had gotten under his skin. I wasn't ready for that. Neither of us could let go; yet we continued our personal lives and spoke weekly.

Our twenty years of long-distance romance and living together at times have taught me that love has many faces. Being accepted as an independent woman with many talents healed my soul. "Angel, you are the smartest, most gifted woman I've ever known," he said whenever he would read my papers. No one had ever praised me in that way before. Our relationship has shown me how a man and a woman with trauma histories can do a dance of stay and leave until trust builds and commitment unites. Separated by life, we reconnected when I returned to New Mexico from overseas. In between our work assignments, we were together until Parkinson's attacked his body. We are still connected in spirit and by my visits and our telephone conversations. *(Note: John died in September, 2019. His last words to me: "Angel, you are my light!")*

CLARITY OF MY FAITH RESTORED

After returning from my assignment in Germany, I had two goals: return to yoga and find a builder for Casa de Paz (House of Peace), a pueblo-style home I had researched for five years. I struggled to find a builder who would share mutual creative designs. Attending a yoga class the week before Thanksgiving in 2004, our teacher began her Savasana visualization: *Picture yourself walking with someone you trust and are close to.* Immediately, I saw unfamiliar brown-sandled feet walking next to me in the arroyo of my canyon land. I looked up into the face of a man with long brown hair and a suntanned face. His eyes relaxed me immediately.

I whispered, "Jesus?"

Stopping, he lifted me up carrying me past the lone tall Cotton-wood Tree on my five acres, stopping at a circle of boulders where John and I had read the Christmas story one year earlier.

"Joan, here is where you will speak of me," he said.

Walking towards the flat rocky pad of my future home, he stopped. In front of us was the most beautiful stucco home surrounded by light. Walking up to and crossing what would become my forty-six-foot long portal, he carried me into a blank space standing in front of two purple wood and glass French doors that protected a small room lined with a wooden floor.

"Joan, here is where you will write about me," he said.

In an instant, he was gone. Alone, I stood on rocky stubble.

The next morning, a builder I had interviewed called me, presenting an offer supporting my house plans. Casa de Paz was completed in five months. Like the child I once was, I was ready to learn more about Spirit, not a religious order. Each time I hiked the high desert land, I knew I could never hide from myself. The desert strips one clean of disillusionment. I see Spirit's presence daily, in the canyon lands, the blue skies, and the people I meet, with a new awareness that it is not about religion; it is about seeing Christ's love in everyone I meet.

When my journey to share my story led me to read *The Soulful Child,* I reached out to Chloe Rachel Gallaway. Taking a leap of faith, I attended the first VOICES writers retreat. Each morning we began our day with yoga. Thirteen years of grounding, restorative yoga classes that revitalized my core body did not prepare me for our teacher's spiritual statement of *knowing* in our Warrior Two pose the last morning. Standing in a forward high lunge, my left knee bent at a ninety-degree angle; my left arm and hand pointed forward, I heard: *As you gaze past your left hand towards the vast land beyond, may you continue to forward focus on this journey through your healing path.*

Turning to look over my right hand, I heard: *May gratitude fill you as you leave the past behind, bringing you to this place of a new beginning.*

With outstretched hands folding to the heart center, we returned to our floor mat, relaxing in a five-minute Savasana. Then, I rolled to my right side, taking deep breaths, I sat up. Suddenly, tears poured down my cheeks and sobs shook my body. I fell into an uncontrollable familiar motion: rocking back and forth while hugging myself, arms crossed like I did when I was inpatient thirty years earlier. A soft light bounced from wall to wall in the room and out of nowhere my blond, six-year-old inner child appeared—blue bow in her hair, carrying me as a blond toddler. They climbed into my lap and nestled into my chest, not letting go. All my life repressed memories had blocked my ability to connect and actually see these younger versions of myself. Now, in this spiritual moment the layers of healing brought each child to me one by one. Joined by my thirteen-year-old inner child, my twenty-year-old self leaned into me, wrapping their arms around me. I had never experienced this inner oneness connection with each inner child and young adult part of me. For the first time we looked into one another's clear blue eyes, and I whispered:

"You are all safe now. I'm so sorry, for years I didn't know you were inside me. I will never leave or deny your existence ever again."

Slowly, my tears subsided and I opened my eyes. My class and teacher surrounded me, unaware they had witnessed a brief, invisible integration—only I could see those inner child parts of me that revealed our truths and allowed me to voice this story so that you may give yourself permission to use your voice.

Author, speaker and Licensed Clinical Social Worker, Joan Teagle Brumage was thriving in her middle-class family life in Colorado Springs as a wife, mother of three daughters, successful business owner and community leader. At the age of forty-two, an inciting family event slowly and painfully derailed her body, mind and faith-based Spirit. Joan's professional village of physical, emotional, spiritual and educational providers empowered her to piece together canyons of highs and lows from years of repressed childhood trauma. Finding her voice motivated Joan to earn her Masters of Social Work in Mental Health. She continues to be a source of strength and healing for all trauma survivors. Joan may be contacted at jbrumage@gmail.com.

The Immeasurable
Gifts of Sophia

Andrea Roberts Parham

"There are no barriers when hearts connect."
—Andrea Roberts Parham

The fruit borne from our greatest pains, the excruciating there-are-no-words, life-defining events, are often our greatest gifts. We don't ask for these gifts, deceptively masked by their wrappings: wrappings shaded with dismay, despair, anger, sadness, uncertainty, and hopelessness, dotted with "why?" and striped with "it's not fair." Some of the most special gifts we receive are also placed in the sacred abyss of primal pain, the kind of pain that poets and philosophers have attempted to express for centuries. Although some have managed to express the essence of that abyss, words are woefully inadequate; one must feel the emotion to understand. We often become so mired in the wrappings of these gifts that we don't realize what has been bestowed upon us for quite some time, months, years, even decades. Yet, the gifts are always there patiently waiting to be discovered.

From the time I was a small child I always knew I was destined to be a mother, the ultimate expression of womanhood for me. Of course, I didn't think of it in those terms. I just simply knew that was part of my future with a gut feeling I would be the mother of two. Like so many young girls, I played with my dolls, carefully dressing them, brushing their hair, pretending to feed them, singing them songs, reading to them, and putting them to bed—imagining what it would really be like someday.

Someday came for me on July 9, 1993, when my firstborn, my son Patton, entered the world. The creation of life is such a miracle: this beautifully perfect baby boy had grown in my womb, cell by cell for nine months and finally I could see, hear, smell, and touch him. He was not a doll. This was real life, and I was completely and utterly enamored with this creature who depended on me for his very survival. From the start, motherhood exceeded my expectations and I knew I was in for a life journey that would fulfill my soul in ways I never before comprehended.

Patton was a mellow baby. He nursed and slept mostly, as newborns do. In the next few weeks he grew and was right on track with developmental milestones. I was home on maternity leave from my full-time job at a large insurance company with plans to go back to work three days a week once he was eight weeks old. In the meantime, I was fully enjoying being home full time with my son, even going to a playgroup that primarily consisted of four mothers talking and the new babies sleeping. The playgroup was really for the mothers at that point. These women became my best friends and were an invaluable support system. It was my friend Jeannette who had asked me to join the playgroup. My husband and I had met her and her husband at a restaurant one night when I was eight months pregnant. Her growing belly was "as big" as mine and the four of us ended up having dinner together. Our boys, the first children for both me and Jeannette, were born one day apart. The playgroup lasted for years and morphed over time.

I did go back to work, three days a week, sobbing when my husband left with Patton to take him to daycare. Reality was that I had to generate some income, yet my highest calling was to guide my child through life, ensuring to the best of my ability that he honored his being and became fully who he was meant to be. When Patton was a year old, we got some exciting news: he was to be a big brother shortly after his second birthday. We were overjoyed! Would Patton have a little sister, or would it be a brother? Although the thought of a girl and a boy was nice, it made no difference. Most of all we wanted that for which most parents desire and prepare, a healthy baby.

August 25th, 1995. Sophia Joy, my greatest life teacher, was born. She entered the world at 11:34 p.m. in respiratory distress and was whisked away to the ICU. I had a nagging feeling, an intuition, that something was seriously wrong, and in fact, it was more than a feeling. There had been a hint during my pregnancy that something may have gone amiss in her development. Yet, despite a plethora of prenatal testing there were no specific issues identified except the amniotic fluid was on the higher side of normal, and her stomach bubble, meaning the fluid in her stomach in utero, was small. The perinatologist said that odds are everything was fine, but if not, the likely scenario was she had some type of issue causing something less than the normal amount of fluids to go into her stomach. It could be an esophageal fistula (hole), a neurological issue with her swallow, or something else. There was no way to tell until she emerged from the womb. Whatever was to be was to be. There was nothing to be fixed or done. At that point, I had decided to focus on enjoying my pregnancy and spending time with my older child, Patton, who was nearing his second birthday.

After Sophia's birth I was panic-stricken and distraught, asking the nurses what was going on. They did not understand my hysteria and basically attributed it to more common postpartum feelings. A sinking feeling in the pit of my stomach voiced in loud echoes that something was wrong. One nurse asked me why I felt this way. I told her about the prenatal testing and my feelings that something was amiss. She replied, "You really do have a reason to be concerned. I understand." Sophia was brought to me to eat/nurse. As I held her in my arms, looking down at her seven-pound body, regarding her tiny hands and her face framed with lots of fine hair that was so dark brown it was almost black, Sophia instinctively rooted and moved her mouth to latch onto my nipple, but she couldn't. She tried repeatedly. The instinct was there. She knew what to do, but she couldn't. My intuition was right. Something was very wrong indeed.

A Modified Barium Swallow Study revealed that Sophia could not swallow: the liquid spilled halfway down her trachea and halfway down her esophagus. Of the possible issues identified by the perinatologist, dysphagia, a dysfunctional swallow, was reality.

My baby, this new innocent life, could not eat. Who survives not being able to eat? This was not the middle of the woods or hundreds of years ago; if it were, Sophia would have starved to death as an infant, or died of pneumonia from aspiration of fluids into her lungs. Thankfully, now there is more than one way to eat, and a nasogastric (NG) tube was inserted through her nose down her esophagus so she could be fed adequately and safely, without the risk of aspirating.

My husband brought Sophia's older brother, two-year-old Patton, to meet her in the hospital. Patton, always a thoughtful soul, kissed his long-anticipated new sister on the forehead. It was less than twelve hours after Sophia's birth, a sunny August day in New England with bright light streaming into the spacious, cheerful hospital maternity room decorated in soothing shades of pink and green. Of the many thoughts rushing through my mind, none of them were soothing or cheerful; the prevalent one was uncertainty. My mind raced in many directions and, while my recovering body lay there, I looked for some modicum of certitude. There was none. I stared out the window in dismay of my life ahead. How would this affect Patton's life and our family's future? I was in uncharted territory and the only thing I was certain of was that this new life that just entered the world was not something for which I was prepared. I was about to find out just how unprepared I was.

One of the great things about living in the Boston area was world class medical care. Two days after her birth, Sophia was taken by ambulance to Boston's Children's Hospital, a facility filled with some of the greatest medical minds on the planet. And she was an enigma to them. Suffice to say that just about every medical test known to man was performed on this innocent little seven-pound baby, constantly awakened to be poked and prodded in an attempt to label her. She never was labeled and it doesn't matter. To reduce her to a medical diagnosis or even a list of such would be to do her a complete disservice. Sophia, this infant enigma, was about to teach me lessons I could have never imagined, and these were not the kinds of lessons I learned in school.

I sat in the NICU at Children's looking at this precious child I had brought into this world, fear overwhelming my body as I wondered how I could handle being this special baby's mother. *What would her life be like? Would she have a happy life? Could I do her justice? What if I fell madly in love with her and she died?* It was clear by now that her life was not going to be an easy one, and the stereotypical family of four with a boy and a girl was not what was happening. This was not the plan. Not the plan at all. I was afraid to love her, afraid that she might die and leave me and I wouldn't be able to stand that pain. But what she needed more than anything was love. She was innocent, peacefully sleeping on her belly in the NICU bassinet, head turned to the side, body covered in a white flannel baby blanket striped with pink and blue, NG tube inserted into her nose and taped to her cherubic cheek to keep it in place. *She didn't ask for this life. She didn't ask to be born deaf, unable to swallow, and more. She didn't ask for it.* What was I to do? Oh, the suffocating panic. I knew how to mother a typical child. I had no idea how to care for such a complex human being physically or emotionally. All children are uncharted territory, but this was like going into the desert without water and being responsible for someone else too. I was in distress.

Eyes wide open
Body frozen in fear
She knows not what to do
Lying still in darkness
Paralyzed

A nurse in the NICU, Louise, upon seeing a river of tears silently flowing down my cheeks, asked me why I was so upset. I told her that I didn't know what to do with Sophia, that I had thought I would have a typically developing perfect baby. She must have seen the agony in my eyes. I was truly at a loss. It wasn't about being unfeeling or wanting a doll; I was truly lost. My mother compass was gone. I will never forget the words of this ginger headed young nurse, wise beyond her years. She calmly said, "You do have a perfect baby. Sophia may be different than what you expected but she is perfect and beautiful." There was love and compassion in this woman's voice. She was holding Sophia at the time with immense love pouring from her heart into my child and me. I felt hope. If she believed that, surely I could too. I have a special place in my heart for Louise.

As I think in most cases when a child is born with special needs, a developmental pediatrician sat down with me and my husband to discuss Sophia. She told us we had options, clearly sensing the hesitancy in me. I was not ready to care for this child. I wasn't sure I could do it. The pediatrician laid out the alternatives. "You don't have to take her home. There are options. You could put her in foster care, or put her up for adoption." In that split second, the mama bear in me rose up on its hind legs ready to attack anyone who would even think about taking my daughter away. I emphatically exclaimed, "No! No one will take better care of her than me and her father. She is coming home." It was not a decision. It just was. From that moment forward, Sophia was simply my child, an indomitable being that challenged me and taught me in ways I never could have imagined.

The social worker in the hospital also met with us to see if there was any way she could support us emotionally or otherwise. As we sat across from her in the second meeting, feeling like it was a waste of time because we both knew there was nothing she could do unless she had a functioning magic wand, I looked deeply into her eyes and realized she felt the same way. She said, "It's clear that the only way I can help you is to fix your child." We responded, "Yes, that's right." She said, "Ok, so there is nothing I can do for you." She said this with the utmost compassion and kindness. It was true. The only thing that was going to make me feel better was to fix my child. In the years to come I would realize that Sophia didn't need fixing at all. She became a gift to everyone who had the honor and privilege of knowing her. She was born perfectly Sophia.

Sophia remained in the hospital for a total of five and a half weeks. She transitioned down to the main floor where I learned things like CPR before bringing her home. She came home on an apnea monitor, to monitor her breathing, 24/7. There were g-tube feedings round the clock. She had a Percutaneous Endoscopic Gastrostomy (PEG) "button" g-tube surgically placed directly into her stomach somewhere around the second week of life because it was evident she would not be able to nurse or eat orally. As someone who had nursed my first child for nineteen and a half months, never giving him a drop of formula, this crushed me into tiny pieces. It cut like a knife on my heart that I could not nurse my second child as I had my first. The pediatrician saw how devastated I was over this and commented that she understood, that providing nourishment was so much of mothering. But, that wasn't it. Not at all. It was more about bonding, the fact that I had memories of my infant son sleeping with me and just waking to eat. It was natural, it was easy. That was the way it was supposed to be and this was not it.

There was grief, a long river of grief that kept coming. All the norms were not the norms and never would be; I felt washed up on the shore of the river every day. The family of four with two typically developing children that I had envisioned for so long was never going to be; a dream was dying right before my eyes, but my child was alive and needed me. I was at once despondent, depressed, dejected, and so very profoundly sad. This is normal and I make no apologies. By no means does this imply that I did not love my daughter; however, to fully accept her and the altered reality, the old vision needed to be released.

I looked at this innocent child, her waking eyes alert and interested in what was going on around her, her hand tightly grasping my finger, her tiny cupid mouth pursing its lips. *It's not her fault. It's not her fault.* Those words repeated in my mind. I never resented her. Some people do resent being thrown into an unexpected situation. For me that wasn't it. I had no resentment or anger. I just had no idea how I was going to handle it. I had reached a point that I knew I would. I had no choice. In my mama bear mind, there was no choice. Sophia deserved the best life she could have and I was going to figure out how to best love and nurture her, to facilitate her to be her best self.

Most days I had to literally force myself to get out of bed in the morning, stumbling down the stairs for a much-needed cup of coffee, or two, before I could function. And, while Sophia needed her mother, so did Patton. I think I needed him as much or more than he needed me. Such a sensitive and tender child, I think on some level he knew that too. Having him crawl into my lap, the weight of his body leaning against me, feeling his breathing, his heartbeat, and smelling his little boy hair felt so normal, like everything was right with the world. Having those moments of normalcy helped stabilize me.

My mother had come from Tennessee to stay with us just prior to Sophia's birth as we had no family in the Boston area. She ended up taking a leave of absence from work and staying as long as we needed her to help care for Patton as we were constantly traveling back and forth from the hospital. In those first four and a half weeks when Sophia was in the NICU, a huge portion of every day was spent at the hospital; we came home to sleep at night and returned in the morning. I was torn between two worlds, like a sailboat in familiar calm waters that kept being pulled into a thrashing sea.

One evening a neighbor, a parent of a special needs child herself, showed up at my door bringing a much-welcomed cooked meal and copy of a brief essay written by Emily Perl Kingsley titled "Welcome to Holland," a metaphorical piece about how you have planned your whole life to go to Italy, but when the plane lands you realize you are in Holland. At first you are not happy, yet once you take pause and really explore Holland, you realize Holland may not be what you planned but it has its own unique beauty. In the moment I read the essay it struck a nerve. I stood silently, not moving, and my eyes welled with tears. This kind woman gave me an empathetic, knowing look. She knew something I didn't. What unfolded in the years to come was infinitely richer and more rewarding than I could have foreseen.

Ultimately, Sophia's medical diagnosis was a generic "multiple congenital anomalies," including the inability to swallow, deafness, and low muscle tone. Basically, her issues all had a neurological basis as there was some "blip" in gestation at a critical point. Yet, even as a little baby she made it patently obvious she was a fighter and she was not only going to live, she was going to exploit life's offerings. In a word she was a little whippersnapper, the feistiest spirit ever to grace the earth.

In early October, we finally said goodbye to long days and nights in a sterile hospital, white walls, beeping machines, and bustling nurses. It was a goodbye I welcomed. And, so Sophia came home. We had negotiated the purchase and sale of a house while Sophia was in the NICU, as if there wasn't enough going on. It was the right thing to proceed forward with our plans to move and so, a couple of weeks after she came home we moved to a larger, nicer house, one that would be a fabulous place to raise our family. I can remember Sophia sitting in her infant seat, connected to her apnea monitor, while I was cleaning the empty house we were selling. Stupid me. I was trying to save money and cleaned the house myself. I should have hired cleaners. I felt like a hamster running on a wheel that was spinning out of control with no way to get off.

Exhaustion was to become my norm. Never enough sleep. Working a corporate job three days a week. Doing for others. My two-year-old. My husband. My daughter. All their needs tugged at me like a heavy weight pulling me down stream. I was physical and emotionally drained and running on fumes. More often than not, I drove the forty minutes to work rolling down the car windows so the cold air would help keep me awake.

Sophia was g-tube fed and had severe reflux which meant that she could not consume large amounts of food at once and it had to go in very slowly. If not, she would projectile vomit. And, that was a fairly common occurrence. Laundry was done daily. While most babies triple their birth weight by age one, Sophia, having weighed a little over seven pounds at birth weighed only fourteen pounds at her first birthday with a diagnosis of failure to thrive. It wasn't because we weren't feeding her; it was because she could not process and absorb enough food. Not nursing her was something I had reconciled a long time ago, but what I would not compromise on was that she was to be held while eating. She was not to be just placed in her baby seat and hooked up to a pump to put the food in her stomach. Her father or I would hold her while a Kangaroo pump slowly dripped in her g-tube feeding, and Sophia loved being held as much as any baby would, enjoying being nestled in her parents' arms and snuggling in to enjoy her time with mommy or daddy. She was a human being, and quite an exceptional one. As she became an older baby, we had a special bright yellow, firm foam supportive seat insert for her chair at the dinner table. We all had dinner together with plates of food in front of us, Sophia with her tube feeding dripping in, licking/tasting food, and slyly throwing it under the table so her plate would be empty also. It was critical for her to have oral stimulation and not become oral averse; plus, never one to be left out, she demanded what everyone else had. Cleaning the mess under the table was a small price to keep my child psychologically whole.

Sophia's reflux was so severe that I had to slowly drip food in her overnight with the Kangaroo pump. *Drip. Drip. Drip.* She slept next to me often with her head on my left shoulder as I held her. And, my son slept next to her. We could not leave him alone as it did not feel right to have him, at less than three years of age, all by himself while his sister was with mommy and daddy all night. My husband slept on the other side of our king size bed. We needed to ensure the children did not fall out. And so, it was a nightly occurrence that all four of us, usually plus some stuffed animals, piled into the family bed together, reading books and snuggling into familial slumber. Sophia's personality was such that she was a bundle of energy all day, never napping save an occasional twenty-minute respite, so she slept quite well through the night as did Patton.

There were constant trips to the Gastroenterology Clinic at Children's. Prescriptions for Zantac (to reduce stomach acid) and Propulsid (to help the motility in her gastro intestinal track) were part of Sophia's medical regimen. We were trying everything we could to avoid surgery to stop her reflux. I felt strongly that I did not want her anatomy altered if there was any way to avoid it as that comes with other potential issues. When she was about nine months old, Sophia's case manager nurse from Early Intervention brought me an article about how craniosacral therapy can help reduce reflux. I had no idea what it was, but if it could help my child and there were no negatives, I was in. I researched it, found a therapist, and drove an hour one way for her to have these treatments once a week. Sophia always fully cooperated, lying on the treatment table and patiently allowing the therapist to release restrictions in her body, primarily the head and spine, with soft touches no greater than the weight of a nickel. Later I found a brilliant pediatric physical therapist, specializing in children with special needs, with over twenty years of craniosacral experience fifteen minutes from my house. Linda was a godsend. Sophia was Linda's patient for years, always looking forward to her sessions and greeting Linda with an engaging smile as she entered the sunny therapy room overlooking beautiful flower gardens. Finally, as Sophia grew and became stronger, the reflux was reduced. There was not as much vomiting, and the washing machine spinning and dryer tumbling reduced to a more manageable pace.

We had abundant professional support, and I took full advantage of it all. In Massachusetts, there was Early Intervention, and many therapists came to our home. My two days off from work were far more exhausting than the days I drove forty minutes each way to my corporate job. Those two days were packed with appointments at Boston's Children's and with therapists coming to the home: speech pathologist for oral motor therapy, physical therapist, deaf education specialist, occupational therapy, etc. Our lives had become a collage of caretakers, appointments and health management; I swam with it all trying to keep my head above water. Then there were the moments I'd stop and watch Sophia sitting in her chair, her head full of dark brown hair, her still eyes gazing out the window at a bird on the ledge, and I'd be reminded that she was growing and developing magnificently in her own way.

Massachusetts also had a family sign language program whereby someone came to the house to teach basic sign to the family and to any friends who wished to attend. We had about three months of those classes. We were determined to give our daughter language. She had a hearing aid in her best hearing ear. One ear was completely deaf, the other was technically hard of hearing. Fortunately, Sophia had an ABR (Auditory Brainstem Response) test done when she was an infant at Children's and her first hearing aid was placed at ten days old. So, from that point forward, she had some sound coming in to stimulate her brain. Yet, her deficient oral motor skills—at that time she could not even stick her tongue out of her mouth—made it clear she would likely be using her hands to communicate with the world. It's not something that I had ever thought about before, how when babies eat, suckling nourishment from mother or bottle, they are developing skills needed for speech. So, we started learning a new language, American Sign Language (ASL), and signing whatever we could to her. Children learn language first receptively and secondly expressively. Before her birth, it had never occurred to me to learn sign language, but as with everything I was to do for her, I jumped in with all I had. ASL is an expressive, robust language spoken with the entire body. When Sophia was just a few months old she realized she could do something with her hands. As hearing babies babble orally, deaf babies babble with their hands, regarding them with fascination, wiggling the fingers, twisting the wrist. One day when she was four months old, she was lying on the floor of our sunny family room on a bright red blanket sprinkled with festive shapes; I peeked in from the adjoining kitchen to see her intently studying her own hands, experimenting with different hand movements and closely observing them. It was as if she was seeing them as a separate entity with a power of their own.

At seven and a half months of age, Sophia signed her first sign. We were all sitting around the dinner table and she looked up at the light hanging over the table, signed "light," and turned to look at me. Gushing with excitement, I enthusiastically nodded my head and signed "yes" validating her. A sense of pride, relief, and joy simultaneously entered my body as I witnessed Sophia make the connection her hands could speak. She signed "light" again, and looked at me beaming with pride. Every cell of my body screamed "yes!" My baby girl could speak! Sophia quickly added to her vocabulary and was able to express herself quite well. At fourteen months she was on track with a vocabulary that was considered developmentally typical for a deaf child, one that was ONLY deaf. And, Sophia had so many other challenges. I could not have been prouder of her!

Sophia was without a doubt the most persistent, tenacious spirit that I have ever known. If you look up the word "determined" in the dictionary, her picture is there. She surpassed expectations; well, everyone's except her family's. I had very high bars for both of my children. I felt, and still do, that as parents it's our job to help our children to become their best selves. They are not carbon copies of us. They are not a second chance at our hopes, wishes, and dreams. They are them. It's up to us to honor their being. It's up to us to nurture, love, encourage, and be the guide that helps them come into their own full being. And, that is exactly what Sophia did. And, she blew minds in the process. For starters, no one would have ever expected her to be on track with any language development for a typically developing child, and yet she defied the odds in that regard.

My friend Jeannette also had a baby girl, a month after Sophia was born. As our boys were fast friends, we socialized constantly. I don't think anyone ever realized how painful it was for me to watch Jeannette's daughter develop typically and see that Sophia, although exceeding expectations as she dealt with all of her additional challenges, was nowhere near that track. Yes, I reveled in Sophia's accomplishments and wouldn't have traded being her mother for anything. Nonetheless language was such a huge barrier, and Sophia's low muscle tone caused physical developmental delays also. Jeannette was one of the friends who came to learn ASL with the family sign language program at my house, and I was so touched and appreciated that she did that.

Overwhelmingly my friends were supportive in the ways they knew how to be supportive. They genuinely tried. I know they did. To this day, I still don't think they have an inkling of the depths of anguish and isolation I felt when we would gather and Sophia was left out because she couldn't physically do or couldn't effectively communicate with the hearing children. I don't mean to imply my friends were callous and unfeeling; they were just oblivious to so much. I don't think it was possible for them to understand.

There is no judgment here, only observation and compassion. They thought I parented with skill and grace and were amazed. It was not uncommon for me to get comments like, "I don't know how you do it!" "You are amazing!" "Sophia is doing so incredibly well because of you" (not entirely true, although I did have a key role). "I could never do what you do." I had many solitary crying episodes associated with socialization, sometimes even holding back tears and turning my head so no one would see the tears welling up during events. It was a lonely path.

The truth is that I would have done anything for Sophia and Patton. I willingly sacrificed myself, almost to the point of my demise. Because I was so consumed with doing what needed to be done, I did not realize what was really happening to me; but living in a crisis for a year was literally killing my being. My inner light was dimming.

We had constant appointments to a multitude of specialists, but it was an appointment with Sophia's neurologist that changed the trajectory of my mental health. Right around her first birthday, I was driving Sophia to Children's for a neurology appointment. She was upset and kept crying, why I am not sure, but looking back on it I think she was feeding off of my energy. I was not in a good state of mind. Crying generates lots of secretions and Sophia really couldn't swallow them. I'd stop the car to clear the secretions and clean out her nose to ensure she did not aspirate. The hilly roadside beamed in the morning light; I had no connection to it or life outside of us. I was consumed with doing, doing, and being the caretaker of Sophia. I got back into the car after my third time of clearing Sophia's mouth, drove looking ahead into the flat pavement, and with a glance over at the ditch and a telephone pole, for a moment I thought about wrecking the car and killing us both. With a jolt of strength I jerked myself back into reality and quickly rationalized that there was no guarantee that we would both be killed and I could make it so much worse. Plus, I could not do that to my son, leave him without his mother. So, I called the neurology office and told them I was going to be forty-five minutes late, asking if I should come or reschedule. They said come. At the appointment, the neurologist, who first met Sophia when she was two days old and had told me repeatedly she was one of his favorite patients, examined Sophia, then turned to me and said, "Now let's talk about you."

I shrugged my shoulders and flatly said, "Ok."

Sitting in his chair, this middle-aged man, sporting a white lab coat and a mane of wavy dark brown hair, leaned toward me, chin lowered, looking over the top of his glasses, and simply asked, "How are you?"

I raised my eyebrows and replied, "Do you want the polite answer or the real one?" (No one usually wants the real answer.)

He looked intently into my eyes and calmly said, "The real one."

I matter-of-factly said, "No, I am not ok. At this rate I don't think I am going to make it to my thirty-fifth birthday." (I was almost thirty-three years old at the time.)

His eyes got a little wide and he said, "Well, you are clinically depressed. I think a policeman could diagnose this."

We had more of a conversation, part of which involved me saying of Sophia, "It's not her fault. She didn't ask for this," at which point he looked at me and said, "You didn't either."

I had no response to that. I was stunned into silence as he had bluntly spoken a truth voiced by no one else, a truth I had not fully acknowledged either. He then proceeded to get on the phone and make an appointment with my primary care physician and made me promise I would keep it.

I came home and relayed to my husband what had happened. I told him I felt like I just wanted to go away and crawl into a hole, that being the glue and holding the whole family together was killing me. I remember thinking that the idea of being in a warm, soft, cozy burrow with no light and no responsibility and just falling asleep forever felt so appealing. My husband immediately showed great concern and wanted to help. I think at that point the realization of everything I had been doing, and the sheer magnitude of it, came into focus. He went to work every day, and did some things around the house, yet I was the one that, in addition to my three-day-a-week job, handled the childcare, all medical appointments, therapies, and administration of medicines and feedings, in addition to a huge portion of the household duties. Perhaps I made it all look much easier than it really was, or perhaps that's what he chose to see. We both coped in our own ways. I could see that he was both blindsided and worried, comprehending that I was in a severe crisis. He softly and quickly asked, "Is that what you want to do? Need to do? You can do that. You can go away for a while. We can make that happen."

I said no, that I really didn't want to go away, but that things needed to change because I could not keep doing everything I had been doing, being responsible for all therapy and appointments and everyday care, and working, etc. Something had to give or else I was going to break. I was going to go get some help, as in go to a therapist, and I was going to quit my corporate job. Somehow, we would make the finances work.

While I was not truly suicidal, I was in a place that I completely and fully understood how someone can think suicide is the best option. I knew I had to do something to preserve my sanity. I did go on a low dose of Prozac and went to see a therapist. I was not so sure about the Prozac as I am not keen on popping pills, and prefer a holistic approach. After about a week of taking the anti-depressant, I stood looking out the kitchen window, noticing and appreciating the beautiful blue of the sky and feeling the warmth of the sun coming into the house, thinking, "Oh, I remember, *this* is how normal feels." It had been a long time since I had not felt like the weight of the world was crashing down on me. The Prozac did help me function in a very subtle nuanced way; I took it for about a year and a half. The therapist, Jeannie, told me my body needed a rest, that I had been living in a crisis mode for a year and that she could not believe my strength, that most people could not have done a fraction of what I did. I say this not to brag, but to say that while we are all stronger than we realize it doesn't mean we need to keep the whole burden on our shoulders. I was carrying way too much responsibility alone. Asking for help is a sign of strength. I don't know what would have happened if that perceptive and caring pediatric neurologist had not reached out to me and I will always be grateful to him for doing so. I saw many doctors who had to surely know that I was in a bad place psychologically. He is the only one who took the time to notice my broken sprit, reach out to me, and take action to help. I am not condemning other doctors who didn't. I just think that most are in their own world. It's a job to them. They see patients, and yes, they care, but at the end of the day they go home. THIS WAS MY LIFE 24/7 and there was no escaping it.

Pain rears its ugly head
In unforeseen ways
Surprise
Not so welcome
Why
Unresolved issues
Such acute pain radiates

By late fall of 1996, when Sophia was one year old and Patton was three, I had fully quit my job with no shred of compunction. Any career I ever had or could have pales in comparison to the endeavor of stewarding my children through life. Being home enabled me to be a better parent to both of my children. Patton deserved more of me than I had been able to give him since his sister's birth. Given Sophia's multiple special needs, suffice to say that it was enormously consuming parenting this willful, determined, medically complicated child. Nevertheless, I was beginning to see the rewards were priceless.

To Patton, Sophia was his sister. Simple. He adored her and she adored him. In her older brother, Sophia was also gifted with the best therapist on the planet. She wanted to do what he did. More accurately, she willed herself to do what he did. She observed. She cogitated. She improvised. She always found a way. She figured out that rolling was an efficient substitute for crawling or bipedal ambulation. Blurs of Sophia, a rolling dervish, whizzed through the family room and kitchen incessantly, an act to make any physical therapist cringe. But we loved it. Yes, she did her physical therapy religiously and progressed quite well, but a girl has to get where a girl needs to go! Sophia never did crawl, but finally walked independently at right at her third birthday.

With an age difference of two years, Sophia and Patton were playmates. If Patton was in the kitchen drawing on the easel, Sophia joined him. If he was working on a puzzle she wanted to help. Sometimes her little sister help was not so appreciated. In between Patton's exasperated exclamations of "So-PHI-a!" "Sophia stop!" and "Sophia no!" to which she usually mischievously laughed and kept doing whatever it was she was doing, he was so very patient and tolerant, an astonishingly wonderful big brother. One day there were several large cardboard boxes in the family room. I vividly remember Patton and Sophia, ages four and two, crawling in the boxes, hiding, poking their heads up and down, looking at each other and laughing in merriment. They went in and out of boxes, turning them over, hiding under them, giggling, both in the same box, each in a separate box. This went on for what seemed like hours. Playing, laughing, happy children.

Brother
Sister
Sibling bond
Rooted in love
Everlasting

Full-time school ensued at age three also, with Sophia attending The Learning Center for the Deaf (TLC) in Framingham, Massachusetts. She had been involved with their Parent Infant Program (PIP) since birth, participating in play groups and benefitting from home visits with the head of the PIP. When I went to talk with the head of the Preschool program to enroll Sophia, I was asked what my goals were for Sophia. I replied, "I want her to have friends and be happy." The Preschool Director smiled and nodded her head. Of course, I wanted her to learn too, that was understood.

Other than home, TLC was always Sophia's favorite place to be: she wanted to go to school even when she was sick, to the point of pitching tantrums about it a few times. From the time my barely-able-to-walk, just turned three-year-old daughter wobbled into her first day of pre-school, she could not get enough of school.

Most of the other children at TLC had no other special needs and were typically developing deaf children. A few of her peers also had their own unique extra challenges to conquer. TLC was an oasis of support and love for her, and by extension me. It was difficult for me to send my child to school full-time at such a young age, but I knew that's what she needed. She was able to have all of her educational and therapeutic (physical therapy, occupational therapy, etc.) needs met by some of the most educated, bright, kindhearted, dedicated staff I have ever known. That Sophia thrived in this environment makes total sense, as she was in her element, where she was loved and understood, both with language and otherwise.

TLC also provided community. Priceless. No one person can stand alone. We are social beings and feeling connected is essential for happiness and contentment. Sophia was happy and content, and so was I. The school offered American Sign Language (ASL) classes free to anyone who had a deaf household member. The entire family, my husband, Patton and I, took classes. Sometimes together. Sometimes not. We all continued to advance our language skills. I was the most proficient signer because I was constantly at the school conversing with staff, other parents, etc. I chose to immerse myself as much as possible.

By the time Sophia was in school, I was fully coming into my own as her mother. There was nothing I would not do to help her live to her fullest potential and the net was cast wide. I had always been open to advice given to me by her therapists and experts since birth. In fact, her Early Intervention Case Coordinator told me more than once that they so appreciated that I tried everything they suggested (and more). Always researching and looking for anything that could help: it felt right and good. I had fully surrendered to this different than planned but richer than imagined life that was taking me down previously unknown paths and introducing me to worlds of which I had no prior knowledge. There was joy, true joy and a peace in my life. The dark hole that I had wanted to crawl into two years prior wasn't even a thought. I was basking in the sunshine of motherhood.

When Sophia was four years old, a Speech Pathologist from the Feeding Team at Boston's Children's told me about an experimental electrical stimulation therapy that normalized swallows. She thought Sophia would be an excellent candidate and gave me the information to call the therapist who had developed the protocol and was doing clinical trials in Cleveland, Ohio. I called and immediately talked with Marcy, the therapist, and got chills—the good kind. My gut told me this was it. This was going to work. We had to go. It was December, just before Christmas. I asked how soon we could come and we made arrangements to go in February. The entire family, myself, my husband, Patton and Sophia, drove to Cleveland and stayed a week at the Ronald McDonald House.

The electrical stimulation did not hurt at all. In fact, it was quite gentle and I was told that babies often fell asleep during treatment. Sophia, always cooperative and undaunted by hardly anything, sat still while the electrodes were placed on her neck. Then Marcy turned on the device and administered electricity. My child who had NEVER been able to swallow more than one or two small bites of anything (and even that was rare), who choked easily, who was born with a completely dysfunctional swallow, and who we had been told was unlikely to ever be able to eat orally, proceeded to eat an ENTIRE four-ounce pudding snack! Miracles do happen and one happened that day in Cleveland. I have never thought of electricity in the same way since. That force of nature, harnessed by humans, that powers our everyday lives illuminating homes, brewing coffee, and so much more enabled Sophia to swallow normally! Yes, after a week of treatment the Modified Barium Swallow Study showed her swallow was NORMAL! When given the results, I clarified, "You mean that she has a functional swallow, right?" Marcy replied, "No, she has a normal swallow." I was flabbergasted. A seemingly unattainable dream came to fruition. All I had ever wanted for Sophia was to be happy and have friends and now it was possible that she could go to birthday parties and eat cake. My heart exploded with fireworks of sunshine and pure joy for Sophia! I felt as if I was swirling in a dream, weightless, my body effortlessly soaring and twirling into the air. Oh, the freedom!

Now that Sophia could swallow, she actually had to learn to eat, a massive undertaking. Imagine never having to consume food, but just having it placed in the stomach. Fortunately, I had heeded the advice of the experts when Sophia was a baby and had always ensured she had oral stimulation and provided her with tastes of food so she would not become orally averse. She had been licking lollipops before her teeth emerged, sometimes eliciting looks from those who had no inkling why a mother in her right mind would give a baby a lollipop. Lemon was her favorite flavor. Being g-tube fed the way she had been, dripping food in slowly, often with frequent small meals because of her reflux, also meant that she had not experienced hunger the way most people do.

I proceeded to work to wean her off of the g-tube. It took several difficult and frustrating months, and I almost took Sophia to a special in-patient feeding clinic in Virginia that did just that— weaned kids off g-tubes. A conversation with the director of that clinic made me realize Sophia was "almost there" and I needed to stay the course of what I was doing with her at home. The specialist advised me not to come, but to continue what I was doing. Sophia was finally fully weaned off of g-tube feedings at age five. No more plugging the Kangaroo pump tubing into the g-tube "button" protruding from her abdomen that went directly into her stomach. Her g-tube was permanently removed close to a year later and the stoma (the hole in her abdomen that had been surgically created for the g-tube to be inserted directly into her stomach) was closed. The surgeon also detached her stomach from the abdominal wall, as scar tissue had adhered the two. Especially with children, extreme caution is exercised when removing the g-tube permanently. It will only be removed when there is absolute certainty the child can eat adequately; otherwise, an entire new surgery would be necessary to create the stoma (hole) for g-tube placement.

Sophia had wanted the g-tube taken out long before the medical professionals had cleared us to remove it, and she was beyond elated when the hole was closed because she had a smooth tummy like everyone else. She would run her hands over her abdomen, feeling its uninterrupted flat surface, nodding her head in approval. Sophia could also now wear any clothes she wanted, including crop tops and two-piece bathing suits, as there was no concern about covering or protecting the g-tube "button". From the time she was a toddler Sophia expressed her, often very strong, opinions about apparel, and she loved new fun clothes, especially things that sparkled and shone. Clothes shopping became even more fun.

I found joy in all of the accomplishments, large and small. It's important to stop and take note of where you have been and how far you have come. Sometimes we can forget. My being expanded exponentially mothering Sophia. At some point, I can't pinpoint exactly when, I let go of the fear and chose to focus on faith that it, whatever it was, would all work out. We don't always understand the full path and I learned to have peace about that. We had become a happy family with mom, dad, boy and girl, doing typical things families do, going out to dinner, socializing, swimming in our pool in the summer, building snowmen and sledding in the winter, and so much more. Sophia would stand on her father's feet facing him and holding his hands, music blasting so she could feel the beat, and they would dance, her feet moving with his. She reveled in that, laughing with glee as she looked up at him. Like instruments in a symphony create beautiful music, all of us together created our family's rhythm, melody, harmony, tempo and texture. Life was good.

My enigmatic baby had become a feisty, tenacious little girl who had defied the odds in countless ways. Who was I to put a lid on what she could do? There was no way I would limit her. She had proven time and time again that she could accomplish the unexpected. So, after watching her brother play game after game of soccer, Sophia announced that she wanted to play soccer. She was absolutely tiny for her age of five years, her body being the size of a child two years younger with her three-foot-tall, spindly frame. And she couldn't hear and had balance issues. I took a deep breath, explained the situation to the developmental soccer league and they said "Sign her up!" It was the end of the fall season when I drove both Patton and Sophia to the office to turn in the applications for the spring season.

Spring arrived and we went shopping for cleats and soccer balls. We bought one of the smallest sizes of cleats made: tiny girl means tiny feet. I introduced her at the first practice and explained that she could not hear, but that she could see just fine and that she communicated with her hands. We taught the other girls on her team a little sign language, Sophia's sign name (the letter "S" shaking), the signs for soccer, kick and goal, how to get her attention, etc. And, play soccer she did, teetering down the field and signing to her teammates with mom as the interpreter. Sophia was thrilled to be a part of the team and she worked hard. Her teammates accepted her with curious affection. The girls encouraged Sophia and cheered her on, sometimes with hugs, always with smiles, and often with gestures and the few signs they knew. Positivity and encouragement abounded. They were intrigued by this imp who used her hands to communicate and they marveled at her intense zest for life. Sophia was not one to sit on the sidelines.

To see her accepted, and realizing her goal of playing soccer was to achieve a happiness victory. Sophia's victory was my victory; in this mother and child were one. In those hours that she was on the field, whether it was practice or a game, she was triumphant and so was I. My child with neuromuscular issues, who had just walked independently two years prior, was now at age five running up and down the soccer field. Overcome with emotion, tears welled in my eyes one morning while watching from the sidelines, the cool spring air blowing across my face as she ran downfield. I admired Sophia.

So often I did not stop to think. I just acted. That was my life at the time. If you asked me what television shows were popular I would have to look it up. "Me time" of any sort was a rare occurrence. While I had quit my corporate job, by 1997 I had started doing some independent work, something in which I had full control of the working hours, both quantity and timing. I knew that a "regular" job was never going to work for me yet I did want to have some adult time and do something that both fulfilled me professionally, and have an endeavor that gave me a little break from motherhood and family. I was slowly learning to take care of myself.

Sophia had fairly regular appointments to see her otolaryngologist (ORL) at Boston's Children's. She was there off and on to have the cerumen (earwax) removed from her ears because when you have an ear mold for a hearing aid in your ear, the cerumen can easily become compacted. Sophia also had ear tubes since before her first birthday because the dysfunctional swallow resulted in fluid going up her eustachian tubes, causing chronic ear infections.

Many times I accompanied her into the Operating Room (OR), staying with her until her eyes rolled back into her head and she lost consciousness for the surgery. The staff at Children's was always so understanding, realizing that she needed me not only as a mother, but as her communication link. They couldn't sign to her. Without communication she would have been stressed and frightened. From that moment in the hospital just days after she was born when we sat with the pediatrician and she said, "you don't have to take her home," from that moment on, a pact had been made inside the beating walls of my heart that I'd never leave her.

It's difficult to maintain perspective when you see your child every day. So, it is appreciated when someone looking in on your situation grounds you in reality, and it's especially nice to hear something positive. One particular visit to the ORL, the doctor remarked, "Sophia is incredible. Seeing her as a baby I never would have thought she would have been able to come near to doing what she is doing. It's impressive. You've done a fantastic job."

I replied, "Thank you, but it's not me. It's her."

Thinking back to the frightened new mother I was, not knowing how I was going to do justice to the innocent complicated new life I had brought into the world, I grasped the realization that it really wasn't me in the lead now. It was Sophia. She was never going to let her disabilities hold her back. She did not see herself as "less than" or "without" at all. She was all about what she could do and she pushed herself harder than anyone I have ever known. It seems I wasn't sent out into the desert without water to care for my new baby. We went into the desert together and Sophia brought ample water. To really say it, she led us to a stunningly magical oasis.

One day I was at the grocery store with Patton and Sophia. Inevitably some of her favorite (and easier to eat) foods were in the cart, Go-GURTs and tubes of peanut butter, along with some other favorites. As we were checking out, the young male clerk started to talk to Sophia, asking her a question. I said to him, "She can't hear you. She's deaf."

To which he woefully replied, "Oh, I am sorry."

I laughed and quipped, "Oh, don't feel sorry for her. She is one of the happiest kids on the planet and she has an amazing life." He just looked at me, somewhat stupefied. What I said was unequivocally true. I felt it sizzling throughout my being. The emotional body always tells the truth.

When Sophia was eight and Patton was ten, we planned a six-day trip to Disney World in Orlando. I had been in Orlando for a conference with my business and my husband flew down with the children the day my conference ended. The family checked into the hotel located in the Magic Kingdom, and what was to be the trip of a lifetime commenced. Disney has an incredible reputation for serving those with special needs, and our experience was nothing less than spectacular. I had contacted Guest Relations, inquiring about ASL interpreted events and was sent a schedule for the week we were to be there. My husband and I meticulously planned the entire week around the ASL interpreted events to maximize accessibility for Sophia. The way it worked is that on a given day of the week interpreters are at one Park, and the next day they go to another, and so on. For us it was Monday at the Magic Kingdom, Tuesday at Epcot, Wednesday at MGM Studios, Thursday at the Magic Kingdom, Friday at Epcot, and Saturday at Animal Kingdom.

Monday morning, we walked through the gates of the Magic Kingdom. We did have a stroller for Sophia because although she was eight she was still incredibly small for her age and we knew she would not have the stamina to walk all over Disney for six days. She was only about forty-two inches in height with a lean build. An average eight-year-old girl is over fifty inches. Always a planner, I ensured Sophia had platform-type boots with her in case she needed a little lift to meet the height requirement for a critical ride or two.

The performance schedule had specific information about how early to arrive, precisely where to view the performance, including where to sit, and other pertinent information. We were welcomed to Disney World with an ASL-interpreted performance of "Cinderella's Surprise Celebration," later that morning attending "Story Time with Belle." It was a revelation to attend performances to which Sophia had full access without me interpreting. Her face lit up with excitement and she was mesmerized, immersed as if the performance was for her and her only. She missed nothing, soaking it all in like a parched sponge dropped into a pail of water.

One of my favorite experiences was in Epcot at the "Diver Lock-Out Chamber Presentation" where a diver goes into the chamber to demonstrate diving technology while someone on the outside explains it to the guests. At the beginning of the presentation, the presenter asked for a volunteer. Sophia's hand shot up immediately and she was selected. The interpreter went up with her to interpret for the presentation. The volunteer does things like ask the diver if he is ok and directs the diver to go up or down with hand signals. It was a total delight to see Sophia, wearing her newly purchased red polka dot Minnie Mouse hat, independently participate in this event, perfectly taking direction and doing everything asked of her. And, it was freeing for me, as her mother, to simply observe and document the event with photos. One of my most cherished photos of Sophia is of her intently paying attention during her stint as a dive chamber volunteer.

A bit of a thrill seeker, Sophia absolutely loved roller coasters and so did Patton. The Seven Dwarfs Runaway Mine was a favorite ride that we rode several times and that was appropriate in so many ways. *Snow White* was a movie that Sophia would watch and enact at home, of course playing the role of Snow White. It had been her favorite Disney movie until *Finding Nemo* was released. At that point it became all about Nemo. I think she related to Nemo with his small "lucky" fin and not being like the others to a point. She was always Nemo. She would direct everyone else to play the other characters, and had many Nemo-related items: computer games, books, clothing. Her birthday party theme choice that year was, unsurprisingly, Nemo.

On the last day we attended the "Festival of the Lion King," a story with which Sophia was quite familiar. We arrived early and sat in the section designated for ASL interpretation. Once the festival began, they asked for volunteers to participate and Sophia did so, being instantly swept up in the performance. She was in her glory parading around the theater with the characters and a few other children. Actually, she was in her glory the entire time we were at Disney World. When I was a child I used to watch "The Wonderful World of Disney" on television; later the title was changed to the "The Magical World of Disney." When I saw the light in my daughter's eyes and saw her experience the wonder and magic in the flesh, I saw a child that was jubilant at the core. I don't think we could have possibly realized how apt her middle name, Joy, was when we named her. Sophia Joy certainly lived up to that name.

Family life had settled into a comfortable dynamic and routine. Mostly school and work during the week and activities on the weekend. Sometimes we went to special events such as a town festival, or places like the Children's Museum. More often than not we socialized at the homes of friends or stayed home, especially in summer, swimming in our pool and playing in our backyard playground complete with a swing set, slide, and sandbox. On Friday or Saturday night we would go out to dinner; Outback Steakhouse was a favorite. In the booth, Sophia was always seated next to me, and Patton sat next to dad. After ordering food, Patton and Sophia were happy to entertain themselves with the crayons and paper offered, or play on their Game Boys. While my husband and I dined on steak, Patton typically ordered chicken fingers and Sophia's standard fare was the Walkabout Soup, tasty and easy to eat. No meal was complete without both of them eating an enormous Spotted Dog Sundae with lots of rich hot fudge sauce and a cherry on top for dessert. We always went home afterwards, our family of four, full bellies, full life, content to be together. It was more than enough.

While Sophia made friends at school, she had a special friend in Anna, the daughter of one of my friends and the younger sister of one of Patton's friends and schoolmates. The girls enjoyed many activities, one of which was playing dress up. Sophia was a bit of a fashionista and so was Anna. The two of them would go upstairs to Sophia's sunlit room replete with two floor-to-ceiling windows, decorated with white bedding and curtains dotted with large, colorful flowers, walls painted a sky blue, floor covered in a soft light colored berber carpet subtly speckled with tiny bits of bright color. This was fashion central, where the girls would pilfer through the dress up clothes, selecting what they wanted to wear, often adding jewelry and accessories such as gloves and purses, then coming downstairs to model for whoever was there to see the fashion show. Sophia's fine dark brown hair and slight build contrasted with Anna's wavy lighter locks and more solid build, yet they were identical in their fervor for fashion. Sophia had a red velvet dress, with white fur trim around the bottom of the skirt and at the cuff of the long sleeves. Anna really liked that dress also, so Sophia and I went to the store and bought a similar outfit. The two girls often chose to wear those outfits, dizzily twirling in laughter as the skirts flared out. There are no barriers when hearts connect.

In June of 2005, Sophia completed second grade, proudly graduating from Lower Elementary with her classmates at TLC. Sophia wore her favorite color, blue, complete with her oval blue-wire glasses and the silver ladybug necklace Anna had given her for her ninth birthday. The students had all made blue mortarboards to wear for graduation and commemorated the achievement with appropriate elementary school pomp and circumstance. They were all delightful children quite proud of their advancement and rightly so. They all had come a long way. Sophia, an enigma at birth, had developed into a spunky, beautiful, thoughtful, sensitive, funny, intelligent, persistent, loving, daredevil, who let nothing stand in the way of whatever it was she wanted to do or achieve. She expanded the consciousness of anyone who interfaced with her. After celebratory snacks and socialization, we went home to start summer break. We loved those relaxed days of summer, filled with days of no agenda, swimming in the pool and playing with friends.

June 28th, 2005. The day started splendidly, when her friend Louise arrived at 9:00 a.m. for a play date. The girls played all day, dressing up in a variety of costumes and clothes from Sophia's rather large dress-up wardrobe, building sand sculptures, one of which was the Eifel tower, doing art projects, swimming and more. Sophia was so very excited for Louise to come to her house for the first time to play. It was school break. The peals of laughter, the thunderous running through the house and out to the back yard to play, are all seared in my mind. To hear those sounds again, what I would give for that. It's priceless.

Tears still stream down my cheeks when I think of that day. I didn't know. I had no idea. It was in so many ways a typical lazy summer day. Yet, it was anything but typical because it was the day that I knew I would never be able to mother Sophia again. In fact, the tables got turned on that day. Sophia became a life guide for me.

That evening, Sophia and I were sitting at the kitchen table after our family dinner. The four of us had devoured grilled swordfish and macaroni and cheese, both favorites of Sophia. I could see Patton through the glass sliding door behind Sophia as he ran around the backyard playing with his new Super Soaker water gun that had just arrived that day. My husband was relaxing in the adjoining family room. Sophia wanted a Fruit Roll-Up, something she had eaten many times and a food that had been recommended for helping her advance her oral motor skills. She expertly pulled off a piece of the Fruit Roll-Up and began to chew it. As I sat there with her I saw her eyes widen and knew she was in trouble. The ball of fruit roll-up that she had attempted to swallow was lodged. She started choking and frantically signing "help." She vomited, but the ball of sticky fruit was still stuck. My mind raced, "*Oh my God, this is 'it,' the moment I have been fearing. She is going to leave me. Please no, please no…* " I simultaneously grabbed her and screamed to my husband. He instantly emerged and performed the Heimlich several times. The ball of death was not moving. While he was working on Sophia, I dialed 911. Next, I slid open the back door yelling for Patton, who gratefully witnessed none of this, to get our neighbor Mary, a nurse practitioner. *The Heimlich didn't work. What to do? What to do?* In desperation, I tried to pull the Fruit Roll-Up out with my finger. *The sirens sound in the distance. Help is coming. Maybe it will be ok. Maybe it will be ok. Please, please, please come and save her. I cannot live without her.* My entire being was pleading for her life.

I was cradling Sophia in my arms when she lost consciousness and her eyes rolled back into her head as they had so many times when I had accompanied her to the OR for surgery. This time was different. This wasn't anesthesia. The paramedics arrived. *Help is here. Help is here. Maybe it will be ok. Maybe it will be ok.* I watched as they desperately tried to save her. She had gone into cardiac arrest. I went from being hysterically powerless to unequivocally distraught. *Oh my God. Oh my God. Breathe, Andrea, breathe.*

The paramedics took Sophia in the ambulance. Mary drove me in her car to follow the ambulance while my husband stayed with Patton. The ambulance stopped within a minute of leaving the house. We stopped too. A strong jolt of energy hit me and pulsated throughout my entire body. *What time is it? What time is it?* I looked at the clock in the car. It was 7:10. The ambulance started moving again and we kept following.

They revived Sophia, and she was taken to a local hospital where my husband and Patton joined me in the Emergency Room where Sophia lay in bed in stillness, hooked up to numerous medical devices. I remember sitting in a small dark consultation room with no windows and tile floors. Several doctors and nurses spoke to us. I cannot remember any of their faces or voices or exact words. I was starting to numb myself and put myself in a protective vacuum to process the inevitable reality. My soul knew Sophia's being was gone already. Sophia's heart had stopped beating for thirty-two minutes and her organs were starting to shut down, but we were told there was still a modicum of hope because children can recover in ways that adults never could. The numbing continued. And, then I looked at my loving, sensitive eleven-year-old son, so very concerned about his sister, and a weight hit my heart like a ton of bricks had been hurled at it. *Patton's little sister is going to die.*

Sophia went by ambulance to a larger medical center and I went with her. My husband took Patton home, both of them desperately wanting the same thing I did.

While Sophia was getting settled into the second hospital, I went to the waiting area. It was after 1:00 a.m. by this time. The silence was deafening, all but for the ticking of the clock on the wall, in this vast room with its institutional tile floors and stark walls. I sat in an upholstered chair, utterly alone in every sense of the word, struggling to process what was happening and, once again, as when Sophia was first born, wondering how I could navigate unplanned and uncharted territory. *How could I live not being Sophia's mother?*

The nurse, a strong-looking man in his 30s with short brown hair, brought me to Sophia. She lay there in the hospital bed much as she had as a new baby, hooked up to machines, appearing to be peacefully sleeping, lying on her back, eyes closed, face framed with her now beautiful dark brown long manes cut stylishly with bangs. Her chest rose and fell with each breath. I wanted to crawl into bed with her. There was not enough room so I did the next best thing, pulling a chair up beside the bed, resting my arms alongside her and head next to her, stroking her head, desperately looking for any hope that she might still be there. She wasn't. I had known since 7:10 p.m. The dam broke and the river of tears unrelentingly gushed. In a pause of the torrents, the nurse encouraged me to go and rest. I told him I could not leave her. He understood, and with great awareness and empathy looked at me and gently said, "You know the body is just a shell."

I whispered, "I know."

He turned and left the room trying to hide the tears welling up in his eyes.

Morning came. My husband and Patton arrived at the hospital to see Sophia. As my husband walked into the room with Patton, who was just eleven days shy of his twelfth birthday, my heart shattered into pieces for both of them. Sophia's blood pressure was bottoming out despite medical intervention and her organs were shutting down. We had no choice but to say goodbye, making the decision to not prolong the agony and agreeing to remove the life support. The nurse tied off a lock of Sophia's soft fine dark brown hair with a white ribbon and cut it, handing it to me. Patton tenderly covered up his little sister with a soft pink fleece blanket sprinkled with hearts, kissing her cheek much as he had done when he first met her as a newborn. Struggling to control his emotions, my husband leaned over to embrace his daughter one last time. The three of us huddled together sobbing uncontrollably in our shared anguish as the heart monitor slowed and then flat-lined. Sophia was now free of pain and suffering. We were not.

We could not imagine life without her. We drove home in shock with an empty seat in the car.

The world stood still. My empty arms ached. The void felt as vast as the universe and all that is and ever will be. Never again could I hold Sophia, feel her arms around tightly around me, feel her head nestled into my shoulder, smell her hair, hear her laughter, see her engaging smile. No more shopping trips for fun clothes or anything else. A part of me was dead. Although I didn't realize it then, Sophia wasn't finished with me. She had more lessons to teach and gifts to impart.

I had been so very afraid to love Sophia, that she would leave me one day if I dared to become so attached to her, this complex, precious being. I had taken the leap and had gone all in. And, there are no regrets. None. As I write this, tears stream down my cheeks, running into my mouth and I taste the salt of grief. Grief is the other side of love; they are partners, ensuring we never forget.

If someone had asked me if I would have taken that leap had I known the depths of primal pain I would experience, the answer is an unequivocal yes. How could I not? However short her time on this earth and however short the time I had the privilege of being Sophia's mother, I would gratefully take it. Every. Single. Second.

As it turns out I had nine years and ten months.

"Lucky, Lucky Me, I'm your mommy," I would tell her constantly, her eyes beaming brightly as she looked into mine feeling my unadulterated love and wonderment. Although I did not realize it the day she was born, good fortune befell me the day Sophia became my daughter. This child was a force to be reckoned with, a mighty spirit indeed. Sophia's spirit lives and the tremendous lessons learned and gifts bestowed on me by Sophia in life are only unparalleled by the gifts that came, and continue to come, in the aftermath of her death. I am still her mother. And, she remains my teacher. Lucky me.

Author and speaker Andrea Roberts Parham is an introspective soul whose calm, nurturing nature helps her inspire and guide others to connect with their own inner wisdom. She believes that if we had a planet full of people who were grounded to their core being and stood into their own brilliance the world would be forever changed for the better. Andrea asserts, "Out of your darkest days come your greatest gifts if you are willing to look for them." For over two decades Andrea has applied her philosophies to leading and mentoring others in business, and to helping people become healthier with lifestyle choices. Andrea is the author of *Lucky Me,* the full story of her journey with her daughter, Sophia, both in life and in the wake of Sophia's unexpected death. Connect with Andrea at AndreaRobertsParham.com.

Snowflakes
Become Water

Nicole "Nikki" Bruton-Phillips

"Wisdom packaged in love is the greatest of gifts."
—Nicole "Nikki" Bruton-Phillips

A thousand moments can be lived in a lifetime. Take the leaves of a tree falling into the roaring waters of a mountain stream or the millions of different snowflakes that gently drift to the ground on a snowy day… we, you and I, are much like those things. Every child, parent, family member, each person in our lives are those same things as well. Sometimes the leaves and snowflakes collect together and other times they drift alone, but either way they reach their destination, having served the purpose that they were meant to while existing in this universe; they leave an impact, an imprint, forever changing the environment and the existence of the lives around them. As much as the presence of a being can affect the life around them, their absence may have an even greater influence in the world.

Many leaves and snowflakes have fallen in my life. At various points I have been both a quiet, floating leaf and a roaring mountain stream at the same time. Other times I have been the snowflake unnoticed in my own uniqueness, with the same beauty and grace that gently causes the leaf to softly fall into the thundering waters of the stream, carving change within the landscape of the universe.

With each alteration to the environment comes a new voice. As a child, I couldn't imagine being a snowflake or leaf, much less a roaring mountain stream changing lives. Between the voices of my grandmother, my children, and my mother, I didn't stand a chance of continuing to shy away from my true soul's purpose in this life. My existence as each of these elements has led me to the ownership of why I am who I am, standing in my divine purpose, unifying disconnected voices so that others may find acceptance of their own soul's purpose. Often, silence of a voice comes early on in life with events, whether they are big or small, that cut deep enough to interrupt the connective nerves of the soul, heart, and spirit. "Soul cuts" (as I call them) and voice silencers are usually created from divorce, abuse, death, bodily trauma, betrayal, and the emotional absence of or disconnection from a parent.

My children, my mother, and my grandmother have been my greatest guides, lighting my voyage back to the waters of self-love and appreciation for the life I have lived.

As I write this, I am sitting in a noisy, eclectically colorful café waiting for my youngest child to exit an art exhibit with his beautiful girlfriend of two years. I am able to be in the moment and take in the feeling, deep within myself, at how far we have come. My son, Michael is on his first date! While the average person might not find this milestone to be significant, for the parent and child who were repeatedly told that they "never would..." I love this moment! I am in appreciation and awe of the strength and resilience both of my living children have shown every step of the way.

❋❋❋ *Snowflakes become blankets of lace-like frost warming under the morning sunlight only to become trickling drops of dew that bring new life into our souls.* ◊◊◊

The day I brought my first child, Devon, home from the hospital, the first stop I had to make was a visit to my grandparents' house. As we pulled our brand-new truck (my fiancé, Heath, had just picked it up that morning before our baby and I had been discharged from the hospital) up the drive, I looked down at my beautiful miracle and whispered, "We are here." A peace came over me, watching this sweet little round face with lavender-blue eyes that reflected the indigo and purple tones of the infant carrier's cover and removable sunshade. As we got out of the truck, one of my younger cousins greeted us with eagerness and excitement to see both his new baby cousin and my new amethyst colored 4x4 truck parked in Grandma and Grandpa's driveway.

When Heath and I walked through the front door during the late afternoon of June 16, 1998, I could smell fried chicken, hoping that it was homemade. I couldn't tell if I was more exhausted or hungry. My grandparents and aunt were sitting at the kitchen table having KFC. Right then it was decided, I was exhausted. My grandmother read it all over my face as my aunt removed the hat from my baby's head and unfastened the harness. She couldn't wait to hold the newest member of the family. The house was roasting; the AC had given out and it was the opening of summer in Belen, New Mexico. Fans were blowing air throughout the house with windows and doors open to create some hope of a breeze; still my aunt was right—it was much too hot for the cute matching hat that had been appropriate earlier when we were still in the chilly hospital two towns away.

The moment finally came when my fair-skinned, cherub-like babe with flame-red hair was nuzzled sweetly in one of the best places in the universe, my grandmother's arms. There began my little love's third life lesson (my mother and myself had already bestowed the first two big talks right after birth). Marveled by her gentleness and warmth, I attentively observed as my grandmother imparted wisdom packaged in love. As she began to weave a tale of life, love, happiness, and destiny, my exhaustion waned, and the voices around her blended, eventually fading away into some distant background hum much like when the sounds of a summer garden are buzzing with bumble bees and cicadas. The realization of what a true gift I had in my grandmother washed over me.

Then Devon was passed to the loving arms of my grandfather. My grandfather held my baby one more time before passing away a little over a month after this day. The imprint of a life without his presence would silence many voices while giving birth to so many others.

I hoped that my child would somehow forever retain the memory of being held by such truth. It had been my grandparents' love, wisdom, compassion, and guidance that gave me such a remarkable mother. Despite the obstacles in her life, she continued to be a strong, intelligent, kind, forgiving, accepting and loving woman. I was now stepping into similar shoes; I had no idea how much strength and courage would be required to be the mother my children deserved and the woman I was destined to be.

❋ ❋ ❋ *Water is love, assurance, hope, and light. Water is air. A single drop of water can move a mountain. Frozen, it will break the mountain.* ◊◊◊

My mom had been a lifeguard at one point and swam most of her life giving her a heightened awareness of how quickly a child could drown. She knew the best time to teach a child to swim is actually after they are born, while they still have a memory of spending nine months growing in water. Her parents' home had a swimming pool, so at three months old she and I were enrolled in a local, private *Swimfant* program (a mommy-and-me swim class). Little did my mom know the true gift she was bestowing upon her daughter. Much like the first breath of air blown directly in a baby's face to make them inhale and then hold their breath before being dunked underwater, swimming was the metaphor for my early movement through the world. The feelings, memories, freedoms and lessons of the pool would end up being vital tools that I carried with me throughout my life. The pool would become the source of my heart until my children were born and even after I would make every effort to integrate the two. Water would be the place that my voice met my gift, where I always excelled and only truly shared with those I loved. These fundamental lessons are still used when I work with families now, creating space for children and parents to be heard.

Water was and still is my solace, my refuge, the one true place that has never failed me day or night. It always accepted me, welcomed me, called to me, and brought to me a peace and strength that I still find when I return to my own private watery oasis. There is a stillness that occurs when I am fully immersed and looking up at the sky from underneath the water that has always brought a great deal of clarity and perspective to my life. Swimming was clearly in my blood, but very few realized how much it was in my soul and spirit. My heart and spirit's security blanket were water; there was nothing more heavenly or divine than the cooling, blue, self-contained, back-yard ocean. And while my grandmother didn't always like it, as she had a great fear of drowning, she would indulge my internal craving to be out there. Facing that fear, she'd take me out to the dreamland of my soul.

Most of my happiest memories are of my life around the water. I'd swim during the mornings while I was at preschool, allowed to have the entirety of the deep end at daycare to myself, because I was an experienced swimmer. The splashing and jocularity that gives way to enormous laughter on a hot summer's day at a family barbeque or quiet calm that comes as I float along the water's surface of the swimming pool, still brings me to stillness this day. However, I really didn't care for the intrusions when the adults took over my pool at night with their afterhours skinny dipping. Yuck! Didn't they know who the pool was for?

During scorching summer days, my grandfather, who was a stoic six-foot-tall, 300-pound Cheyenne Indian (the last blood Chief, it was said) would become my island and float buddy both in and out of the water. His five-foot-five, slender yet curvy, brown-haired, Irish wife would lay out in a white leather bikini; she could be found on a nearby deck chair reading and drinking scotch, while her long, manicured fingernails held a filter-guarded cigarette, as smoke clouds formed around her perfectly coiffed hair. This woman would become my first unknown guide in the journey to my voice.

Yes, my grandmother was a stunner and I never saw her beauty go to her head. She honestly was the total package. She was up before the sunrise every morning cleaning the house and it was practically immaculate. Her genius level of intelligence complimented her physical beauty and poise. She was the embodiment of everything that I would strive to be later in life. My grandmother's life, or what I knew of it as a child, was exactly what I knew life should be if you were a married woman.

Her academic knowledge was vast, much like walking through the greatest libraries in the world. She always had books stacked around her. Her private "pools" were the walls of books where I would play as she spent her leisure time reading. I hated reading, especially if the books were without pictures. Reading was up there with adults thieving *my* pool in the evenings. With the look of impatience on my little round face, I'd ask, "Why are you reading all those books, Grandma? They don't have color or pictures."

Her reply was almost always the same. "There are million different colorful pictures and voices in *these* books. What will yours be?"

✳ ✳ ✳ *Water washes over me after breath blown in my face. This is love, this is home. If I stop breathing, "always remember your body is meant to float." At three months old I can't walk, but I can swim. Swim for the edge when I am choking. Swim for the edge when the waters are too overwhelming. But I hate the edge because that means my time has come to an end...* ◊◊◊

I dreamed of a life near water, a life living in the water, a life where my special "gifts" and voice would be accepted. While other little girls were longing for a new doll at Christmas, I was longing for the time when the pool cover would come off. I pictured myself as a mermaid and truly couldn't imagine being anything else. They were free, living life in unending oceans. Swimming since I was three months old fed my mermaid spirit and belief that *water is the song that feeds my soul.*

Voices…what did Grandma know about voices? My favorite voices were the songs I heard under the water. Sometimes if I was lucky and really careful, she would get one of the conch shells for me and allow me to hear the voices of the ocean still trapped within. Those times brought me a great deal of comfort: especially when there were voices keeping me awake at night, whispering throughout the darkest hours. I would cover my head to stop them from talking all night long. Some were mean and malicious; others were kind and soothing sometimes lulling me to sleep.

My grandmother had tried out just about every organized religion. By the time I had come along, she'd discovered that her own special "gifts" occurred within the realms of metaphysics and astrology. Naturally she had already spoken with clairvoyants and psychics about our entire family's past lives and possible futures. With me being born a Pisces, she told me at an early age that water was my element and my calling in life would be to teach, heal, and empathetically create.

❋ ❋ ❋ *Accepting the cold snowfall leaves leap from frozen branches trusting the unforgiving rushing stream will cradle in the journey to fulfilling the end of their purpose.* ◊◊◊

I was born with the gift to heal. Placing my little baby hot hands on foreheads to remove my family members' headaches and pain became a secret home remedy among loved ones. No one was aware of how much I was absorbing of the world around me; it was just a beautiful, unique gift that provided relief to others. I was too small to comprehend the strains my little spirit was going through. No one made the connection between me often being ill, or, the "zoning out" spells I would have (later discovered to be seizure activity), and my intuitive gifts. Anything metaphysical or psychically inclined was known as *gift* in my family and *gifts* like mine weren't to be shared with the rest of the world or for profit. My childhood was practically blissful once my feet touched the water, my sacred space of rejuvenation and release.

By the time I turned two, my "gifts" had grown now appearing as clairvoyance. My mom and first stepdad, Daddy Phil, had rolled his CJ-7 while driving back from a day in the mountains. Someone called my grandmother to report that her daughter and son-in-law had been in an accident while coming out of the nearby canyon. My grandmother walked into the dark, wood-paneled den of her home where I was playing by the fireplace. Her face was snow white, soft and stoic all at once. She was wearing a flowing turquoise linen blouse that brushed against my arm as she knelt down, as she had many times before, to meet me at my eye level. I was playing with the little cast-iron cooking set that she had played with as a little girl. Her gentle brown eyes like that of a doe looked at me, trying to hide a mother's worry, taking a deep inhale to set her resolve and remain calm as always because that is what children need and their need is always much greater than that of parent or grandparent. But before she could get a word out, I saw in my mind where my mamma was and exactly what was happening.

Looking at her I said very sweetly as if nothing were wrong at all, "It will be alright, Grandma. Don't worry the men are getting mommy out now. It's all OK. Don't be scared. Mommy is hurt but she is alright. We can fix it." I hugged her, patted her like you would when trying to soothe a baby, and then went back to playing.

I was a shy and well-behaved child who didn't cause too many issues, but the closer it came to summer, the more restless my spirit would become. I was a spirit searching for a connection to my own voice. My grandmother often saw that in me, so she in need of her own connection and peace at the time, would show me ways to calm the rushing stream within myself.

One spring, she took me out to her garden of irises. They had such bold, beautiful colors and stood so tall that I could get lost among them. The giant, bearded deep purple ones were incredibly dark, they would sometimes appear black, depending on the angle and the way the sunlight bounced off their soft petals. Those were my absolute favorite; their blossoms would reach just right at my nose, making it practically impossible not to be lured in by their intoxicating fragrance. I often thought that my grandmother must be some sort of wood nymph or fairy because, no matter where she lived, one moment an area of her yard would be bare and the next it seemed would be filled with greenery and flowers. As I grew older, I would learn that she wasn't just trying to help me connect with my spirit and quiet my mind but she was attempting to regain a sense of order within her own heart and spirit.

Like the leaves of fall, great changes would come in my life and my secret ocean, the place of release would be gone as a result of my grandparents' divorce. Once my grandmother moved away, the "value" that children are to be rarely seen and never heard was being dialed in more and more. Feelings of helplessness, anger, and rejection began to trickle through my heart, eventually carving out vast crevices with the passing of each year. Still absorbing the energies of the world around me, a fiery rage burned through every inch of me, screaming to be unleashed.

By six years old, I had stabbed a cross-eyed, dark haired, class-mate with a pencil while he was standing near me in line to sharpen my pencil. In the first grade, I was told that all of the things that I thought were special about me just made me strange and foreign to other children. "What is a Puerto Rican?" "What is a Cheyenne… That isn't a real tribe." "Why do you have so many dads?" "Why does your dad have nigger hair?" "Is your mom even your real mom because she looks white and you don't." You name it I heard it and when you are a child it is damn near impossible to answer your peers' inquisitions. It was an immense struggle making an educator understand without getting side eye or being questioned further on your home life.

I couldn't take much more of the children standing all around, taunting me, laughing at me, calling me names, their fingers point-ing, as the boy waiting to sharpen his pencil leaned in to kiss me while professing his love. I just wanted to go home to be with my mom or family, anywhere but with these kids who constantly picked at me. "Please be quiet," I said softly.

The boy just kept coming toward me. My family had taught me not to be mean or cruel to anyone, even though the world had already shown me that most people didn't share that same belief. Again, a little louder this time I said, "Please leave me alone. Please be quiet." I was raised with manners and saying "please" and "thank you" were always a must. He wasn't turning away, and by now the majority of my first-grade class had crowded around me forming a mob of unrelenting children. Much like a cornered animal, I lashed out with the only weapon I had available: my freshly sharpened pencil. I could feel his skin break and the muscle pop under the pressure as I drove it home before breaking the lead off. He screamed out in excruciating pain. My boiling frustration and fear had begun to burn through me; now not only was I in trouble but I became terrified of myself. Kids are taught that anger and frustration are *bad* unacceptable feelings that only troublesome people have.

Surprisingly, that wasn't what won me daily rides home with the school principal, who kept a bottle of cheap vodka in her desk drawer, which she regularly pulled out as I waited for her to drive me home. What actually won the lovely opportunity of daily after-school rides with her was throwing a table at my teacher, while I was once again being taunted by other classmates. This time the ridicule came from my inability to read. Unfortunately, the moments of being humiliated and bullied would last for the next few years as I moved from school to school each year. Every school day until the third grade, I could not wait to get back to the safety of my room.

※ ※ ※ *Glistening silent snowfall... Roaring freight train avalanche plowing through the forest... not all leaves gently fall. Some flakes are too cold, with razor edges to their intricate lace patterns, these bite, freezing the life from young golden greenery. What was once soft and flexible becomes hard and rigid as it crashes down into the flowing waters of the mountain stream.* ◊◊◊

My mother had challenges with finding her own internal balance, and with speaking her voice, as it too had been silenced as a child. As beautiful, intelligent, and courageous as she was in raising me on her own for the most part, her unresolved deep pain led to conflicts and issues within relationships that would result in multiple marriages throughout my childhood. Those marriages led to deep-rooted feelings of abandonment in both of us. It was difficult for me as child to come to a place of acceptance, appreciation, and compassion for my mom. My father made it a point to mention her shortcomings, flaws, and weaknesses as he saw them. With each new relationship, questions, observations, and evaluations of her choices would come from not just him, but the woman he was with as well. My mother's imperfections were seen as mine. A far cry from who she actually was, I learned to view my mother as he did: careless, weak, incapable, selfish, simple and inferior.

It was a drizzly evening and the New Mexico desert sky was filled with the final minutes of the pink and purple sunset. Seven-year-old me had puppy-dog ears because mom didn't know how to style my hair the more it grew. I sat in the front passenger seat of our burgundy '76 Chevy Monte Carlo, tapping my feet as mom sang to a song on the radio. Her hands on the wheel, her subtle emerald green to mostly brown eyes looking over at me, she reached for the knob on the stereo to turn the sound down. Smiling as her straight blonde hair brushed over her shoulder, she began speaking, "Nickle, hey monkey, I need to talk to you about something for a minute."

"Yeah, what mom?" I said while trying to stretch my legs far enough so that my feet would reach the floor board of burgundy carpet.

"Well, what do you think of Allen? You like him, don't you?"

"He's alright. He tickles too hard and his breath is yucky because he smokes a lot. But he is OK. Why?"

As the question left my mouth, a feeling began to emanate that this was a more serious talk than what her smile and my thoughts had indicated. Talking about her latest boyfriend couldn't be good. I was just getting used to my "Daddy Larry," my mom's third husband, no longer being with us and her dating again. I still wasn't sure why they had split up. All I knew was that I went to visit my father one weekend, left on a Friday, returned on a Sunday, and all of "Daddy Larry's" stuff was gone. No understandable explanation was given, just that he couldn't and wouldn't be there anymore, but just like with "Daddy Phil," if I wanted to see him arrangements would be made.

"What do you think, Nic, about the idea of him and I getting married?"

"I don't... no."

"You don't what, Nicole?" my mom said with a bit of impatience growing in her voice.

"I don't want you to get married again. I don't like it. I think it isn't a good idea."

My face looking up at her and then turning away toward the car door window, hoping to become lost in the wet road and street lights as we drove by. Street lights, stars in the sky, cars going by. I wondered what my grandparents were doing. Would I be able to swim soon?

The patriarchs of the family had instructed me to listen and observe; whereas the matriarchs taught me how and when to speak. Unfortunately, candid honesty often goes unappreciated by adults to say the very least, especially when a child is expressing an unwanted truth. My honesty tended to get me in trouble, and clearly that was happening again. Why had I gotten in trouble so often for speaking the 'truth"? My grandmother would explain that it wasn't the truth that got me into to trouble, it was my age. Wisdom in children was often unappreciated, and perhaps it was my delivery that warranted a talking to. I guess I had done it again...

My thoughts continued to wander under the growing oppressive silence... *Where was the blonde-haired, skinny, blued-eyed boy that I had met the day before while playing at my friend Brandy's house; what was he doing right now?* I wanted to see anything or be anywhere but where I was.

Finally, I looked back at my mom. She had instilled the importance of always making eye contact when someone, particularly an adult, was speaking to you as a sign of respect. I tried to respect her as much as I could. Eye contact was painful for me. Fortunately, I had learned ways to cope with making direct eye contact such as talking to myself, coaching myself that it would be alright to just get it over with because the more I turned away, the longer it would be commanded of me.

The look on her face was far from pleasant. Hurt, disappointment, and anger washed over her once singing, smiling face. A transition of stern resolve eventually gave way as she turned her eyes back to the road in front of her. "Well, I think you are wrong and it is too bad you feel that way because we are getting married."

I sat there as those words burrowed their way into my mind. There were so many things I wanted to say, but *do I dare say them out loud?* I mean, really, what the hell did she even bother asking me for then? This was bullshit!

※ ※ ※ *Water flows through ice and snow as each unique flake graces everything that it has touched with irreplaceable life. A leaf floating through calm and roar... Do not fear the water as you reach the delta's shore.* ◊◊◊

When I became a young mother and wife myself, I accepted limited guidance from anyone, especially the women around me. I have always been pretty headstrong and determined to do things my way even if that meant walking through hellfire first. I did things the hard way while longing for the easier or better way, particularly when it came to being a mother. Frequently I have felt like I was failing. That feeling of failure would begin to worm its way into my natural-born intuition, blocking me from the ability to trust my own voice and hear the voices of my children. When you are the parent of two special needs children and are disconnected from yourself, it becomes incredibly difficult to advocate for the testing, services, and other things that those children need to grow into the people that they are meant to be.

My first child, Devon, and I spoke the same language, so it was easy for me to tap into my inner child and figure out most needs and wants even before the *silence came* at eighteen months of age. Tapping into and figuring out my second child, Michael, wasn't so easy. Much like my childhood, it seemed like once again I was being forced to be a single snowflake that should be part of both leaf and stream. I had postpartum depression after Michael was born and a marriage that I was rapidly outgrowing. Tuning into his voice felt incredibly difficult most days.

❄❄❄ *"It isn't breaking for your own self, Nicole. It is breaking because as always you love and hurt deeply for others. Just like your mamma has had her heart break because of the hardships you have gone through, so will yours with your own children. That is the most difficult part of being parent."* My grandmother was always honest with me and could often see my emotional side even when it played against her overly logical sensibilities at times. ◊◊◊

On the first Mother's Day that I was a mother of two, the weight of postpartum depression fully closed in on me. Heath was working yet again this Mother's Day, and everyone else was busy with other plans. I was exhausted and dealing with the grief surrounding another year without my grandfather washing over me. With my grandfather's and Uncle Rick's birthdays falling on or around Mother's Day, it had always been a jovial time spent with the whole family. I missed my grandfather and the connection of being with family. I felt isolated and lost among my new normal. The longing for my floating island was astounding.

It was 9:30 a.m. when I stepped out of the shower. As I was dressing, a deafening shrill cry came from the nursery. It was so loud and startling that it woke Devon up. Pulling a shirt over my head as I ran into the room, the recognition came that Michael's cry was of complete pain. I quickly picked him up, and spoke tenderly in an attempt to comfort him. Following the normal routine of a diaper change, we headed downstairs. I grabbed a bottle and bowl of cereal for Devon and went back upstairs and into the nursery for some typical tummy time and rocking. Unfortunately, that isn't what happened. The crying that had only slightly subsided during our walk downstairs revved back up. Back down the steep staircase we went. A head full of strawberry curls bobbed along behind us, trying to satisfy a three-year-old's curiosity. Much like animals in a forest sensing the impending storm, Devon quickly retreated back up the stairs. That should have been my clue to what came next. The shriek came again as my baby's body writhed and agonizing defeat filled my heart. This tiny gentle soul was in excruciating pain and there was nothing I could do.

In an effort to exhaust all the options to soothe an upset baby, I removed all his clothing but the diaper. Collapsing in the gliding rocker, I began rocking feverishly trying to deliver some sort of relief to an unknown affliction. Michael had been born with an inability to maintain his body temperature and failure to thrive, all of which led to frequent illnesses and reflux. It seemed like around two months old he had become this baby that was inconsolable.

There we sat with a patient Devon whose big, indigo eyes looked up at me with empathy and concern while reaching up with soft, little three-year-old baby hands, placing them on baby brother's little forehead, and reciting over and over, "There, there, brother, it is OK. I am here. Mommy is here. We gotch you. Shh… Baby shh. Don't cry. It's OK."

A sudden admiration swelled inside me with the epiphany that this incredibly loving child, who had seemingly been mentally locked away from much of the world, was coming out of mental seclusion to ease their baby brother's agony. My eldest child's voice and compassion were acting as the calm in the storm, the *pool* my new baby needed. I would like to say that the crying stopped but it didn't. Devon momentarily disappeared, returning with the cordless telephone. My sweet child's bright empathetic eyes met my weary tear-filled ones with comfort while handing the phone to me. "Call Daddy."

The casino phone operator could hardly hear me over the screams of my baby. Michael had now been crying for four hours and his little round cherubic face was broken out in red blotches with puffy eyes. By the time my husband's boss finally picked up in the casino's main kitchen, I could hardly speak clearly as I teetered the blurred lines of desperation and hysteria. Irritated by my intrusion into the extremely busy holiday, he reluctantly agreed to retrieve my husband as soon as possible. I was broken. There had never been a baby or child I couldn't soothe, connect with, or pacify. Why now was I so inadequate at being the mother my baby was screaming for?

Soon another voice, a female one, came on the line (later she would turn out to be one of my dearest friends). Maria was compassionate and eager to assist us. She enlisted another female co-worker to find my husband while she remained on the line. I don't know if she was trying to keep me from being disconnected or she was genuinely concerned for the distressed people on the other side of the phone.

Finally, a frustrated familiar voice came on the line. I tried through cries of defeat, exhaustion, and despair to explain the urgency of the situation. The reply that came in return gave me little comfort. "It's Mother's Day, what do you want me to do? You know I can't leave. I will try to get out of here as soon as I can but you know it won't be until late. I'll see what I can do, but that is the best I can do. I've got to get back, my timers are going off." There was a click and that annoying tone of a phone left off the hook came.

My children and I were on our own. I reached out to other possible resources, including the Ask-a-Nurse hotline. The Ask-a-Nurse line was at a loss, as my baby was still accepting a bottle, not running a fever, and hadn't endured any physical trauma or injury. I placed a call to my parents. They were busy volunteering at a fraternal organization in another city and unavailable to help. I had nothing left, no lifeline. No one was coming.

I was losing my mind. The suicidal thoughts I had fought during my adolescence were starting to swim around me. I placed my screaming baby in his crib before falling to my knees. I doubled over in fetal position; I had totally failed. Devon curled up next to me, little fingers wiping away my tears. I had pleaded with the heavens to bring my child relief and compassion for whatever was going on with him. I was only on the floor for a few minutes, but it seemed like hours as the waves of abandonment washed over me. Not only did I feel abandoned but I felt like I was deserting my children by lying there in a puddle of my own tears. I needed my mom and they needed theirs. I eventually got back up and reached in the crib as my baby was still screaming, his chestnut hair soaked from sweat and tears. I bounced and walked, then sat back down in the glider with a newfound effort and awareness to rock slower this time. My heavy eyes began to close as I felt my son's body shudder and sob in my arms.

Unexpectedly, Devon began talking to someone. Hearing a masculine voice and a little voice chattering, I thought I had for sure lost it at that point. Fighting to open my eyes, I tried to listen more intently over Michael's continued crying. Following the sound of a bottle shaking as heavy footsteps climbed the stairs, Heath's hands lifted our baby from my worn-out arms. The two female co-workers I had spoken with earlier had rallied behind him, making it possible to leave early from work. Within minutes the screams lulled and then all was quiet; my baby had finally found salvation. I was spent as I walked back to our bedroom. I don't remember if I thanked him for coming home early or if I even said anything at all. I just had to get out of there. I ached for my grandmother's irises and the cool waters of the backyard private ocean to dive into.

✳ ✳ ✳ *So many leaves and snowflakes have long since moved to the water's edge and their time is done. Yet the roar of the mountain stream keeps carving its path through unbreakable rock and stone. This is life, this is my heart...*◊◊◊

A few days after we found out about my grandmother's cancer, and her life expectancy being extremely short, my children, my boyfriend, Barry, and I had gone to visit her in the hospital. She was now on the hospice floor awaiting transfer to a rehabilitation/ nursing home. Such bullshit! No one gets rehabilitated once they go to those shitholes.

The room was softly lit in an effort to hide the fact that this was the place people come to die. The two-foot Christmas tree that my Aunt Li Anne had delivered earlier that day was now taking up the small dining table near the drafty window, adding a combination of holiday cheer with a touch of hovering heartbreak. Sitting upright in her hospital bed with her now shallow cheeks (she had always appeared full of life and youth), sunken eyes, and gray-streaked silver hair, she asked Barry if he would run to get her a Diet Coke. The whole scene was a lot for my twelve and nine-year-old kids to take in; after hugging their "little grandma" while saying their hellos, they opted to venture off with Barry to search for her soda. After removing my grandfather's WWII Naval pea coat, I started to pull a chair closer to her bed.

With my back turned to her she started speak, "You know I will never forgive him for that."

I finished pulling over my chair, "What? Who are you talking about?"

Staring off at the television hanging on the wall, glasses dripping down her nose, she replied "Your father."

Rolling my eyes and then cocking my eyebrow, I asked, "What did he do this time?" I had long since grown tired of conversations surrounding my biological father. I knew better than anyone who he was, after all I was his daughter.

"He never wanted you, you know. The day you were born, he said if you came out black, you wouldn't be his." She spoke with a pain and anger that had been carried for the past thirty-two years.

Several years back a similar conversation had taken place in the presence of my grandfather and mother. The question of me being my father's child was absolutely asinine; I was definitely both my parents' child as I had looked like each of them at various points in my life. I said, "Apparently, according to him, he was joking."

With a sharp turn of her head like a whip extending out and landing its mark, her gaze set upon me. With a dead seriousness in her soulful smoky quartz eyes locking on mine, she stated matter-of-factly, "No he was wasn't and that man never deserved you or my daughter. Your Grandfather Robert knew that."

My grandfather had never liked my father, believing he was always up to something. I had never seen that look on her face or heard that tone in her voice before. I didn't know what to say. Thankfully, Barry and the kids arrived back with Diet Coke, full of conversation and cheer. The silence in those few seconds of our last "real" conversation was painful. As painful was the wound that would fester for years to come as a result.

❋ ❋ ❋ *Even a snowflake has the capability to burn as it bites with a frost that has the power to shatter the last leaf that is desperately holding onto the tree.* ◊◊◊

For months my grandmother's words to me would replay over and over in my mind. Those words and the memory of my voice, my very being repeatedly told to be silent would swim around my thoughts.

My father was the master of control. He possessed ways to instill insecurities masked as character-building "life lessons." This education must have been created to break one's spirit and silence any voice on every level possible that wasn't his. Everything was so contradictory to what my grandparents and mother were hoping to teach me. However, my father was the one man that I constantly sought approval and acceptance from. As a child I would do anything to make him smile. Life being an emotionless game of chess, my sisters and I would constantly strive to best one another. It was as if being better than one another wasn't good enough; emotional and mental annihilation was the game: we were like his rats in a cage.

The voice of my father echoed as his footsteps approached from down the hall. Ever observant, there he now stood as I sang along with the song playing on MTV.

I was six years old with big round hazel eyes, unruly curly brown hair, and golden olive skin. I was proudly singing my heart out for the whole world to hear in the middle of my stepmom's living room. Standing at the hallway opening was a slender, six-foot-one man with an afro perfectly picked—not a hair or curl out of place nor a nap to be found. From beneath his sly grin and furrowed brow, condescension left his lips. "Who is killing cats out here?"

My older stepsister looked up with a matching wicked grin and a roll of her dark brown eyes. "Nic is," she answered like a cat that had just cornered a mouse.

I looked up at the hazel-eyed man who I completely admired and said with a big smile on my face, "Me, Papi, I'm singing!"

With an ice-cold calm, much like something you would expect to see on the face of an evil genius, my father said, "Oh no, Nic! Don't sing. You can't sing. Yesterday you tried to draw and well, you couldn't do that. Let's just stick to learning how to read for now, because you can't do that either."

Feelings of embarrassment and shame began to expand within me. Shame cuts deep, bleeding into self-doubt and feelings of never being good enough, injuries of the spirit like this at such a young age planted the paralytic seeds of silence. Simultaneously another seed was taking root deep inside me, resilience. *I could strive to be better, to be something more.* Earning my father's love, approval, and acceptance would remain a focus well into my thirties.

❄❄❄ *How does a snowflake stay part of the snowfall when it is forced to be both part of the mountain stream and the leaf still on the tree?* 💧💧💧

The need for refuge was tremendous by the time I became seven years old. Teachers as early as preschool and continuing through middle school had often reported to my mom that speaking with me was like having a conversation with an adult. I had made the transition from being outwardly expressive of my pain through violence to frightened, silent, and just trying to keep from being noticed in places that didn't feel safe. School, my "stepmother's" home, unfamiliar people and new environments made me long for the days when I could just be left alone to swim. Much of my child-like spirit had already been broken at age seven when my grandparents had rekindled their lifelong commitment to one another. I had seen and experienced things that no child should ever have to go through. It was at this point when my own personal philosophies around marriage, life, love, extended families, parent-ing, and placing a child's needs before all else started to develop.

The insecurity and fear I felt around my peers as a child was just the tip of the iceberg in the growing list of adversities I would deal with throughout my childhood. The world around me was overwhelming and even more difficult when people's expectations varied from place to place. Each school was in a completely differ-ent part of Albuquerque than the next one, so the demographic and economic needs were always different. The way every school functioned was different both in the classroom and on the play-ground; building friendships and trust was stressful. Every year was different; new homes, new families, and new schools. The struggle to keep up with the differing rules and parenting styles (none of them could ever agree on anything or how I was to be raised) was overwhelming. Two couples, two households, four totally different sets of rules and expectations with each one.

Years later when I began struggling in middle school and fre-quenting the counselor's office, it was suggested that our family attend private family therapy sessions. It was there that twelve-year-old me expressed my thoughts of the day aloud. This should have been the beginning of healing. It was a little too late; but I was finally getting to speak, or at least I believed I was. The problem was this: my family didn't know that once you left the session you weren't supposed to go home and continue to dig into the issues and at each other. Our therapy sessions were never fun or productive. We had been fired by two therapists before family mediation was suggested. Again, mediation was another seemingly pointless route for us. It made Allen feel powerless, and my mom left feeling exhaustively hopeless after each session. I, on the other hand, often left each meeting not understanding why we were even bothering, we were just going to argue and fight the entire drive home. One hour once a week wasn't going to fix us. *We were fucked up!*

❀ ❀ ❀ *Becoming a parent is like staring into the water looking at your reflection before you dive in. In order to reach your destination, you have to both face and pass through yourself...* 💧💧💧

There are many pieces of Devon and Michael's childhoods that I look back upon wishing I had done better and been healthier. I would silently apologize over and over to my children that I had been working with limited knowledge, unresolved grief, and a lot of fear. Impatient as I often was, the one thing I felt at my core was that I was their voice when they needed me to be. I was doing my absolute best to see the world through their eyes and hear their needs. The correlation between my childhood struggles and their movement through the world wasn't lost on me.

My grandmother always said I would be a teacher, guide, and healer. I would try to run from those key pieces of my purpose, but I would always be brought back to it and there was nothing more revealing to that than my own children's diagnosis of Autism. Devon was extremely verbal early on, but went silent after a time. Michael would start off life non-verbal, but eventually reach a point when he couldn't stop talking. Having a special needs child that suddenly went silent, their inner world locking them away from me, was not only confusing; I found myself walking lines of strength and insanity. Then when I had another child who lived in constant frustration from the moment he first attempted to verbally communicate, I discovered new levels of heartbreak. And then the flood of self-defeating questions forced me through uncharted waters.

For the longest time I believed Heath had some deeper connection or understanding with our youngest child. I thought that he had some sort of magic touch that caused our son to need him more; only his arms appeared to lull the seemingly relentless cries. The reality of the situation was Heath was usually incredibly exhausted after work; the crying had no effect on him. I had mistaken his fatigue for an unattainable level of calm. He was unaffected by the crying and would fall asleep holding an equally exhausted baby. This change in focus and energy shift would be just enough to get our little one to center in a space of silent stillness.

I was trying to open a jar of jam one day and under pressure to make lunch. The frustration of trying to get this jar open was building with each failed effort of twisting, and banging the lid with a butter knife to loosen it. I tried every trick I could think of. Eventually succumbing to the fact that I would need my husband's assistance to complete this task, watching him open the jar with little effort sparked a connection. My new baby was the jar of jam that I couldn't open without the help of his father and somehow that fed the self-defeating feelings of being inadequate as a mother and woman. Looking back now, I see that was a moment when a *higher power* in the universe was trying to get me to hear my voice. I was just as connected to both of our children and I did hear them. I not only heard their voices; I felt their needs, pains, and joys almost as acutely as I could feel and hear my own. However, when I was caught in the darkness being lost and not knowing who I was, it was difficult to see the good signs placed right on my path.

My childhood traumas and baggage kept me locked within a chasm of fear. These fears eventually became my new swimming pool: a pool that I had begun to slowly drown in. I don't know if it was my upbringing in such extraordinary environments or I just simply was a young mom too wrapped up in my own shit, but I apparently wasn't the typical special needs parent at first.

A twenty-three-year-old mom, I was sitting in the diagnosticians' office with a team of physicians and a therapist, Heath's arm around me while I rocked Michael against my chest. Our Devon played within a world few were allowed to enter. Various testing methods were strewn about the table that separated us from the professionals who had spent an entire day with Devon a few weeks prior to this moment.

"Mr. and Mrs. Bruton, you need to understand and begin to plan for your child to live with you the rest of your life. Devon may never be able to function without you and will need a lot of specialty services both in and out of school."

The first time you hear that speech, you have a million questions, and you feel your heart begin to break like ice on a frozen stream cracking under the pressure of burdens much too heavy for it to hold. Little cracks spider outward giving way under the strain, eventually allowing greater deeper fractures to form. It isn't one quick break, like that of a love ending, no this was some immeasurable lingering pain. Apathy attempts to freeze your mind as every dream you had is blown right out the window. The second time you are given that same speech about your other child, an icy numbness has taken hold of you. Life becomes completely about necessity.

After receiving Devon's diagnosis, my husband and I would begin our search for connection and support with other families with children on the spectrum. At the time, we weren't the type of people to join organizations and support groups. We were young parents and a married couple of only three years with minimal financial resources compared to the families we were meeting. When our Michael was diagnosed, it was a bittersweet relief; the questions of his constant crying were answered. Connecting with families like ours with two children diagnosed on the spectrum proved to be challenging. We were intimidated, overwhelmed, and confused as to what direction we needed to go. Both of us were working, though fortunately I was able to work from home, and so I was more available for finding services that we were told our children desperately required. My days were abruptly filled with work, therapies, school programs, and doctor appointments. Naturally each child was unique and their diagnoses followed the same rule. The things that created stability and regularity for one child often set off the other child. I was constantly pushed beyond exhaustion. I had been blessed with two wonderful snowflakes, internally I *knew* that, externally I was forlorn. They needed a mother who mirrored their distinctive spirits. Revelations that my children and I were so very similar were the first drops of hope and connection in my new pool of refuge.

❋ ❋ ❋ *Life's various losses are like the unseen fallen trees in the forest... They happen every day. Some we aware of, some we are not; but few of us fully grasp the ripple effect or permanent impact on life.* ◊◊◊

I had lost babies, a marriage, an ex-stepdad, three other grandparents, great-grandparents, friends, so many friends including my best friend, Heather. All those losses outside of my babies and mom's father wouldn't shake me to my core like losing my grandmother would. Her death was like having the wind knocked out of me. I was there the moment she took her last breath as the final gasp of air released from her body, stopping her heart and all physical life left this earth. Much like that first dunk in the pool as a baby it was both beautiful and terrifying all at once. My grandfather was the foundation, the structural core in our family and my island when my mother couldn't be, when I was too tired to swim in the deep end, and couldn't swim through life anymore. He kept me and my entire family from drowning most of the time.

Having been my safe harbor, my grandmother was the spiritual heart my children and I had through the roaring waters of life. What the hell was I supposed to do when she was gone? She had unknowingly been there through my boyfriends, failed parenting moments, addictions, mental breakdowns, and physical health crises. How would I find my way now? This was the woman who had taught me how to build my soul and seek my best self. She lit a spark when questioning my voice. She had cared for my cousins, my children, and me when we were small children, exposing each of us to the incredible world of books and the knowledge contained within them. What were we to do once she was gone?

On January 17th, 2010, my grandmother went to dance with my grandfather, moving on to the next life. Three generations of women—my grandmother, my mother, and me— were the only ones there during her final hours of physical life. I had been filing her nails and beautifying her all night as she lay in a comatose state, while my mother talked to her in between giving the family updates on her declining condition. I just kept hearing this Okie twang running through my head, her voice, "Don't square them off. I don't want my nails to look like feet. Now there you go. Make'em pretty now, Nicole. I can't look like the wreck of the Hesperus." In those hours, it seemed we lived an entire lifetime and still the time was too short. *Could we have just five more minutes?* I held my grandmother's cold, frail hand as tight as I could, like a little child, while whispering words of gratitude down close to her ear. As I noticed the contrast between the strength in my grip and lack of in hers, I realized we were almost done. She had begun to swim for her edge. It wouldn't be long now…

It was time for me to lean down over the edge of the water just as she had done for me when I was a child, handing me a towel then sending me off to run free among the iris garden.

Suddenly her oxygen tank ran out, and my mamma said, "Just hold on to her I am going to find a nurse. Mamma, wait we'll get you another tank…" My mother left the room at light speed in search of assistance.

Leaning into grandma's face and then pulling back in hopes to meet her beautiful brown eyes one last time, I saw closed lids peacefully resting, as I had seen many times when she would nod off during her reading. I spoke quietly, "Thank you for being my grandma. I know that I didn't always believe you or hear you, but I am hearing you now. You have always seen me, you know who I am. Thank you for my mamma, she is *my everything*, and I wouldn't be here without either of you. You have always known exactly what I am and know now. I will be alright, they will be alright. We *all* will be alright. Do you see that handsome man waiting for you? You know what time it is. Love and hold my babies like you did for me. It's time… Mamma will be alright. You can go home now; they are waiting and I will be there too. Do you see me yet… my indigo light, my scales, my fins now? I am there, they are there. I love you."

Her eyes flitted as she lightly squeezed my hand one last time.

❊ ❊ ❊ *Walk long enough in a forest and either you will grow to appreciate the beauty and life around you or you will become deaf to the sounds of the mountain waters calling you and blind to the shade protecting you.* ◊◊◊

My mother had come back in the room. I got up to give her space to make sure she had her place. I was a little girl again as I observed the light in my mamma's emerald green eyes dim, her lips moving, the lines of exhaustion and wisdom showing in a fleeting moment. She too knew the oxygen wouldn't arrive in time. And suddenly she was the little girl sitting by her mamma as she wrapped her hand around my grandma's hand one last time. "Oh my mamma" left her mouth. One last breath and all the life, spirit, soul was no longer in my grandmother's body. My mamma's shoulders fell with the realization that her mamma was gone.

Everything slowed like the hush that washes over a forest after a fresh snowfall, and then my vision blurred. I was now sitting in an ocean of numbness and pain with this strange calm. I had spent all night at the nursing home away from my children and boyfriend. I was physically, mentally, and emotionally drained. My hands were on the steering wheel. Crying out in pain couldn't happen yet, I had to get home.

There isn't much I remember between taking the car out of park at the nursing home and placing it back in park under the carport of my driveway. Thoughts—thousands of little leaves and snowflakes—flashed through my mind like a movie reel, every moment every second with her. I no longer had someone to talk with about the universe or connections of the spirit and soul. There would be no more cheesecake afternoons while I cut her hair and did her nails. No more days of delving into the family history. The keys to the vault of family history and knowledge were now mine. Her stories would become pieces of my story and her voice would live as pieces of my own. I missed her uniquely discreet way of hearing my inner voice and supporting my beautiful individuality. Trips to the library with my kids and their "Little Grandma" were lost. Now I was walking through my front door, collapsing into Barry's arms, preparing myself for how I would tell my sweet children that their "Little Grandma" was gone.

❋ ❋ ❋ *Just like when I was a child having underwater tea parties with my friends and listening to the distorted sounds we each made, I dive into a child's imagination to hear the*

voices that long to be heard. Now with magical silver platinum
curls that fall around my still round hazel eyes I meet them at
eye-level as sign of respect, acceptance, and assurance just as my
grandmother had done with me and my own children. ◊◊◊

Even through my grief a particular memory kept creeping forward, burning, searing, and engraining itself within the forefront
of my mind: my last verbal conversation with this grand soul. Her
voice was gone in that final breath and now I was clawing at my
brain in a sudden urgency to hear it, but all that came was that
damn conversation. This memory was total bullshit! Why out of
all her teachings, beliefs, and special moments was this sticking
out in my mind? *Fuck,* I hated him for this, my father once again
robbing me, silencing a voice in my life. This man who never
wanted me, had denied my existence many times, and had used
me as a pawn in his real-life game of chess. Children were voiceless
pawns. This man didn't deserve to be the last conversation that my
grandmother and I would share. I hated my father's words and ego
being embedded in my memory of our last verbal exchange. "If
she comes out black, she isn't mine," she said he said. My grandmother was at least now free of the space those words had taken
hold of so many years ago in her heart and mind.

Following the death of my grandmother, the children and
I began to participate in both individual and family therapies
to cope with all of the losses and traumas that we had endured.
Not only was I the woman with daddy issues, but having parents
remarry/commit several times to multiple people throughout my
life, I became the woman with what I call *"parent issues."* When
I entered romantic relationships, I took one of two paths: sup-
pression of my voice or my constant attempts to drown out my
partner's. The lessons that imprint on us as children shape our
world and influence how we navigate the relationships in our lives.
Sadly, this carves a path into our children's lives as well.

As much as my grandmother had impacted my life while she
was alive, it was her passing that became the key to unlocking my
mental and emotional prison from much of my childhood trauma
and oppression. My anger and hatred gave way to understanding,

forgiveness and release. With all of that emerged the realization that I no longer was in desperate need of my father's love, approval, or acceptance. He was no longer GOD to me. My mother had loved me and given me more than I had ever longed for. Her flaws and weaknesses were actually her strengths. Through the process of many therapy sessions and self-care work, I'd come to a comfortable understanding that many of my father's flaws were hardwired and he was just as broken as the next person.

I tried to get the world around me to hear me, understand me. Eventually in my longing to be heard, I would turn away from— at times denying, my intuitive abilities in hopes of finding just one person to listen. Yes, from time to time the universe stepped in, practically moving mountains to bring me back to the intuitive gifts I had been blessed with. GOD, the universe and my angels were always trying to get me to appreciate and value my place in the world, the greater purpose I was born for. I was so busy chasing approval, understanding, acceptance, and love that, all too often, I would completely miss the signs that the universe was giving me.

When I finally sat still in self-imposed isolation, I began to hear my true voice once again. It had been screaming for years through the struggles and hardships. My voice, my spirit, had been speaking through my children and the lives of all the children around me my whole life. The thing is, while some people struggle to have a strong voice, that is something I have always possessed. It could be heard through my silence, play, dancing, art, swimming, and most of all my children. My children have been personified reflections of my voice through the experiences of life, proving that once again moments and points of realization are a lot like those snowflakes and leaves. Their battle scars are much like mine and even intertwined with mine and yet there is a beauty to be found within those scars. I see the scars now as attempts to silence a voice that was to be heard, respected, and honored. I find beauty in that each healed trauma is a mark of resilience, growth, and a deep inner self love with such immeasurable strength and courage.

I am humbled and in full understanding of the future barriers we will, they will, shatter as I suddenly remember how small my seventeen-year-old son felt to me when he reached for my hand as we entered the exhibit today, needing my reassurance that he could do this and that it would all be OK. As I hear families, couples, and ladies chatting around me, I wonder how many of them are living their true purpose. How many are empowering their children to use their voice? How many can truly relate to how unique and precious this moment in time is? How many of these people are snowflakes being forced to be part of the leaf and stream while being part of the snow? How many are snowflakes leaving an impact and changing the world around them? How many are truly reflective of the change that a child's voice can make when it is finally heard? *Children should be seen and always heard.*

Through blowing winds, rushing waters, and waves that pull you under I have become the glistening snowflake, the floating leaf, the flowing mountain stream, and the guardian mermaid as I was meant to be.

Mother, *Intuitive Family Champion,* and writer, Nicole "Nikki" Bruton-Phillips is devoted to enjoying a silly* life with her family through her soul's calling and passion. As she walks in her purpose, Nicole is writing her complete story, "A Mermaid's Soul." As an *Intuitive Family Champion,* she loves working with children to release their voice while creating deeper connection and healing with their parents. Presently, she is engaged in building a family advocacy company, concentrating on the power of unified voice between parent and child.

Being their biggest fan, Nicole supports the voices of her children and living their dreams. Her children remain the greatest blessings and inspirations in her life.

The Old English meaning of silly is happy, blissful, lucky or blessed.
Contact Nicole at nbphillips.writer@gmail.com.

Blue Skies, Blurry Vision

Karen Ann Boise

"To be present in life is to be free."—Karen Ann Boise

The ocean waves were crashing into the beach, with the sun sinking deep into the sea. I watched in wonder at the splendor of it all—orange, blue, purple, all shades of the rainbow, brilliant. The big ball of fire sank and disappeared and with it my sense of being. Unhappy, scared, confused and alone, I sat in my truck looking straight ahead.

I watched the couples on the beach walking hand in hand. They were laughing, hugging, kissing and looking so free, the sand being kicked up under their feet. In the paved lot, I sat safely in my small Mitsubishi Mighty Max truck, high up in the driver's seat, listening to Don Henley sing "The Boys of Summer" straight from the cassette deck Velcroed to my dashboard. This is where I went every evening after dinner. I'd hop in my truck, roll the windows down, blast my music and drive the exact same streets to the beach. This was as adventurous as I trusted myself to be, not knowing my way around this huge city of San Diego; it was the most my anxiety-ridden body could handle. Tears streamed down my face, my heart aching, dreadfully lonely and desperately longing to not be alone in this beauty. And yet, there I was every day, wishing and hoping it could somehow be different. To say I felt lost would be an understatement. I felt as if a huge wave crashed against my chest every time I took a breath.

How would I ever escape the pain, fear and craziness going on inside of me?

How does one choose their future when they don't even know who they are?

The cautious smile and sideways glance of a young man wore into my memory as I sat alone, watching the waves tumble in and out to sea. I had up and run away from him and what had quickly become a serious relationship. I recounted in my head *the man I might love.* When we first met, I wasn't sure if he was painfully shy or if I just made him nervous. He was always super kind to me.

The days went from casual hellos as we passed in the hallway at work to him lingering in my office trying to find something to chat about. Soon he was bringing me a breakfast burrito every day. He was sweet, but outside of that, *what was he?* I didn't know.

Spring was in the air and one evening after many months of casual banter and flirtation, he suggested hanging out at my place and ordering carry out. I was twenty-two years old and living in a teeny one-room converted garage that had a small dorm room fridge and no kitchen. The woman I rented from offered me use of her kitchen any time I liked but I didn't want to feel like a bother, so I either ate out or didn't eat at all. Mostly the latter, as I typically did not have money for food. In those days I wasn't good at taking care of myself and this thread seemed to follow me for years.

We ordered pizza and together we scarfed every last crumb. This was the first time we had ever spent time alone and away from the office. Most of the time when we talked, we were surrounded by others and constantly interrupted by our co-workers walking in and out of my office. On this evening with no disruptions, we talked for hours, learning anything and everything we could about each other. We seemed to come from very different yet similar pasts. His parents had divorced when he was young, leaving him to travel back and forth between his parents' homes in separate towns. He described how by the age of six he had been left alone, both physically and emotionally, and how abandoned he had felt. He was now twenty-three and had been on his own since he was sixteen. He was fiercely independent and had learned to rely on himself at a very early age, as had I, just in a different way.

We discovered so much common ground. Everything he said resonated with me and for the first time, it felt like someone may actually understand me. Talking with him was like wrapping myself in a soft, warm blanket on a cold winter's night; I wanted to sink right into the comfort of his voice. Hanging on his every word, I watched his mouth and I found myself longing for his touch. His soft, blue eyes staring into mine as we shared stories of our youth was the beginning of me wanting to be the one to make it all okay for him. Conversation and laughter flowed easily between us and the acceptance I felt was something I had never known.

Soon it was time for him to go and as he was leaving, he turned to me and asked very politely if he could kiss me good-bye. Sweet, slow, seductive, it symbolized the beginning of many more to come. From then on we began navigating the days and nights together learning the good, bad and ugly of each other. I learned he was an amazing cook and loved it and that I wasn't and didn't. He had a serious side while I was flirty and sarcastic. He was quick to anger and I was quick to defend. We were both passionate when we fought and passionate when we made up. This became our dance. I tried to keep things upbeat and fun so the air wouldn't feel so thick, and he tried to keep me fed and showered with trinkets as our dance swayed through summer and fall, only to take a turn come winter.

Here in San Diego, I had been working as a temp for a few different companies and no matter where I worked, I felt like an invader. It was just like being in school again, being stared at as I would walk by, seeing people huddled and whispering as they looked my way. I tried to convince myself that their chitchat had nothing to do with me, and yet it was always so obvious. I learned as a small child how to read people. I didn't realize until I was much older that I had learned this as a way to mitigate and avoid being in the line of fire at home as our household was one of unpredictable temperaments. It had become a protection mechanism of sorts and I could sense disingenuousness a mile away.

In high school I had been fortunate enough to have a couple of best girl friends that acted as a buffer for me in uncomfortable situations. I hated how much I wanted to be liked. I hated that I cared, and yet, I cared so deeply that I spent a lot energy and time consumed with other people's thoughts, opinions, and rumors about me. It was a spiral down a rabbit hole that could leave me buried under piles of my own emotion within minutes and go on for hours. *Where did this pattern come from?* I never stopped to ask myself because I was too buried in it.

I loathed how I looked and no amount of primping, curling my hair or makeup could change that. Still I tried so hard. My coarse and wavy strawberry-blond hair that grew like a lion's mane around my face and head was to be dreaded every morning. This self-hatred had roots in elementary school, where I had no buffer at all. Not even from the teachers. I was bullied and chased until I fell to the ground from running too fast or tripping on rocks the teachers used as door stops. I was pushed around, teased and tormented until I was crying hysterically begging my tormenters to stop. It never occurred to me to stand up for myself or fight back.

My thoughts were only on trying to understand why others were so cruel to me. The only thing that made sense was that I must be flawed. I did not see myself as different from others but in their mind, I was different, so different in fact that I was given the name Yellow Head Monster. My parents had moved to a small rural community in northern New Mexico when I was four. They had purchased a few acres of land and set out to build an adobe home and farm. For five years my mom, dad, brother and sister labored on the house and land while I would come home each and every day in tears begging my mom to please dye my hair brown. I was absolutely convinced that if only my hair were brown, I would be liked. When my mom told me no, I'd lash out at her screaming and sobbing from the depths of my being. Uncontainable tears poured down my beet-red, snotty face, as I tried to make her realize that dying my hair brown was *the* only answer to my survival. What part of my first-grade logic didn't she understand? Didn't she get it? We could solve this! Instead, she would fold me into her lap while wiping away my tears telling me again and again that all would be okay.

When I was nine, we moved back to the town we had originally lived in. I felt optimistic and excited at the change until I was smacked with the reality that nothing had really changed at all. I didn't know how to have friends or be liked. I was so used to wearing the identity of *the loner nobody liked* that I wore it like a shield. Even when kids tried to be my friend, I'd push them away.

Now, here I was living in San Diego longing for someone to hang out with. Some of the people I met in my temp jobs were superficially nice enough, but I wanted no part. My life was simple, really. I spent my free time playing games and watching TV with my niece and nephew, whom I adored, but the now twenty-three-year-old girl in me was dying of boredom. I grew more confused and unfulfilled by the day and no matter how I tried I could not calm the storm raging inside me.

My anxiety had been on high alert since I had arrived in San Diego and it was getting harder and harder for me to manage. I had become frightened of nearly everything. Driving, eating, interacting, even existing had become terrifying. I lived in fear of having a panic attack because I had no idea what triggered them. I existed in a continuous fight or flight mode, yearning to be somewhere, anywhere, that I could just feel safe. Safe, loved, wanted and protected. I had yet to find that, not even in my sister's home surrounded by family.

After six months of trying to escape from the stronghold of anxiety, I was ready to go back to the security of what I once had. I picked up the phone, dialed his number and waited to hear his voice on the other end. I asked him to come get me.

"No," he said.

It wasn't a soft no, but rather a sharp ringing one that stung my eardrum. Apparently, he wasn't going to let me back in so easily.

I didn't give up. After many phone calls of me apologizing and begging, he eventually said, "I will think about it." He was still enraged that I had left him to run from our life together and start a new life on my own in San Diego. I could not erase the memory of the Christmas we shared prior to me leaving. He had proposed to me on Christmas Eve with a delicate gold ring and a Lhasa Apso Terrier mix puppy. Diamonds and a puppy! I couldn't say no.

Within a couple of weeks of saying yes, I panicked and quickly made the decision to move to San Diego with my sister and her family who were relocating there. I was once told by a co-worker/ friend when I was just nineteen that I was "wishy-washy," and was proving this to be true. But with the wishy-washy comes a backstory that, for most of us, takes years to figure out. The inner battle raged on no matter what decision I needed or wanted to make; I didn't trust myself to make the right one. My life had been so aimless, I had no idea what I wanted and tempted by the idea of a fresh start, I felt certain I would find it in another state. It didn't take me long to realize that, as the saying goes, "wherever you go, there you are."

In June 1990, after many pleading conversations on my part, he flew out to San Diego and drove me back home to Albuquerque to begin our life together. It was official; I had decided on my future before I knew who I was. All the time I spent running, fearing, and not knowing which direction to go, I had landed here. There was some temporary gratification in making a decision, but *was it the right one?*

Our oldest son, Zach, was born in September of 1991. We hadn't talked a whole lot about marriage since I had moved back. I think he was still hurting and feeling burned from the last proposal and since we were living together, there wasn't really any point. I was okay not being married and I did not want a baby to be the reason we said vows. Telling my dad I was pregnant was one of the hardest things I've ever had to do. I hadn't done too much to make him proud and I knew this was icing on the cake.

Hi Dad, it's me, your baby girl. You know, the twenty-four-year-old one that failed college miserably, has no money, is unemployed, is shacking up with a dude, not making anything of my life and oh yeah, guess what, I'm pregnant.

I had lived up to what my father had been told about me when I was in high school. Many of my teachers had told him that I basically would not amount to much. I can only guess what his face must have looked like as he held the phone on the other end. In no uncertain terms he told me I must get married right way. He was positive that, otherwise, I would end up raising this baby alone.

The rebel in me instantly said *no*.

The day I held my baby boy in my arms, the whole world felt complete. I had never in my life felt that kind of deep, unconditional, unwavering love. I lay there in the hospital room, the lights dim, alone, and the most beautiful child I have ever seen was lying beside me in his bassinet. He was a big, healthy boy, coming into the world at a plumb 9 pounds 2 ounces, no wrinkles and a silky soft even skin tone. He was perfect in every single way. As I stared at him, I was both petrified and resolved. I couldn't look away from him as my heart wanted to burst out of my chest. The room grew even more silent, the only noise being in my head. *Don't screw this up. This child just saved your soul and you must get this right.*

I immediately knew we had to get married.

It was time to complete the circle and give our son a family.

Four months later, all was complete. *I do, I do too,* where once there was one is now three. We married in a charming chapel on a snowy January day. All the pews were filled with our family and friends, as my father walked me down the aisle in my off-white wedding gown to seal our fate. As we stood at the alter sharing our vows, the creation of our love rested in a basket between us and upon conclusion, the minister pronounced us a family.

Our relationship up until then lacked good communication, connection, and problem-solving skills. We didn't know how to talk to each other without one of us becoming offended, hurt, or mad. Misinterpreting took the place of clarifying questions, tears took the place of just asking to be heard, doors slamming became the answer to anything we could not solve, and the silent treatment came in to play way too often. At times we didn't even care what the other was feeling. I think we each knew deep inside us what the other wanted and needed and yet, we couldn't find the path there. It was easier to accept the anger than deal with the truth.

We were young twenty-somethings with no role models of what a loving, nurturing, honest marriage looked like. Book and movie romances were my only gauge, and nothing ever looked or felt like that in my life. The shared experience of chaotic, dysfunctional upbringings initially glued us together. His crazy matched my crazy and we somehow found solace in that.

Now with vows said, the giddiness of being first-time parents and newlyweds renewed us and left us with butterflies in the tummy, lots of hugs, long kisses, bodies tangled, morning coffee brought to you in bed, cuddles, long talks, long walks, hopes and stories shared, and what felt like the beginning of all our dreams coming true. We were now complete as we marched to the drum of each workday's beat. My husband had gotten his dream job at the university working in a large theater venue just before the baby was born. It was all he had ever wanted to do and he felt fortunate to find a job like this locally. He would rise early, come home late, and would often work seven days a week since weekends are when most performances happened. On top of that, he would pick up side jobs to make extra money. He was hardly ever home and when he was, it was for a quick dinner and to sleep.

From the start I grew resentful. I had never expected or wanted to raise a baby alone. Yes, I was married. Married and alone, all the time. I reflected back to all those earlier years where I was alone, longing for that just right love, and now here I was alone again. He promised me it was just until we could get on our feet and I held on to that every day wanting it to be true.

The first year of our child's life, I stayed home with him during the day and went to school at a tiny, non-accredited business college at night to earn a certificate in accounting. I didn't necessarily like accounting, but I knew that was what my sister had been doing and she had money. She was the one person in my life that was living life on her own terms and was successful in my eyes. I had admired her my entire life. To copy her, to *be* her in any way, seemed to be the only compass I had. I wasn't skilled in much and I had no formal education other than that little accounting certificate that ended up costing us $5,000 and not meaning anything at all. The school was shut down for illegal practices and with it being non-accredited, the credits would not even transfer to a reputable school.

When I had gone to college right out of high school, I had declared a major in Psychology. I thought it would be cool to talk with people and help them work through their problems. I had always had an interest in people and their stories and at the same time, I was scared of them. With college not working out and now this fiasco with the business school, all I had earned were more failures to put in my pocket.

In the end, it would all come down to getting any job that would pay enough to make a small difference and not just all go to daycare. As a couple, we fell into the same trap that many do when we don't know who we are and inevitably don't know which direction to go to make life better. We were always broke, barely surviving from paycheck to paycheck. His job at the university only issued paychecks once a month and with rent, truck payment, diapers, etc., it was gone within a day of receiving it. Once a month we would go the store and load up on cheese, tortillas, hamburger meat, bread, and few boxes of mac and cheese. Tacos, enchiladas, tostadas, and quesadillas were our mainstay meals and for a treat, we made mac and cheese. When we had depleted our monthly supply of food we'd head to my mother-in-law's with baby in tow to rummage through her refrigerator for leftovers. Three-day-old pot roast, a half loaf of bread, cheese slices, expired milk, you name it. The luxury of being a picky eater was long gone.

I lived in angst everyday with feelings of unrelenting unhappiness and boredom. There was no one for me talk to, laugh with, or share funny stories with of what the baby was doing. So many times I felt like a doll that had been placed on a shelf. Every once in while I would be taken down and played with and then placed back on the shelf until the next time.

My sister-in-law lived with us but she was busy living her own life, and since she worked nights her days were spent sleeping. Without extra money to put gas in the car, even going for a drive—one of my saving graces—was out. I lived in a city with a bus system but the mere thought of using public transportation was nerve wracking. I had grown up in a small town of 18,000 people, with virtually no crime. We didn't lock our cars or homes, and you certainly didn't worry about watching your back as you walked down the street. Now, I resided in the crime-infested heart of the student ghetto, close to the campus. I literally had to ask the prostitutes to please take their business across the street and away from our front door steps. The mere thought of trying to navigate my way around on foot to the nearest bus stop was enough for me stay home in isolation and misery rather than subject myself to the extra distress.

My husband being gone all the time was our number one fight. Like two swans drifting apart at sea, we lived separate lives even though we had this precious baby together. All I wanted was companionship. Someone to spend time with. But the more I asked him to spend time with me, the more distant and defensive he became. I'd tell him I missed him and he would shut down. I'd try to make plans with him and he'd shake his head no, he had to work. I'd try to stay up late just so I could see him and instead he would go out with his friends rather than come home. I lived for his days off just so we would have some time together as a couple, as a family. Some days I would stand tall and strong and express everything I felt, and other days I'd be meek and defeated with no energy at all to even try. I knew we were drifting further and further away from the married life I had envisioned and like a beat-up, abandoned ship, the tide was pulling us out to a deep, dark sea.

My only confidant was the blank pages of my hard-bound journal. Here I would fill up the empty space by spewing my victimization and despair. I'd write about all that I wished for and wanted. My ever-honest heart began to speak as the pen translated its full emotions into words. It knew what my mind did not. I'd write endlessly of the life I longed for and imagined. A life free of fear, and full of light and love. I'd write of laughter filling the empty crevices of our home, while joy bounced from the walls as my son's face beamed up at us in delight. But this was not my life, it was a dream far out of reach. From junior high on, my journal was my safe space though when writing I was still nervous someone would read it. My words were cryptic and carefully chosen as to not go too deep into what I was *really* feeling and thinking. Surface level would suffice just in case I was ever called on it to explain. Holding back was safer than having any type of thoughts, feelings or emotions that were not were not in agreement with those of others. I had learned that to have my own thoughts and opinions was taboo. I walked around day after day, feeling very small and knowing that for me, there was no real escape or safe outlet. My voice was buried deep inside the walls of my chest.

The body has a way of communicating with us and most often this comes through a broken state of painful imbalance. Not that I knew it at the time, but since my thoughts and feelings had no voice and no safe place to land, they started taking up residency in my body. I suffered with constant stomach issues that often ruled my day. I had debilitating migraine headaches, which got so bad that I could not get out of bed for days at a time. Colds and bronchitis were a common affair and soon, not feeling well was just my way of being. I'd drag myself through every day and I did this for years. On top of being sick frequently, I was plagued with symptoms from stress and anxiety; and the more out of control of my life I felt, the more rapidly they increased.

When Zachary was sixteen months old, we had a random opportunity to purchase our current landlords' main home under a real estate contract. They had decided to up and leave the state and were selling their home and the rental house in which we lived. We would have to move. With no idea what we were doing, we made an offer on their main home. We did know that with our current state of affairs it was a long shot but with not having to qualify for a mortgage, we thought we'd try. I had been applying for jobs and had recently interviewed with a major airline to work in their call center as a reservationist. We desperately needed the money and I needed to work.

The house we wanted to buy was in a beautiful old neighborhood, with big trees that lined the streets, still close to the university where my husband worked and out of the student ghetto. The basement of the house had been converted into a two-bedroom, one-bath apartment and already had tenants that would come with the home. With tenants, this was a house we could afford and if I were to get the job with the airline, we might actually be able to make it work. Now, I was motivated. A glimpse of hope for my future had arrived and I danced around the living room holding my baby in my arms and singing out loud.

I remember bargaining with God that if he would allow to me get this job, I would never ask for anything ever again. I asked my dad for the down payment and after a lot of back and forth he called to let me know that my grandmother would give us the money. In January of 1993, right after closing on the house, I learned that the airline wanted to hire me. Even writing about it now I can still feel the gratitude and shock of it all. We were a married couple, parents, homeowners, and I had landed a good job. I remember thinking, *Wow, maybe I am finally growing up.*

I worked for the airline for about eighteen months before I left to work for an attorney's office. They say be careful what you ask for and I was quick to learn that lesson. I absolutely hated working for the airline. The "family friendly" airline was a far cry from that, and I found myself not being able to miss any work to care for my son when he was sick with pneumonia, and unable to leave my shift when my grandmother was in the final hours of her life. I cried every day on my way to work and then counted down the hours until the day was over. I knew I had to work, and I knew for sure that I couldn't keep working there.

I wasn't particularly picky about what I would do if I were able to increase my hourly wage just a little bit with each move. This was the lowest state of being I had resigned to, *just find something and make it work. Just get paid enough to pay the mortgage, just get by and somehow life will work out.* Over the course of eighteen years, I had worked as a reservationist for an airline, a legal secretary, and an office manager for an economic development company, where I challenged myself and got my real estate license. Even then, I felt like I was still running, always running.

The crazy thing is when you are running you can't see it.

Everyone had told me I would be good at real estate because of my personality. I despised it, mostly because I was trying to be someone I was not. It was during this time that the disconnection in our marriage took its toll. I found myself wanting to know when the craziness was going to stop. I had spent practically my whole life wishing and hoping for life to get better. I told myself, *It will get better when my parents divorce. It will get better when I graduate high school. It will get better when I go to college, when the baby is born, when we get the house and so on and so on.* After years of living on hope, which I still do by the way, I realized that hope also requires action and faith. So, after too many years of arguing and not living up to each other's expectations, we mutually decided it is probably best to split. We were at a point where we had no more civil words to say to each other.

From the very first time we shared our stories, we had become allies. Now, two wounded soldiers once joined together to conquer this battle called life, had somehow become enemies on opposite sides of the battlefield. *Where had our love gone? Was it even love?*

After many dark nights of separation, we mustered up a fake forgiveness and decided to try again. It was the classic never-ending seeking of love without fixing the core of the human self. We were both on our best behavior, we tried, we gave, we shared. I became pregnant with another sweet boy who adds to this newfound joy. The nights were soon spent together sharing in the care of this newborn cherub, working together side by side as the infant cries turned into toddler giggles and belly laughs, and fun hide-and-seek created the wonderful pitter-patter of little feet running around on the oak wood floors. We were good and back on track, at least marriage-wise; my anxiety, though, was spinning out of control.

Throughout years of this up and down, how does one block their voice and truth for so long, until one day the moon peeks through the sky and wakes that person up? It's a terrible waking, because she realizes the only way out is alone…

Alone, that one thing I cannot stand!

Then one night, *enough was enough.* My fourteen-year-old son had been invited to travel to Greece and Turkey with his best friend and his mother. The mom was salt of the earth and very well-traveled. She adored my son and I knew in my gut that he was in good hands. From the moment they left, panic rose in my chest and there was no way to escape it. I didn't have a way to contact him the entire three weeks he was gone and with each passing day my fear spiraled more and more out of control. Bedtime was the worst and I'd spend the whole day dreading it. The moment my head hit the pillow, every impractical and insane thought would bombard me, stealing my sleep and leaving in its place a feeling of doom. I was dying inside.

I needed this torment to end.

It was undeniably time that I address this anxiety head on and begin to regain control of not only my thoughts, but of my life. Every day up until then was a living hell. *How had I lied to myself this long?* This night, I paced back and forth in the faintly lit hallway as my husband and two-year-old slept. The hardwood floors creaking beneath my feet was the only comfort I had. I tried to focus on the creaks so that maybe I wouldn't hear the thumping of my heart in my chest, as each beat came faster and faster and echoed in my head. I could feel my throat closing up, making it hard to get air. Panic set in with each shallow breath I took. I couldn't breathe. My chest was getting tighter and tighter as I began to hyperventilate. Sweat was beading up on my forehead and I swore I was going to die. No matter what I did I couldn't seem to gain control.

Dropping to my knees I pleaded and prayed for Him to help me. *God, please, please stop my mind. I'd been down this road many times before often landing me in the emergency room. Each time I was told it was just stress and would be sent on my way with Xanax in one hand and a fist full of feeling like I was nuts in the other.* I sat down on the living room floor, pulled my knees to my chest and began to rock myself back and forth. I had no idea where to turn for help or what I was going to do but I did know this was it! This had to end, right now.

The path to self care and self discovery is a steep hill to climb.

I stayed in my marriage, but started a new way of being. I stopped watching the news. I did not need to hear about all the evil in the world; my mind could make up worse. I needed to hear good things, positive things, happy things. Every time I had a thought that did not serve me I would challenge it. No longer would things be true just because my mind said so. Saying thanks took the place of worry. Staying present took the place of antici-pating what could go wrong, and feeling good became a conscious choice rather than a rare occurrence. I became super aware of all the blessings and gifts in my life and started to focus on them. I began a gratitude journal and started writing about the day's bless-ings, giving me space and time to sit in the gratitude and feel the swelling of contentment in my heart. I found gratitude to be the gift that grounds me and discovered that the comforts of life we often take for granted are the very things that bring me the most joy: the roof over my head, a comfy bed, blankets, warm water, hot coffee, food, clothing, transportation. Whenever I started to forget how fortunate I was, these were things I remembered.

I also started to *really* hear people when they spoke and found that bearing witness to someone when they shared was one of life's greatest treasures.

I learned that to be present in life is to be free.

I started waking early and going for runs, with friends no less, and going to the gym. The endorphins made me feel good and the added energy I now had added to the optimism and excitement I was beginning to feel with each new day. I corrected each "what if" thought with an opposite thought and it made me smile at my cleverness. I stopped saying I "have to" when I was tasked with something I didn't particularly enjoy and started to say "I get to" because *how beautiful is it to be alive and given an opportunity that many are denied?* I started holding my shoulders back and my head up high. When passing someone, anyone, I would make eye con-tact, smile and say hi. Helping myself was the moment I learned to truly help others and thus I began to be the voice that I had so desperately wanted someone to be in my life. A voice of love, a voice of encouragement, a voice of acceptance, and a voice of hope.

Our youngest son, Sam, was now four and life kept rolling along as usual. We had gotten comfortable and given each other space and then, from out of nowhere, *déjà vu, here we go again.* Tsumani-like, the past came crashing in and all the demons came full on to play. The here and now have no room where dark past shadows loom. Love could not conquer all when clouded with distrust, denial and fear. In a flash, it all imploded. Shattered matter, debris and dust were everywhere we once touched. I had to bolt—run, not walk—and start anew. Tragic endings, cavernous wounds, ugly scars left only in their aftermath the strongest thing we ever shared: the deep, unconditional love for our children and a desperate longing for hope.

Up until the day I moved out of our family home for good, I had lived each day of our marriage waiting for "someday." It was time for me to accept that when it came to our marriage and the dreams we had, someday would never come. I had held on to my marriage with everything I had. I didn't trust myself to be okay and now years later looking back, I don't know what I feared.

I had been preparing for this my whole life.

When my parents first divorced, my mother fell apart. The roles reversed quickly, and I was all of a sudden an eleven-year-old parent to a thirty-seven-year old woman. I was her confidant, her friend, her companion, and the one whose shoulder she would cry on. She had never been alone before and now it was just her and me. I made it my job to make sure she was okay and there I believe set the stage for the next thirty years of my life. I made it my responsibility to make sure everyone was okay and if they weren't, *it must be my fault.* This was how it was in my marriage. If my husband wasn't willing to come home when I asked, or willing to change, or agreeing to try something I suggested, and if he wasn't happy, then I must have been doing something wrong. I put so much energy into trying to fix him, save him, and comfort him that I totally lost myself, all while being a martyr and placing the blame on him.

I read every self-help book I could find. My bookshelf looked like a counselor's office. I had just about every topic covered from co-dependency, anger management, marriage counseling, effective communication, childhood trauma, workaholism, etc. You name it and I probably owned and read it and always with someone else in mind besides myself. I was going to read myself into solutions for everyone else and solve all their problems. It took me years to realize that the only person I could help and save was myself and wow, what an aha moment that was setting me free like a white dove flying from its cage.

The first night I slept in my new rental house alone I remember feeling like I had many times as a child. Like when there is a creepy sensation that washes over you. You're not exactly sure what you are afraid of, but you are. You feel frightened to walk down a hallway, given the sense that something is at your back. You imagine its scary face. You can almost hear the background music of a horror movie playing as the terror intensifies. It's unsettling and sleep won't come because you can't lose the prickly feeling coursing through your body or the way the hair is standing up on your arms. Your mind is of no help with its incessant chatter and there is nothing you can do to calm it.

I really believe the only thing that got me through that first night was my yellow lab/retriever Sadie, my friend, my companion, my hero. It's funny because Sadie was the sweetest dog ever and a complete fraidy-cat. She would hide behind me when someone came to the door wanting me to protect her and yet on this night, I felt protected by her very presence.

The next day my sister came to town and helped me move and get settled. By the time she left, my new little rental house felt almost like a home. My kids were now there with me and our new lives began. It didn't take me long to figure out that we would be okay. I instantly felt different. All the worry and uneasiness of not knowing what to expect from day to day was beginning to diminish and mostly, the realization that I had control over me—and that I always had—was the greatest gift I have ever received. There is being alone and there is being lonely. I was finally getting to know me and it wasn't nearly as scary as I'd thought.

That said, the first year after leaving my marriage there was plenty to navigate and figure out. For almost twenty years of my life, there had been two incomes and two daily parents. Now, I was a single mom to a sixteen-year-old and a pre-kindergartener with clearly different needs. I was making just enough to get by working as an executive assistant for a community college and was shocked when my first paycheck rolled in after the divorce was final. Now single, the amount of taxes coming out of each check had doubled. I remember bursting into tears at the cruelty of it all. *God, really?* Some days were too much to bear as exhaustion and fear would take over, leaving me to wonder how I'd ever make ends meet and manage a teenage boy's hormones and a four-year-old's tantrums. It seemed the punches in the gut just kept coming and yet I had made a decision: I will endure whatever comes my way with grace and gratitude and I WILL rise above. I knew in my very core that I had no choice but to make this work and fortunately, alone or not, making things work was my forte.

As a child I was accustomed to being alone but I didn't like it. When my parents divorced, I was eleven and my older brother and sister had already moved out and on with their lives. It was just me and my mom. For the first years after, my dad fleeted in and out of our lives and the time I once spent with him slammed shut like a coffin. While my parents were married my dad was my playmate, my friend, my companion. We were inseparable until the very day he left. Sitting at Overlook Park, we stared out over the canyon as my father tried to find the words.

"Your mom and I are getting divorced," he said.

I had known something was up because that day's car ride had felt different, it felt planned, and my dad didn't usually plan anything. He did things when he felt like doing them. As I heard his words, a sense of relief washed over me. I was not surprised, and in fact, I was happy. This was good. I shook my head yes. *Yes, yes, this is okay. The constant tension, anger, fighting, and yelling will stop now.*

"It's okay Daddy, it's for the best." I said. "We will all be okay."

I didn't know it at the time, but this would also be the end of our weekly trips to the library where my father's love of reading became my own. No more walks in the woods behind our house, no more bedtime stories or cuddling with him before I slept. The day he told me they were divorcing was the day I received a purple ten-speed bike in exchange for my dad's daily presence in my life. Never in a million years did I know just how pivotal this would be to my life, my confidence, and my sense of how I fit into this world or didn't.

My dad moved out and into a small apartment in town and my mom and I moved out of the big two-story house with the park-like backyard and into a small trailer in a trailer park. It was the beginning of many moves we would make all while staying in the same town. The yelling and fighting that I was so sure would stop once my parents divorced continued and never really did stop. It became a way of life and soon I understood that the only way to avoid it was to never allow my parents to be in the same room.

I often landed in the middle of their arguments, either as a translator or a mediator trying to get them to just stop fighting. My mom was upset with my dad for not spending enough time with me and my dad would yell at my mom for blowing the child support money. My mom didn't have any money, of that I was sure. She had been a stay-at-home mom my whole life and after being married to my dad for twenty-two years had to go to work. Her first job after the divorce was working at a hardware store earning minimum wage. The middle-income life we once enjoyed had come to a screeching halt. I had never really asked for many material items but now I knew for sure that I couldn't. A slow death swept across my insides, the brokenness molding itself into my body. I'm pretty sure this is where I vowed that if I had ever had kids and divorced, I would do whatever it took to put my kids first.

I took this lesson to heart and thankfully my ex-husband and I are both constants in our kids' lives, blended families and all. What we could not give them in our marriage we could at least give them being apart. My parents had been very young when they married. My mom was sixteen and my dad just nineteen. They were kids themselves when they had kids. Now in divorce they were each experiencing a freedom they had never known and with me being the straggler child, I was just in the way. I never faulted my parents for this. I think somewhere deep inside of me, even as an eleven-year-old, I understood. I just missed having my dad around and although I could not articulate it very well, I felt abandoned by him and would lay in bed at night with a heavy weight of sadness on my chest.

It was the same weight I felt while watching those waves crash in and out at the sea that night in San Diego. I was running for a reason, because my soul wanted a way out. But our story never leaves us; we just transfer it to a new thing and it keeps showing up. I had transferred all this hurt to my relationship without knowing myself or how to heal my wounds.

My father had been my one constant, the one who made me laugh and made me cry. I adored him and was crushed by the realization that our once joined-at-the-hip relationship was no longer. This became clear when I moved in with him to finish out my last two years of high school. My mom had moved to another city and I didn't want to leave my friends, especially now that I finally had some. My dad graciously let me move in and live with him and my grandmother and eventually my now stepmother. They say you can't go home again and boy this was true.

This did not feel like home. My father was strict, no nonsense and had accumulated many rules. Nothing resembled the time we used to share together before the divorce when I was daddy's little girl. Ever since he had moved out, all I had wanted was his affection, validation, his approval. For him to accept, like, and love me unconditionally as he once had. I wanted to be good enough for him to want to spend his time with me and thankfully, I did get moments. He taught me to ride a dirt bike, throw a mean Frisbee, and play a crazy-competitive game of Uno. I was so happy to get some time back with him.

Now that I had this opportunity to live with him, any time I had with him was precious but also scary and hard. I hated making my dad mad at me and as a moody, mouthy and sarcastic teenage girl, I seemed to do that often. I walked a tight rope of wanting to be with him and wanting to be nowhere near him and this is where I finessed the art of walking on eggshells, which I continued to do for the next twenty-five years. It took me forty-plus years to feel worthy enough of any man's attention and time.

Fear is a crazy beast and it wreaks havoc on the very things that matter to us to the most. It thrives on telling us untruths and weaves itself into our every thought, robbing us from really knowing what we are capable of in this life. It even steals from us the ability to question it so we blindly believe what fear tells us, make it true, and therefore deprive ourselves of the very thing we want the most in our lives. I wanted my dad back and yet I was always too afraid to just tell him that. I know he loved me. I know he only wanted the best for me and I know now that I'm a parent why he was so strict. Looking back, I can see where I let fear stand between us and how I had allowed it to create the story of me not being good enough to receive his love.

My daddy died not too long ago, and, in his death, I felt all of the love and acceptance I had longed for. When I got the call that he would not make it through the day I was on my honeymoon with my now husband and hundreds of miles away. By the time we rearranged flights and I arrived in Phoenix, a good eight hours had passed. Upon landing I turned on my phone and there was a text from my stepsister telling me to get there as soon as I could. He was barely hanging on and with a sinking feeling in my gut, I was sure I wasn't going to make it to him in time. I arrived alone at my parents' retirement community and was met by my brother-in-law who showed me the way to the skilled nursing unit my father was in. I had left my husband at the airport to get our luggage and rental car and I proceeded to take an Uber. I had to get to my dad as quickly as I could.

As we walked down the corridor to his room I could almost hear the strange quiet of death and each step I took. When I walked into his room I saw my stepsister and stepmother sitting there distraughtly. With a sigh of relief they looked up at me. He had waited. Oh thank God, he had waited.

As I glanced over at his bed I did a double take. That wasn't my dad. The man I was looking at was small, frail and looked so weak and, he had no facial hair at all. My dad was not small, frail and weak and he had worn a full beard and mustache as long as I could remember. When I was in high school, I was constantly told how much he looked just like Kenny Rogers. This was no Kenny Rogers and I had no idea who the man was lying in that bed. My stepsister had warned me that they had given my dad a shave but never in my wildest dreams did I picture this.

I took a deep breath, steadied myself, and walked over to kneel beside his bed. He knew I was there. The moment he heard my voice, he raised his eyebrows. His eyes were closed and he could not speak but he still found a way to say hello. I was given the gift of being able to tell him how much I loved him and that I would be okay because I knew he would always be with me. I told him I knew he was more than ready to go, thanked him for waiting for me, and softly kissed his cheek. Within moments, my daddy took his very last breath.

My stepsister and I sat at his side, her holding his hand and I with one hand on his head and the other on his chest. I could feel each of his final heartbeats as they became slower and slower until at last, his heart just stopped. Being with my father when he died was one of the most beautiful moments of my life and I will never question again whether he loved me. In that moment I received it. Time stopped and the years of pain washed through me, a calm feeling rushed me and it was love, *I finally got it.* I feel his unconditional love wrapped around me all the time now and he likes to show me regularly that he is with me. Be it the hummingbird in the backyard, feathers placed in my path, or a penny found in a parking lot, I know he is never far away and just when I am missing him the most, he will appear in my dreams just to say hello.

As I look back now it is in wonder and awe that I made it from where I once was to where I am today. The little girl of yesterday is at last happy, accepted, and at peace and the woman I've become is independent, strong, and not afraid of much. I stand up for myself and what I believe in unabashedly. I face things head on, I speak my truth, and I admit out loud when I am wrong. I now have boundaries where there once were none and I am very clear about what I will and will not allow in my life. I am a public speaker and ironically this was a very real reason why I flunked out of college all those decades ago. Back then, just the thought of speaking in public would make me want to hide and throw up.

All my life and I do mean *all* my life, I had been fighting to get what I want, fighting to get what I need, fighting to get ahead, and fighting to stay ahead. Somewhere deep inside of me I believed that was how you got and received love. You fought for it. I was wrong. Love is the one thing in life we shouldn't have to fight for. Love does not require giving up our dignity and self-worth or living against our values, morals, and beliefs. It does not require having your boundaries repeatedly broken down, trampled upon or disregarded. What love does require, though, is loving yourself enough to not compromise on any of the above. It means honoring yourself enough to ask for what you want, what you need and what you deserve. It means it is okay to be unapologetically yourself. It means that you only compromise when it is a conscious choice and not because it is driven by fear. It means that you love yourself and therefore can receive love from others. When I finally learned to love me, stop being scared all the time, and stop focusing on what everyone else was doing or not doing, I laid down my sword and my shield, surrendered to what was, and started living life on my own terms.

It is hard for me to pinpoint the moment this transformation became my normal. When I think back to where I was and how far I've come in this life, I feel like a superhero. A marvel who truly had it within her the whole time. Now, exactly what was the marvel moment? Of that I am not sure. Was it taking the action and doing whatever it took to overcome my stress and anxiety? Was it moving out of the home and house I loved after living there for eighteen-plus years and starting over in a friend's rental house? Is it striving every day to come from a place of grace and forgiveness while co-parenting with my ex-husband? Was it deciding to go to college and receiving my degree in Psychology exactly thirty years after my high school graduation? Was it when I said to myself, while sitting in my first coach training, that I wanted to be a coach and facilitator and now I am living that dream? Was it taking one full year after my divorce to date myself and not anyone else, so I could figure out who I am and what I really wanted and then, articulating it to the world and expecting to get it? Was it putting the caption "Looking For Someone Worthy" up on an online dating site and fully expecting no one to reply? Is it believing in love again and knowing it is true because I have the courage to ask for what I really want? Or, is it as simple as not playing the victim anymore, taking responsibility for my own happiness and well-being, refusing to give my power away to anyone, and realizing that to be hopeful and grateful in all things is to be a lifelong learner and appreciator of all we experience in this life?

As Maya Angelo once said, "When we know better, we do better." I learned so many lessons from my first husband and marriage and I am extremely thankful. I learned that we all do the best we can with what we've got. I learned that we sometimes hurt the ones we love, and I learned that forgiveness is the best gift we can give ourselves and others. I learned that with hope, just about anything is possible; and I learned that when we are true to ourselves, and hold ourselves accountable to that, then we have no trouble being true to others. I learned that I can love and trust again. I learned there is not one moment of my life that I would change. Not a single one, as each experience was crafting the person I have become. And, I learned that dreams do come true.

In January of 2019, I packed up my downtown office filling a small box with all my little trinkets, books, coaching tools, and a ton of amazing memories. This was my last day of working for a community college and the first day of giving myself permission to work for myself, live my truth, and finally trust, love, and accept myself in a way I never had. And, I had given myself a celebration gift that seemed indulgent and yet something I was being called to do. I was headed to Sedona, Arizona, for a writing retreat. I had no idea what to expect but from what I knew of the writing coach and others who had attended prior, I was in for something beyond amazing.

When I drove up to where I was staying it looked like a scene from a movie. A big, beautiful, picturesque house was sitting just beyond a gate entrance at the bottom of a dirt road. The home was wrapped in large green lawns, brilliant red rocks, and in one section of the grounds there was a lovely pond that beckoned to show you your reflection in the glassy water. Big trees all around whispered, "Sit on me," and the sound of chipmunks and squirrels eating their daily feast harmonized with the birds bantering back and forth. I would have sworn I was in Heaven.

Early one morning I ventured out back to bask in the Sedona sun. The weather was perfect as there was no chill in the air on this warm and beautiful January day. The brilliant red rock commanded my attention the moment I stepped outside. As I looked up and around at all of the majestic beauty, I was instantly taken captive by the vibrant, clear blue sky and in that moment, *I knew.* I knew I had finally made to it where I was being guided to all along. Tranquility ran through my entire body. Tears of love and pure joy sprung from my eyes and a sense of true belonging washed over me. My vision had been blurry for most of my lifelong journey and, at many times I had no direction or idea where I was going, yet standing there, I unquestionably knew that I had finally found my way.

Karen Ann Boise is a coach, trainer, and consultant who works with individuals to master confidence. As the owner of Compelling Exploration, she offers her propriety H.O.P.E. Intensive Group Program and facilitates workshops that open the conversations of *honest, open, possible exploration.* She believes that being self-assured and confident at work, in our relationships, and in our lives is the key to reaching goals and fulfilling dreams. On the personal side, Karen loves hanging out with her husband, Scott, and sons, Zach and Sammy, and close friends. She enjoys traveling, trying new things, and reading, and she strives to always enjoy life and be happy. Connect with her via email, karen@compellingexploration.com, or visit her website, www.compellingexploration.com.

The Lady in Blue:
Unveiling Soul Magic

M. Jacquelyn Simpson

"They tried to bury us. They didn't know we
were seeds."—Dinos Christianopoulos

The first time I attempted to die was by swallowing prescription
pain killers. I was only twelve, but I knew my pain could not
be relieved with one or two tablets. My pain needed the full bottle.

I was birthed into all manner of darkness. My being born,
during the darkest part of the night, was a telling coincidence. The
other forms of darkness would not be resolved with the rising sun.

My mother had been nannied by voodoo queens, where she
learned the power of séances and casting spells and curses. During
her childhood in New Orleans, she gathered with her mother and
nanny in a darkened room. The black candle would flicker as the
Ouija board was anointed with oil to conjure the lowest spirits.
They would read the litany of the dead, send curses, and ultimately
pledge allegiance to the dark forces.

She brought those talents and alliances with her when she
married. They were waiting for me as I matured in the womb.

I would hear the story of my birth often. The story of my
mother screaming in anger, because her obstetrician refused her
medication, so close to my birth. The pain was not too intense,
but the anger at being denied what she wanted made her cuss and
yell. My mother's anger overshadowed my birth.

Four days later, we went home in a cab, because my father refused to pick us up at St. Joseph's Hospital. I don't know how she explained that to the nurse who rolled us out. I am sure my mother covered her humiliation with a lie. My mother was used to living with humiliation. She already had two sons, whose birth had dragged her into motherhood, which she described as *frustrating* and *degrading*.

She vented her frustration on my brothers with a belt.

When I was born, everything changed. I brought beauty into their lives, with smiles, a head full of black hair and my eyes that studied faces with deep concentration. I was an inquisitive baby that learned quickly.

My father declared me the most beautiful baby in the world. He would carry me in his strong arms for hours as he paced the floor.

My mother nursed me at her breast with the contentment of a mother's job well done.

I imagine I felt loved.

By the time I was three, I was feeling the slap of the belt on my naked thighs.

My mother loved babies, but didn't like children. Each infant she brought into the world would enjoy a few years of idyllic babyhood, then we would abruptly become the enemy.

She would go into a rage grabbing a paddle or hairbrush, hitting us wherever she could reach. I was slapped across my face, so many times as a child that I could not stand to have my face touched, even by a friend, well into my adulthood.

Too young to know what the word "jealous" meant, I could feel it with the sharp sting across my face. Whenever my mother's friends would comment on my beauty, it meant a slap as soon as they left. Jealousy, a short fuse, and frustration all intermingled as I was hurt without cause.

I did not cry out in pain, so another slap would follow the first, as she tried to break my will. Years later, I would discover the magic that kept my tears from flowing and my face from being scarred.

Mom was the most vicious, but she did not stand alone.

Every Saturday morning my father would spank us. Cartoons would be interrupted as he stormed into the room yelling at us to be quiet. Then with his electrical-engineer precision, he would start with the oldest. This basement with cinderblock walls and concrete floors looked like the other normal suburban houses, but as it shrunk around me, I knew I was alone, unsafe from the rage of my parents.

I trembled as I waited. By the time it was my turn, the room was pressing in on my shoulders. I was defenseless, as dad's big, powerful hand would smack against my underwear with fierceness.

The hitting never let up, even into my late teens. My mother blamed her "temper" for the beatings. Sometimes she would come to me late at night, crying and asking for forgiveness, her brown eyes deeply pained. I wanted so much to believe she loved me. She wanted to emote her pain, without relieving mine.

I grew numb inside, as I learned that words are empty and actions are truth.

The abuse that cut more deeply was the humiliation and ridicule.

My mother had a searing way with words, sometimes sarcastic, often cruel. She'd scream that I was lazy and stupid. That I was a whore, long before I knew what that meant. She used weird deep southern racial slurs, including her infamous line: "They wouldn't let me have slaves, that's why I had children."

My mother and father were matched in their darkness and I was far too young to understand the story behind this. My father was not a loud man and his words were few. Often, he would look at me with disgust and mutter, "You are too pretty for your own good." None of this was questioned, because we were taught to treat our parents with blind obedience.

I lived trapped in a maze of lies and ridicule. *What does a child become when this is their normal?*

The food pantry was always running low, to the point that we would eat sugar sandwiches for breakfast. Lunch? It was out of the question. We usually went to school with an empty brown bag. We carried that bag and pretended to eat, so we would not have to admit that our parents didn't supply us with bread and peanut butter. I often volunteered to help with school chores during lunch to avoid my lack of food from being discovered by the other kids.

We were not poor, we were just not cared for.

I felt unloved, like a dog left in the streets. This was my life and only glimpses of the outside world said to me, "This is not a normal family."

How does one survive all this pain and still find the light?

Even with all the abuse, my early childhood was not totally miserable. I played with my brothers in the morning, while my mother slept past noon. Our toys were usually household items, making forts made out of blankets and spaceships out of over-turned chairs. One summer my favorite toy was a pile of bricks, which we made into a variety of challenge games by assembling them in our yard. The bricks knew no boundaries. They doubled as a path to Utopia and a wall of protection. With them I could build an imaginary world reflecting my dreams and it left me feeling accomplished.

Unsupervised we were allowed to do anything, as long as we didn't wake my mother. "Swashbuckling pirates" was a game we played, sword fighting with long kitchen knives. Being smaller and younger, I never won the game, usually just dropping the knife and running out of the kitchen.

Except, one morning my brother, Eddie, grabbed my knife, up close to the wooden part and I pulled it toward me, leaving a deep cut between his thumb and finger. I got in trouble for that, because his screams woke my mother and my parents needed to take him to the hospital for stitches.

Many years later, Mom and I sat across a small cafeteria table and she asked me if any part of my childhood was happy. I looked at her brown eyes, now dulled by depression brought on by years of torment by her own shadow side. Part of me wanted to flippantly slough off the question with a joke and another part wanted to be honest.

I thought back and told her about the happy days I spent in the hospital when I was five. I wasn't sick or really seriously injured; I had been admitted to the hospital for observation after tumbling off the back of the couch onto the concrete floor, during another game of fantasy. The blonde nurse treated me so nicely and brought me real toys to play with in my "high crib." I was well fed and cuddled.

She always smiled at me and never once hit me; even when I hugged her so hard, she couldn't get away. I felt liked, maybe even loved. She showed me I was worthy of being cared for, not just "the trouble" I was at home.

I didn't know I was a healer, but even at five, I knew I wanted to grow up to be just like my blonde nurse. And because she showed me I was valuable I believed I could.

As I sat in the cafeteria with my mom, even though I was an adult with children of my own, I dared not tell her about my greatest childhood joy, because I did not want her to diminish my memories of visits from "The Lady in Blue."

I remember her first visit. I was just three or four, scared, and cold, as I lay in my bed in the dark room. Then suddenly, somewhere in the restless night, the light behind my closed eyelids started to brighten. I began to feel warm, as if a loving mother had placed a cozy blanket over the thin, scratchy army blanket covering my trembling form.

I felt "washed" by love. I giggled a bit at the thought of love being able to wash you, like soap and water in a bathtub.

But it did. I felt I had been washed of the pain and fear.

I lay there feeling warm and safe.

Then I opened my eyes.

The Lady in Blue stood at the end of my bunk bed. She made no sound, but said everything. I felt her love for me and *knew* I wanted to be part of the stream of love.

Another friend came to me from the heavens: I knew him as Angel John. And he was quite talkative. I loved his grand lessons of universal wisdom, explaining about earth life and how it was a part of heaven life, but people didn't always understand that. John also talked to me about my personal path. He assured me I would grow to be a healthy, loving mom and that he would always walk by my side.

Although, my spirit friends usually came to me in the night, I learned to wait for their voice or presence when I was sitting alone in a tree. John would encourage me with his words, and The Lady in Blue showed me visions of my future life. She would open her robe and allow her gown to become a backdrop, what looked like a foggy movie. I'd see my future self as healthy, happy and fulfilled. The details were hazy, but the story line was clear. In the future, I would be talking to people and angels at the same time, by interpreting heaven language into earth language. They both told me the world was changing and I was to be part of the change.

One late afternoon, I lazily laid against the crook of the maple tree, when I heard John's voice. It was a bit sad and apologetic, not like the upbeat tempo I was used to since I was a baby from my wise teacher.

John explained to me that he was doing his best to lessen the pain from my mother's blows.

Years later, I was able to fully realize that it was my spirit friends' protective haze that allowed me to hold strong, without tears. I believe it was the way my mother understood that I was of the Light... just as strongly as she was of the Dark, which pitted her against me.

I didn't know how, but I did know why. I was chosen because My connection to God was completely natural. Using today's lingo, I was born "hard wired" to spirit.

The Lady in Blue visited me often and told me that someday I would become the brightest light in the night sky, allowing other children to find their protector in me. The feel of her love and steady presence brought me through many beatings and beratings of my childhood.

I soon learned my protector to be the Blessed Mother of Baby Jesus. I still call her My Lady in Blue.

She told me over and over that I was loved.

I believed her.

The spirit world had stepped in to save my human life. It was all I had and felt absolutely natural to trust it. This spiritual communication was a type of growth, just like learning to walk or talk. Blessedly, in my earliest years, I was taught by the Blessed Mother, the meaning of love and integrity.

Does one fully escape darkness when they have found the light?
When I was eight, I made a mistake that paralyzed me for years.

I realized that not everyone had ongoing communication with the angels. I grew concerned about my being so different, maybe teetering on crazy. I had no one to ask, except my mother.

So, I asked, "Mom, John is an angel I speak to about my future. Is he real or am I just imagining him?"

My mother instantly scolded me, saying of course it is my imagination and I should never tell anyone about John.

I wasn't sure if she was right, I just knew I should keep it a secret.

The next day I overheard her say to a friend, "Oh, she is such a stupid girl! She thinks her imaginary friend is real."

Those words sent icy cold shivers through my body. Now, I was scared. The love was disappearing into thin air. The one friend I could count on for truth and guidance was Angel John, but now he was a liability. I was a young child and I had to choose my battles very carefully.

In my family being stupid was the lowest level you could sink to.

Stealing, lying, cheating were small crimes, compared to the worse, which was always, "You were stupid enough to get caught."

Being stupid was dangerous.

So far, I was smart enough to avoid some of the most severe beatings by knowing hiding places when mom was on a rampage. I was smart enough to be aware that a wrong answer could bring on pain and to never, ever question my parents' methods.

I stopped communicating with my Angel John, not because I outgrew him or stopped believing. I stopped talking to him because stupid could get me seriously injured. My mother's response may have been cruel, but in fact, it was my own shutdown of my spiritual gifts that paralyzed my growth for a number of years. I stopped listening to John and totally lost my sense of security.

I still prayed and felt great comfort in sliding into the back of the church before school, as well as going for Sunday mass.

I had a special devotion to The Blessed Mother, but I no longer felt like she was my personal guide or protector. The amazing spiritual connection I felt with The Lady in Blue was now stunted into basic religious views of spirit and human being disconnected. I would beg for help, but not expect it, because "bad girls" don't deserve unconditional love.

How does darkness try to take over?

Groggy and disoriented, I walked to the bathroom in the middle of the night. As I took a few steps my underwear dropped to the floor. I was too groggy to figure out how. I stepped into the bathroom, where my older brother was sitting on the toilet with his underpants down around his ankles, but oddly the toilet bowl was covered with the lid.

I became the prey.

When I told my mother that Eddie had cut my underwear as I slept, she told me that brothers get curious and often touch their younger sisters. She warned me not to tell anyone, don't yell, and just wait it out. Her older brother used to wake her up in the morning by straddling her and playing "bouncy-bounce" against her bottom.

My mother's advice against incest to this tender, naïve nine-year-old, was to wait it out and if he gets too far, just pretend you are waking up, so he will go away. Not only was I my brother's prey: I was set up by my mother to be *easy prey*.

I later learned that my mother had a childhood of being easy prey. My grandmother allowed older men to caress my mother's young budding breast for money. She also had her dance burlesque style in scanty outfits as a small child of only six or seven.

My mother's life had been filled with darkness and she expected I would carry on the family legacy.

When my brother would stealth into my room and touch me or rub his body against mine, I felt like I had swallowed glass and it was ripping apart my insides. So, I would count slowly to ten, then start over again, until the numbers had no meaning and I was numb in body and mind.

For three years, I was unprotected in my own bed. There was no Lady in Blue, no Angel John. There was no one, and I slipped into a deep cave of despair.

My mother's beatings had escalated to blood. My brother's touching was becoming so aggressive, I feared being raped. I had no one. Killing myself was the only way out. It became so overpowering that it was all that was left inside of me.

After I swallowed the pills, I lay on my bed with the wisdom of my twelve years and celebrated. I would never again feel the slaps to my face or the kicks to my stomach. I lay in the bed that had witnessed my humiliation of being a helpless female and now it would give witness to my one act of bravery. I did not fear death, even death by suicide. Even though I had stopped talking to the angels years before, I remembered their lesson, that God was pure love. I was going to get to this love if it meant leaving my body behind.

I didn't die.

There was no big rush to the hospital or stomach pumping. I woke up with a bit of disappointment and a lot of determination. I figured if narcotics couldn't kill me, I was much tougher than I was being told. I knew I had one true friend, confidant, and powerhouse: myself.

I felt so much larger. I shed the feeling of helplessness and lack. I suddenly felt as if a new woman had entered into my life and was taking charge of my desperate situation.

I realized I truly was a child of God and God would not abandon me, even though I was born into darkness to a family consumed with regret and suffering.

I would never become them and knowing that gave me great strength.

I took every morsel of self-respect I could muster and added it to my inner strengths, much like a savings account of self-worth. I felt free.

I had evolved from despair to anger. Despair wanted me to die, but anger gave me the propulsion to live.

This Divine Intervention, showed on my face and in my actions. I was not a new person; instead I was a greatly enhanced version of myself. I was creating my own reality and I would take no prisoners.

My mother noticed my new powerful attitude. She scornfully spit out the words "the worm has turned" to Eddie, realizing that I would no longer be such easy prey.

Immediately, without my saying a word, my brother stopped molesting me.

I also started to stand up to my mother, at least behind her back. I started writing my own rules of what was morally correct and no longer accepted anything she said as valuable or even truthful. This was still a defense mechanism but one that worked well.

I didn't yet have the physical or mental power to make her stop hurting my body, but she never hurt my psyche or heart again.

I started drinking with purpose. I would slip in and take a hit from the bottle of rum before I had to have a conversation with my parents. Without them seeing I'd slide the rum bottle back under the counter where it stayed, the burn of the rum still on my tongue; I was now on fire and nothing could stop me. This bit of liquid courage was the only sort of self- medicating I fell into. Drugs were widely available in my school, but I always turned them down. I knew I wanted to have children and wanted my physical temple to be healthy for my babies.

I became an avid liar, mainly out of self-protection, but also so I could slip away and visit with my friends. When I was fifteen, I would use those same talented lies to slip away to date an older, married man. Luckily, I still had my virginity to give to him.

The system I had crafted to keep me "empowered" started to break down. It was like the alcohol, liquid courage. I was surviving the dysfunctional family I was born into, but I was now creating my own suffering. Even though the brief glimpses into my "later path" encouraged me, I was so far off that I was truly lost in the woods.

Everywhere I looked I saw anger, fear, and dishonesty. I had no mentors. I saw family harmony as a rare bird that I would spot at a friend's house or in books. I read as much as a could, but *never* ran across a book that showed a girl going from being beaten and molested into a happy life. In the books, girls that were abused became hate-filled and wild. They became prostitutes or if they were very lucky and beautiful, they became someone's wife and had their own children to beat.

Walking was the best therapy I had access to. Walking away from my house, alone or with my sweet, furry blonde mutt, Chow-Chow, I felt free and light. Something so simple as walking and distance can change a life. On my walks, I made plans for the future and found my encouragement with every small flower or butterfly. When I returned within view of my house, my heart became cold and the words from so many years ago rushed into my head: "Don't Be Stupid." I knew I was residing in a prison without an exit.

I knew I would leave the house as soon as I turned eighteen. But leaving the house, would not free me from this self-imposed prison I was building around myself. It was against my code of ethics to date a married man or even have sex before marriage. I was scared of any addiction, as I watched my mother smoke three packs a day. I was locking myself into a cell of pain and self-destruction with alcohol and heartbreaking confusion. What had started with a clear, empowered vision was now murky. I had lost sight of the path toward Love.

With the same determination that bolstered me to take pills at twelve, I went face to face with this downward spiral. I would rather be dead than descend into the abyss of self-hate and psychogenic suffering. I had found power in distancing myself from those who didn't understand love, but I had not found a way to live from love, the pain inside was overbearing.

It was a warm, cloudless day in May when I dropped to my knees. I felt the wet grass on my legs, soaking through my jeans. I knelt there and looked up at St. Bernadette Catholic Church.

The white marble of the church blared its purity against the green grass before me. I prayed out of frustration and fear: "Dear God I know this is not my path. Lead me to where I am to go." I paused, trying to conjure a more complete, more articulate prayer.

Nothing came to my mind or my heart. Silence.

I walked away, not knowing that I had just opened myself to Spiritual Guidance and changed the trajectory of my life.

Spirit does not show us the full road map and expect us to remember all the twists and turns along the path. Spirit gives us one step, and as we take it, we are laying claim to our life path and declaring our trust in divine wisdom. I was given a few steps, without any immediate reward. I went to an audition for a local play and didn't get the part. I went to Gino's Hamburger shop and met a nice man, who didn't ask me out. I kept listening and kept stepping and knew the path was lighted... all I needed to do was keep paying attention.

I stand at the edge of my front yard, the summer grass deeply green and the air sweetly fragrant with the smell of honeysuckle. My mother is inside, and for these moments I am away from the angst. Within a week of my surrender to God's Will and the Divine Guidance along my path, something has happened to me. I didn't realize the vastness of these changes, but for the first time, I am truly happy.

I had met a young man named, Tom, and now I see a different side of love. Sandy blond and muscular, he is tall with the perfect posture of a young Marine. He smiles easily and often laughed at his own stories. It turns out, he wanted to ask me out when we first met at Gino's Hamburgers.

Two months later I'm poised there on the grass with a smile slowly coming to life, because I know that Tom will be driving up soon, as he has every day since we started dating on June 20th. As I turn my back to the street, he rounds the corner. I am so excited and so overwhelmed by his love for me, that I am afraid that I will jump toward the car as it comes alongside the curb. In rapid succession the engine cuts off, Tom jumps out of the car, the door slams and he is holding me in his arms. This is the most delicious, most amazing experience I have ever had. The caterpillar is about to burst from the shell.

Too good to be true?

He holds me, kisses me and we exist truly in the bliss-filled bubble of young love. Our bodies respond to each other with the delicious tingle of romantic heat.

"I love you," Tom whispers in my ear as I become immersed in joy.

"I can't wait until we are married, so we can be together all the time," I say, feeling lifted by the prospect of us creating a life together. I am only seventeen, but I know he is The One. We had already gotten engaged, just two weeks after our first date.

"I want you to be the mother of my children," he tells me.

I have wanted to hold my own babies in my arms since I held my baby sister when I was five, and yet I hesitate.

This I need to answer, *this* I need to address with Tom.

"Tom, I don't know how to be a good mother."

All this is said and we are still standing in the front yard.

"Don't worry about it," he answers me with the simplicity that I will learn to appreciate. "Until they are five, we just need to love them and by then we will figure it out."

The simplicity and logic hit me… he's right. Parenthood is complex, but when it is based in love it is doable, even for us, two kids, raised by wolves. Tom's mother used to beat him with a high heel shoe and kick him out of the house when she was in a drunken rage.

Tom and I tried to elope, but it imploded.

We had dated for five months and ached when we were apart. He had been at my house every day and we always talked long into the night. We were carefully chaperoned by my mother. It was a weird dichotomy that she was concerned about my having sex with my fiancé, but never protected me from being molested as a child.

When we did get out alone, there were fireworks!

Even with all that heat, we would communicate our hopes and plans, in between our love making. We understood and accepted each other's past, although I never mentioned to him that I had been molested by my brother and felt unloved by my parents. Some secrets are just too painful to bring out on a date.

My relationship with my mother was still dismal; she was the dark and I had cut the cord long ago. Tom had met me shortly after one of her tirades where she had dug her fingernails into my cheek, drawing blood, and kicked me in the stomach, bruising my spleen. He was not shocked at the violence, because he had grown up with a violent, alcoholic mother.

When Tom proposed at my house on the Fourth of July, we planned to wait two years to get married. But Tom was ready and just three months later he said, "Let's get married today". We didn't get married that day, but we did get our license.

Now the race was on. Tom was eager and I had been ready for years to say goodbye to my biological family, and the world I grew up in.

Is True Love a way out of the darkness for good?

We were married at St. Patrick's church with a hodge-podge of immediate family, who had found out just the day before that we were going to elope by meeting with a priest there to marry us. Just twenty-four hours before, my mother discovered the small suitcase I had packed. She screamed and cussed over the phone to everyone she could reach, including Father Callahan, who was to marry us the next day. She didn't want to permanently stop the marriage; she just wanted control. She threatened to lock me in the basement and tried to manipulate me by yelling, "This is so embarrassing! What will I tell my friends?" She saw my planned elopement as a direct defiance of her power to threaten me with pain or shame.

In a weird twist of parenting, my father stood up for me, saying I could marry Tom. Then he let me down by looking directly at Tom and adding, "You know she can be a real bitch to live with."

I was seventeen, marrying a twenty-three-year-old marine I had dated for less than five months. No one even tried to fake "loving concern" for me.

My father was grateful to get rid of a daughter, especially one who was "too pretty for her own good."

On November 6th, he drove me to the church, without a word. I sat in the front seat, an unusual feel since kids belonged in the back. My prayer was simple, as simple as the one in front of St. Bernadette's, just six months ago: "Dear God, if I am to marry Tom, let us get there safely. If I am not, stop me now."

The car stopped in front of the bell tower of my church. When I saw the bell on the church steeple waiting there in silence, my heart beat faster and faster. I was ready.

Father Callahan tried to placate my mother's seething rage and calm Tom's mother's alcoholic tantrum, without success. Our wedding had brought out the worst in each of them.

Perhaps a true elopement would have been easier, but for me, my married life needed to start with a commitment to God, not to the state, so a priest was necessary. I decorated the church with two roses, one yellow and one pink, which I had cut from the front yard as I was leaving with my father. I placed them at the feet of the Blessed Mother statue with a whispered and tearful "Thank you for Loving me" to Mary, my Lady in Blue.

Father Callahan's Irish face broke into a reassuring smile, as he started the quick ceremony. Standing at the base of the altar, I could feel the daggers being embedded in my back coming from both moms. Those daggers just took their place alongside the others and they would remain there, relatively quiet for a number of years.

Tom and I moved to an apartment, which we mainly furnished with hand-me-downs. I enjoyed being able to create our home with used furniture, by dyeing old curtains and decorating with whimsical wall hangings we had bought during our honeymoon in Pennsylvania Dutch country.

Tom had reenlisted for three more years in the Marines, so we had a steady income, although it was not a generous one. Luckily, it included full medical, because we would need it.

By Christmas I was expecting our first baby.

Other people may have advised us to slow down, but I was listening to my inner spiritual guidance, not to popular wisdom.

When I strode across the stage for my high school graduation, Tom, my sister, Irene, and my father applauded, while under my gown, Baby Nichol kicked within me. My mother was still spitting mad. Not even the upcoming birth of her first grandchild was going to get her to forgive me for crossing her.

I had restarted my life in many ways. I was truly loved by this man.

I was speaking with my spirit guides again and I felt empowered. The "later path" was illuminated for me. The calling to be a healer became grounded within me, because without the darkness of my birth family, I was a new person with endless possibilities to blossom.

That May afternoon when I kneeled at St. Bernadette's had opened a door, one I'd feared had been bolted shut by my anger and shameful family karma. I had lowered my human ego and given permission for God to guide me. However, this was not a "big bang" that erased my past and locked me into the narrow path of goodness.

Not at all. Rather it gave me the tools to hear the deeper truths. It gave me the awareness of spiritual nudgings. My spiritual reawakening was a gradual incline of learning and on-job-training.

Step by step, day by day, I chose to become enlightened.

That short prayer at St. Bernadette's was the catalyst, which set "Us" in motion.

Over the years, I have learned that every human is constantly manifesting, though Universal Forces and Spirit Guides who love us unconditionally. Those guides are often Ascended Masters, who have walked this earth many times. They hold no malice toward us or negative judgment of our actions. They happily assist us to create whatever we are looking to embrace.

In addition to unconditional love, our Guides know what we want. They listen to our words, watch our actions and most importantly feel for our vibrations to get a complete picture.

Spirit Guides know the path of least resistance to receiving those desires into your life.

They see the world and all its being with all the moving parts, so they can create the path that aligns with your desires, with a pattern of quickest possible responses.

"*Dear God, I know this is not my path. Lead me to where I am to go*" was the short prayer that gave my spirit guides permission to intervene on my behalf. Indeed, to totally change my life, as I was gifted with their guidance, immediately and beneficially. Spiritual Communication is an ongoing process of speaking, listening, and acting. Whenever Spirit gave me action steps, I walked with faith and then I would receive the next action step. So, it required continual trust and forward movement to secure our spiritual connection.

I asked God to lead me and I met Tom within a week. We married within six months and over the years, raised four productive, happy children into adulthood. Our life has been adventurous and abundant; healthy and joyous.

We have had pain, because it is part of the human experience, but not long-term suffering.

We have made mistakes, but none of which became insurmountable problems.

We have been poor, but not hungry for the basic necessities.

We have been financially abundant, without becoming arrogant. It was not "too good to be true." It was the truest form of love firmly embraced. Through it all, we were loving, caring partners. Through it all, I listened to Spirit. I kept a pillow in our bedroom closet, so I could sit in the darkness and feel my spirit guides' presence, without distractions.

For three decades, my primary role was to be a protective mom. With each baby I was filled with love, gratitude and spiritual wisdom about their life path.

When I held my babies, I would drink in their smell and promise them my love and protection.

My firstborn had a full head of black hair and long toes. My arms wrapped around her tiny body, as I held her to my breast. Immediately, I was overjoyed with love for Nichol and gratitude to God. I knew I would always protect her.

That same night I had a terrifying nightmare.

I dreamt that my parents were trying to hurt me and my baby. I took a hairbrush and smacked them hard in their faces. Their faces started to crumble like an old china doll. They were lifeless.

I woke with a start and could feel my tears streaming down my face and onto my pillow.

Spirit explained to me, "You didn't kill them, you just uncovered the truth within them. They are hollow and hold no power over you. "

The nightmare had turned into an amazing gift of self-empowerment.

Every night I would kneel at each child's bed and whisper the same prayer: "Let them know the love of God." Although I raised them in the Catholic Church, my goal was to encourage a bond between The Divine and my child, regardless of which church, if any, they attended.

As our family grew, I would regularly hear the voice of divine guidance, although I had not developed the ongoing spiritual communication, which would more fully expand later.

The guides would tap on my consciousness with answers, about where to live or how to help a sick child. I could find wellness for my family through prayer. My family was my first practice zone for my healing gifts.

Often, I would hear Spirit counsel me about my marriage. It was clear that my past still lived in me and I wasn't yet completely free.

At times we argued, and within a short time, I would hear from Spirit:

"Jacquelyn, go to him."

My response was understandable. "No, Tom was wrong and he should apologize to me. He always does this, he never listens to me. Why am I *always* the one to break the silence? You never tell him to..."

My guides would speak clearly. "Jacquelyn, you don't have to apologize, just go to him, with a hug. Your togetherness is too important not to."

I knew it wasn't mathematically fair and I knew it was for the absolute best. So, without apology, I would hug Tom. The tension would be over and we could move forward.

Free will gives us the choice to accept the guidance or ignore it, without punishment. I listened and one night the directions from Spirit were crucial to my daughter's life.

Being a spiritually guided mother required much attention to the quiet nuances and connection to the sacred. Motherhood had taught me to hear the different inflection in people's voices and when I received a call from a teacher I heard fear in his voice as he explained that my Nichol, now sixteen, had been in an accident.

In absolute silence, I rode with Mrs. Apple down the dark, windy country road from our house to get to Nichol. Mrs. Apple was a wonderful neighbor and I had no car with me at the time. The only illumination was from houses lit with Christmas lights.

As we rounded the curve, the bright lights burned like bleach into my eyes. So many blindingly bright spotlights, staring down into one small area of the narrow road. It was eerily quiet, as no cars other than the one I was being escorted in were allowed on the road.

Upon turning the curve, I saw that our car was crushed, but worse, the windshield was shattered, where a tree had crashed through to hit my child's face. I stumbled from the car and ran in a panic to the ambulance. There were so many paramedics surrounding her gurney, they didn't notice me. Their hands and instruments moved fast and their words were sharp. Again I recognized the fear.

Blood streamed down her face, with a crushed eye socket, her mouth oddly tipping to the side, like a stroke victim.

"I'm her mother," I called out to the medics. Not one person acknowledged me; not one set of eyes would meet mine; not one word of encouragement, only a fearful warning: "we have to leave NOW."

Nichol couldn't see me but she could hear me... "I'm here Nichol. I am going to ride up with the driver. I will not leave you." The nearby hospital was not equipped with a shock-trauma unit, so once she was stabilized the hospital would transfer her. I had my hand on Nic's shoulder as she lay in the emergency room; I wanted her to feel my presence, hear my reassurances, and know I loved her.

A nurse with a clipboard looked at me and asked, "Which shock-trauma center do you prefer we send your daughter to, Johns Hopkins or York?"

This question had no basis for an answer. I had decided on virtually every part of Nichol's life from her name to the decision to let her drive dad's car tonight, but never had I thought I would have fifteen seconds to answer, *Which hospital do you trust to repair your daughter's crushed face, eyesight, teeth and maybe her chest and lungs?*

As I had so many times before for lesser requests, I asked for divine guidance. My vision quickly pinpointed down to one nurse. My intense focus blocked out everything else, as I asked her, "Where should I send my daughter?"

Without hesitation, she said, "York Shock-Trauma. Johns Hopkins is more well known, but York is better for this." I knew God has spoken through this earth angel. I agreed to York and then she added, "My husband is head of trauma and I will call him right away and give him all the details."

At York Hospital, there were so many decisions, for which I was totally unprepared. As each question came up, I breathed into the fear and handed it to God. *Who, what, where and when?* It was so complicated in scope, because of her multiple wounds and broken bones, yet it became clear, as I listened to my spirit guides, who cradled me with assurances that she would heal.

I would slip into the quiet hospital chapel, close my eyes, and ask for a miracle. There are an amazing number of Spirit Guides and they have their specialties. Archangel Raphael would inspire the surgeons, perhaps even directly assist their hands. The Blessed Mother would comfort me, with her warm hugs and soothing words. Many of the guides I didn't know by name, but I learned to feel for their presence and vibrations of love.

Even as the plastic surgeon asked for Nichol's school picture, so he could reassemble her face, I trusted through the pain. It was my job to explain the surgical process to her father. He was Tom to me but for this devastating conversation, he stood as her daddy. I prayed for the best words and spirit whispered them in my ear as I spoke them to Daddy-Tom. We stood facing each other cornered in by the sterile, white-washed walls of the hospital. I had stepped into the hall, so Nichol wouldn't hear the gruesome details of her upcoming surgeries. Tom's eyes showed fear and I knew it was my work to help him let that fear go, to let the light come into him. He was so protective of Nichol and now I was asking him to step aside to let God handle our greatest family trauma.

I took a deep breath, locked my eyes onto Tom's, and spoke. The words flowed through my mind and out my mouth. I had lived for this moment. At that moment, spirit and human melded into one consistent flow of wisdom.

I knew the angels were assisting the various doctors to suture her wounds, reconstruct her face and carefully lift shards of bone off her optic nerve. She was no longer in critical danger, but it would be a year before the vision in her eye was clear. They let me take her home early, so she could be home for Christmas. The presents were stacked under the tree where I had left them almost a week before.

Nichol was a beautiful sixteen-year-old girl, who spent quite a bit of time with makeup and hairstyles in front of her mirror. Her little brother's gift was a small ornate mirror. Nichol gasped when she saw her swollen face filled with stitches. Again, I asked spirit for the perfect words of comfort. Nichol and I walked silently into my bedroom and stood in front of a full-length mirror. Spirit guided me to start by showing her the strength of her body, which had come through a life-and-death accident, very much alive and healthy. Her mind was sharp and there was no brain damage. Finally, after many assurances, Spirit said it was time for her to acknowledge her face. As I looked in the mirror, I saw her face morphing from infancy through now and into the future.

Sadly, Nichol could only see the now. Nichol is not one for fluffy words and Spirit nudged me to speak as a healer, rather than her mother. I gently traced where the scars would shrink and become fine white lines and how her eyes would align once the swelling was down. I told her that her jaw would be wired next week to bring the bottom of her face into its natural balance. As a healer I had learned how to put things in perspective, to step back and let my inner guidance evaluate each circumstance; now I was to lead in this way as a mother. Though this might seem like a challenge, it helped me a great deal in mothering my earth children. Nichol would grow to be beautiful and strong.

THE LATER PATH

Eventually came my plunge into listening from the inside, where my guides could reach me with more succinct messages. With that clarity, I trusted more and began to have deeper experiences.

One morning, I woke up and told Tom we needed to move to Nebraska for a job he had turned down two weeks earlier. He asked me why and I respectfully told him the truth, "God spoke to me in my dreamtime." *Tom worked in Lincoln for eight lucrative and productive years.*

When one of the kids had a tummy ache or Tom had a headache, I would speak to them in a very soothing voice, relaxing them. Then I would pray over them, asking for wellness.

This meditative healing practice would cure a headache, bring down a fever and calm an anxious heart.

When a child asked for prayers for a test in school, I would promise to pray for whatever was for their best and highest good. Usually, they would protest, saying I should just pray for them to get an A. *I explained that asking for what was best for you was far more valuable than a test score. Often our greatest lessons are learned in the pauses and redirecting that detrimental actions cause us to take.*

These were the foundations of my daily spiritual life and a precursor to the life I, once the children were launched, would more fully develop as a meditative healer and a spiritual coach.

Unfortunately, there was still one massive destructive force blocking my path.

Katie, was the first mystic I knew. Young and bubbly, she was born with the gift to speak to spirits. It was divine intervention that I met her, at that time, when I was already studying religions, yoga, and energy healing. My children were all living on their own and I had the time, talent, and temperament to launch my newest rendition of being me.

Katie was smiling as we sipped tea and chatted, until she asked me, "Why are you so sad?"

I started to cry, because my daughter, Nichol, was in an unhealthy marriage and as always, I wanted what was for everyone's best and highest good, especially my two very young grandchildren.

The information she gave me was amazing and amazingly accurate.

Over the next few months she opened my eyes to the very wide expanse of deep spiritual conversations. Before Katie's lessons, I had misunderstood that spiritual communication was to be only Spirit-directed, seldom initiated by me. Spirit would give me advise or answer a simple request. I was playing small, because I didn't know any better. Once I embraced the power within me to be able to have full conversations, with nuances and details, I saw the "later path" start to open more fully.

One evening, I mentioned to Katie that my now deceased parents had hated me. The words seemed harsh, but what else would you call that sort of neglect and abuse?

Katie explained that they were doing "the best they could with the tools they had," a phrase I would repeat often to many people. Instead of placating me and moving on, she said "Jacqui, I want you to see the therapist who helped me a great deal to work through my childhood difficulties and be able to open my heart."

Katie must be wrong, I thought. I left home over thirty years ago and discarded all that pain, like you would an old, tattered doll. I promised her I would see the therapist, Helen, for a session or two, to clear up any lingering bits from my psyche. But I had my doubts. I had buried my past so deep I was certain it was gone—dead—and there was no way it was still alive inside of me.

I can't say Helen "saved my life," because I was no longer suicidal.

The first time I tried to die I was twelve years old, because my life was filled with evil, pain and abuse. The first time I tried to die was the last time, because God saved me from despair, by showing me my own power as a human and as a spiritual being.

I *can* say Helen "gave me a new life," but first she had to dig through the rubble of my old one. She had to help me unearth the darkness and hold it up to the light; it was only then that I could free myself completely.

Of course, it was not one or two sessions, it was a weekly session for two years and then a monthly session for two more. Helen asked a bunch of personal, direct, zinger-type questions, which I was not prepared to answer. Starting with my name. When I explained that I had legally changed my first name, so that I would not be continually reminded of my mother, whom I was named after, she was not surprised. She did ask why I still carried around my mother-induced scars if I didn't want to be reminded of her and my painful childhood.

If I didn't want to be reminded of my mother, why had I lowered my own expectations of self-empowerment? Why had I agreed to be neutral, when I was scheduled to be a spiritual guru and mystic? Now, Helen did not ask all these questions during our first sessions, but these and others surfaced quickly.

I remember when the sessions really sped up. I had lied to her about my sexual past. Just a bold-faced, scared-child lie. I had only told Tom and never in great detail. I called her later that day and left a voicemail:

"Helen, this is Jacqui. I lied to you in therapy today. I panicked out of fear and shame. It makes no sense to see a therapist and not be honest to her. I want my childhood to be cleared out of my system. I will never lie to you again."

Therapy with Helen included talking about my childhood and unearthing the self-destructive traits I had bought into my adulthood. I realized the tightly knotted rope with which I had tied down my childhood was fraying. I was having ugly dreams and anxiety attacks, of screaming, while I beat my steering wheel. I had leapt from being an occasional drinker to five-plus vodkas a night. In hindsight I see the depression and fear was surfacing, as it often does when we decide to clean out our emotional closet. My adulthood was so much more loving and abundant than my early years that I hadn't considered the possibility that I could be even happier and more spiritually productive.

Helen thought it was unhealthy that I had absolutely no friends. I never really thought about it. Tom was my friend; did I need others? I went to yoga three times a week, but never asked any of the girls to grab a coffee with me. I had left a few friends behind over the years, and never kept in touch.

Somehow the shame I felt during my childhood still echoed within me, so I kept people at arm's length. I was likeable and engaging, but no one could get close to me.

Helen knew I was a determined warrior, so the battle to establish my new life began.

I was still talking to Spirit, asking for simple answers and listening for simple directives, but I now knew that I was leaving my spiritual brilliance untapped.

One day she told me about channeled writing, which I was sure I could not do.

"Jacqui, just set your timer for twenty minutes, ask your spirit guides a question and write whatever comes into your head."

I still have those pages, which start off with "I can't believe Helen made me do this, it is so silly!" and I vent for a few paragraphs, as my brain wears itself out. Then, the pages change and I am writing with a voice and vocabulary that is not my norm. After an hour, I have several pages that outline my future life, including writing books so other women will see that their purpose of to live amazingly fulfilling lives, not just to survive. I used channeled writing quite often to get a more complete answer from Spirit than the simple "yes" or "no" I was used to with a pendulum.

Another time, Helen took my hands in hers and asked me, "What do you see?"

I immediately saw a bright yellow ball of light and heard that a baby girl was to be born through Helen. Helen was too old to be having a baby, so, sheepishly, I told her what I saw and heard.

"Jacqui, you know much more than you give yourself credit for. My daughter is having a baby girl in April."

I realized, *Oh yes, that is a baby born through Helen.*

The more we worked together the more I unearthed the gifts I had tucked away.

I told Helen about a dream I had never shared with anyone. When I was about fourteen, I dreamt about the Blessed Mother. In the dream scene, there was a very large pink, square gift box, with a beautiful pink bow, as large as the box top, the sort of present I never received as a child.

The Blessed Mother, showed me the beautiful pink-on-pink box for a long time. It just sat there, filling my dream vision. Finally Mary quietly said, "I have this gift for you."

I now know that box contained all my spiritual gifts, that were under wraps until I was ready to step into my full power as a Spiritual Leader.

I had to wait until the childhood trauma was erased from my cell memory.

I had to be well myself, before I could create wellness in others.

I had to clear the sounds of anger and hatred out of my ears before I could accurately hear the words from Mother-Father God.

I was now ready to open the box that the Lady in Blue, Mother Mary had given me. It had been waiting for me all those years, as I was coming home to myself with my wounds all sewed together by the woven fabric of love.

I met my oldest friend while working with Helen.

I was driving my bright red, two-seater convertible, the perfect car for Clearwater, Florida.

It was summer and I heard this deep, masculine voice next to me. I turned my head with a startle, envisioning that some man had just dropped into the seat next to me. And he had....

My Angel-John returned to me! I pulled the car over and had an amazing conversation, right in my car.

John explained, with that old familiar joyous voice, that we were never apart. He was "proud" that I had broken so many generational patterns that had plagued my family lineage. The more I released the pain of the past, the more clearly I could learn the word of God and connect to the heavens. He explained that "Angel John" was my baby name for him. In fact, he is Uriel, the Archangel of wisdom.

Early one morning, I called Helen from my home in Singapore. She asked about my healing work with the women. I told her that I was getting an ongoing stream of information from my spirit guides and the spirit guides of the women, filling my life and theirs with the ability to manifest from a place of power.

I used different energy healing modalities as divinely guided, incorporating Spiritual Counseling for women, as the words just came to my mind through my soul.

Helen encouraged me to read her soul messages.

Without hesitation, it flowed through me to her. I had tapped into her auric field, connected to her guides, and was sharing the information with Helen at a rapid pace. At the end of the session Helen thanked me for the "information from the heavens," as she called it.

The most amazing words came out of my therapist, teacher and mentor, "Jacqui, would you please allow me to honor you and your gifts, by paying you for my soul reading?"

I bowed my head.

"Jacqui, I see the student has become the teacher."

Helen gave me gifts of clarity, peace and joy… the same gifts I now offer to my clients and students. To her I am most grateful.

I will never be the licensed family therapist that Helen is, however from her own words I received the validation that I was now a Spiritual Oracle. I could hear the voice of Spirit and give people the action steps from spirit to help them along their path.

I was sitting in quiet meditation and spirit told me to go to India. I wasn't surprised, since I had already studied the Bible, Christianity and Buddhism, I figured Hinduism was the next step. Also, I was an advanced Deeksha Giver, which is a type of Blessings from the Hindu priests. The pink gift box from the Blessed Mother was about to be opened again, to show me more spiritual talents. Without much planning, I flew into Delhi and explored India for three weeks.

I stayed at the Golden Temple, the Ayurvedic school, and ashrams. I rode the trains, ate the food, and absorbed India into my heart and soul. I was immediately connected to its spiritual center and embraced this beautiful culture with friendly people. I have since led many spiritual retreats to this blessed country.

My most prized experience was with a Brahmin priest, whose small brown body and sparkling eyes greeted me at the door of his rustic study. The room had only a small wooden table, three straight-backed chairs, and many palm leaf-bundles of astrological knowledge. I had read that these astrology observations had been passed down, to the Brahmin priest, through oral tradition for over 5,000 years. In the past several hundred years, they have hand-written insights on heavy cardboard made from palm leaves.

I went to him, because two of my Indian born girlfriends, who lived near me in Singapore, had insisted that it was one of *the* most mystical experiences. It took many tiring hours to find my palm leaf, but once the priest started reading, my weariness flew away and my eyes grew wide, with the remembering. Much of what he spoke of was told to me as a young child, from the Blessed Mother and other guides.

His gentle, lilting voice spoke about my healing thousands of people of physical disease and emotional trauma. He told me about writing books that would inspire people to open to their true potential of greatness.

He spoke about me being called a guru, which is a teacher, then a guru Ji, which shows the highest level of reverence. He told me, "If I read a thousand more charts, none would be better than this," before he paused.

"You are to bring Heaven to Earth."

I had so much more to learn, so Brahmin priest directed me to wear a yellow sapphire ring on the pointer finger of my right hand, as a mark of my dedication to acquiring knowledge quickly and directly.

As a final act, he took me into his tiny temple. There were no chairs, only a few woven mats on the floor. The altar was crowded with neatly arranged statues and holy cards. Upon feeling the vibration of the temple, I dropped to my knees, as my eyes welled up with tears of gratitude. The Brahmin priest, prayed in Hindi, then turned to me, with a generous gift. He took a strand of India Rudruksha prayer beads, from around the statue of Ganesh, and placed them in my hands. I was grateful and also encouraged, because even though my task may be difficult, I have beads from Ganesh, the Hindu god and remover of obstacles with me.

Divine Guidance sped me along, as if I was being scooped up by the hands of God and placed in front of many great masters and teachers. They confirmed that I was to "bring heaven to earth" and cautioned me that if I did not do my divine work, a "charlatan" would take my place. After all my blessings and gifts, I could not let that happen. I felt a great responsibility to fulfill my destiny as a healer, teacher, and leader, which the Brahmin had explained "was written."

Anyone can become hardwired to spirit. Anyone can become a continual presence on both earth and in the heavens, by stretching through their heart chakra.

Anyone can learn about their spiritual lineage, even directly connecting with their Ascended Master tribe. Anyone can live with great love and abundance and everyone will, once we create The Golden Age of Peace.

I was guided to the light and out of the darkness from the Lady in Blue, who later was known to me as Mother Mary. I was saved so that I could remain in my body and bring this light to others, no matter what the circumstances have been.

I stood outside the door, about to be introduced to two Master Coptic Ministers, a married couple in their mid-sixties. I was eager to meet them, to express my respect and gratitude to them for bringing ancient Egyptian wisdom to modern mystics.

They opened the door and looked at me with the surprise of immediate recognition, although we had never met.

"You are from Archangel Raphael," he blurted out to me. They spoke quickly, as their words excitedly tumbled over each other, about being told to look for a mystical healer who was being sent to them from Raphael.

What I planned to be a brief, cursory visit turned into a number of sacred lessons, including some ceremonies of ancient Egypt to infuse and expand spiritual gifts within people.

As we were sitting on their screened-in porch to enjoy the warm weather, I learned to guide trapped entities to the light. With great love, I called to souls who had been trapped between heaven and earth to come forward. The room grew warmer and I felt the pressure around me as the room filled with trapped souls. I asked the Transitional Angels to light the path to the heavens and open the portal, inviting these lost souls to finally return to their heavenly home.

When I opened the space between heaven and earth, and started guiding the lost souls, the Coptic Ministers saw a shocking sight. They described in detail the earth-bound spirit of a woman, standing next to me.

I felt icy-cold fear run through me, as I realized it was my long-dead mother.

Even in death, my mother was still clinging to me. I had long ago forgiven her and thought our story was over. I realized it was not my responsibility to save her...and yet I felt I should.

The Ministers gathered around me and helped me to find my peace in that moment. I was no longer an abused child, who quaked with fear. I remember thinking, "I am an adult of God, a woman who has helped many souls to find the heavens and many people to find their heavenly path."

I spoke my belief out loud to the ministers and to my mother's soul. "I know that if I judge one person, I judge all peoples. I cannot judge you. I will not judge anyone."

With that decree, the Transitional Angels welcomed my mother into heaven. I lifted my arms into the air and let their grace pour through me as she went.

M. Jacquelyn Simpson is a divine channel of Heavenly Chi, a teacher of sacred lessons and a spiritual leader. She is the founder of "The Healing Trinity" and facilitates worldwide retreats for quantum healing. Jacqui is an expert in energetic and spiritual therapies. For over twenty years, she has combined these sciences with Divine Guidance to bring health and happiness to thousands of people. Jacqui and Tom have relocated to Belize, where she continues her work in-person and online. She proclaims, "I am an Angel of Peace serving my highest purpose; helping all of humanity live a life of love and peace." Jacqui offers her spiritual wisdom to you: www.TheHealingTrinity.com

Publisher's Note

Thank you for reading *VOICES: Women Braving It All to Live Their Purpose, Book One.* Please pass the torch of connection by helping other readers find this book. Here are some suggestions for your consideration:

- Write an online customer review wherever books are sold

- Gift this book to family and friends

- Share a photo of yourself with the book on social media and tag #VOICESmovement and #BravingItAll

- Bring in one or more of the *VOICES* authors as speakers for your club or organization

- Suggest *VOICES: Women Braving It All to Live Their Purpose* to your local book club. Request the Book Club Discussion Questions from www.CitrinePublishing.com/bookclubs

- Contact us to find out how you can become involved *(Details on the next page)*

Are You an Event Planner or Are You in a Book Club?

If you are interested in having a live event or a video conference call with any of the *VOICES* authors for a book club, or would like to invite us to speak at your event, as a group or individually, please reach out to author Chloe Rachel Gallaway via email:

Email: speakinginquiries@voicesmovement.org

Are You Looking to Tell Your *Braving It All* Story?

Wonderful! Please reach out to author and editor Chloe Rachel Gallaway for an interview about becoming a published author with the *VOICES Braving It All* book series.

Email: write@thewingedriverwriter.com

Visit: www.voicesmovement.org

www.VoicesMovement.org

CPSIA information can be obtained
at www.ICGtesting.com
Printed in the USA
FSHW011256311219
65626FS